Motorcycle Vagabonds – Around the World

Part 1: The Americas, New Zealand and Australia

ISBN 978-1533187055

Copyright/Author:
Frank Panthöfer
aka Motorcycle Vagabonds
Venloer Str. 601
50827 Köln (Cologne)
Germany
www.motorcycle-vagabonds.com

Translation: Janna Ernestitani
www.dontbelievethetypeva.com

A Once in a Lifetime Adventure

3.5 years, 183,475 km, 64 border crossings and endless encounters, adventures and experiences.

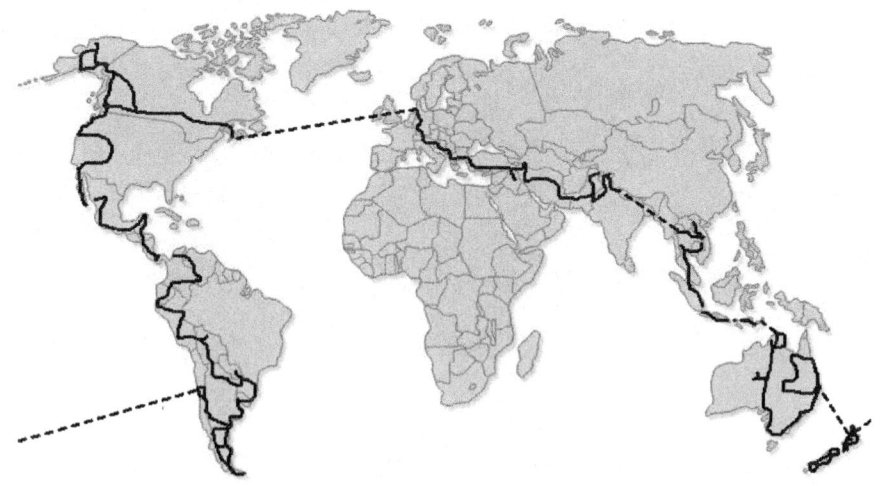

Who are the Motorcycle Vagabonds?

"Motorcycle Vagabonds" is the English translation of our original name: Krad-Vagabunden.
Krad is an old fashioned German word for motorcycle.
It´s not a MC or MCC, it´s just the two of us.
Frank is the writer and Simone is the photographer of the team.

Frank
Born 1968.
Used to work in a suit and tie as a manager in charge of 50 people at a financial institution. Survived several nasty mergers, outsourcings and financial crisis until he understood that the latest disaster was a chance to change his life.
Now he writes books and articles for magazines and is a well-known presenter for motorcycle travel themes.

Simone
Born 1974.
Was a florist in her former life and still is a passionate expert for plants. She has a big heart for animals.
After our return from the atw-trip she wanted to do something more social and has become a nurse.

Besides the social aspect, this profession has the advantage that there is a massive overdemand, which makes it easy to leave for a few months of Motorcycle Vagabond life and get a new job as soon as we are back home.

This Is the Symbolic Meaning of our Logo:

The wings embody wanderlust and the urge to explore the world.
The anchor stands for homeward bound, friends and family.
The (north) star shall help to find your way - on the road and in life.

Prologue

What has all the audible qualities of light rain caressing our tent, rouses us from our light doze, rain? We wish. When Simone is finally driven out of her sleeping bag by increasing bladder pressure, she finds the world around us has suddenly turned white. What may seem romantic at first sight causes our hearts to sink into our boots. How are we supposed to ever get out of this place?

We find ourselves in the Indian Himalayas - on the deserted Muray Plains at 15,630 feet, to be precise. We are a few miles off the road and still need to make it to the second-highest pass of the world, if we prefer not to spend the winter here. Thanks to a lack of good ideas, we simply decide to crawl back into our cosy and warm sleeping bags, and proceed to solve our present dilemma by dozing a little longer. Unfortunately it isn't long until I also have to follow nature's call, only to be immediately confronted with my very own version of altitude sickness: constipation! "Not in this place, not now." rushes through my mind. While snowflakes are gently melting on my bare behind, the air is being filled with my undignified panting and gasping upon every desperate squeezing attempt in an altitude like this. After a few minutes I finally give up in despair. I swiftly pull up my warm pants and flee back into the tent.

Time creeps by, minutes turn into hours, and my thoughts drift on to how distant our current life is from the one we left behind. How happy we are despite all the challenges and hardships we are facing on an almost daily basis. Just a few years ago the world looked slightly different...

If Not Now, Then When?

Cologne, Monday morning, 5am. The alarm clock starts blaring and snaps us out of our sleep, getting up at this unholy time of the day requires all our strength. As per usual on this weekday, especially at this hour, my thoughts are somewhat morose. Once again the weekend has flown by too quickly and it also means the end of our time spent together. Simone is facing her working week as a florist in Germany whilst I have to embark on a fight against narcolepsy and bad weather on a 3-hour-ride to my job in the neighbouring country Luxembourg.

Bad news is an integral part of my typical working day. What awaits me today, though, is a particularly low blow, the onslaught of outsourcing. My department is to be sold to another company, which is notoriously renowned for poor treatment of their employees. Previous experience tells me that being the manager of an affected team makes me a particularly undesired individual in this context. I've already been through similar situations in the past, including year-long vindictive pressure by the overtaking company, which often sees former management as a bitter pill to swallow in order to get the deal. On top of everything else, last year manifested another variation of the already known drama: merging. Two departments doing similar activities are merged to drastically cut down personnel and costs. Roughly this meant for me: we don't need two managers. Pull your socks up and get ready for a competitive race to see who comes out at the end. Of course while you are struggling for survival, you also have to maintain the course of a sinking ship. Great.
Leading 50 employees in such difficult times, in which work-performance is affected by the pressure of facing an uncertain future, is no walk in the park. Am I really supposed to go through this hell for the third time in my life? Is it worth it? To my surprise the answer to this comes easy: Fuck no!

These are dark days. Even my dream of an early retirement has become an unrealistic fantasy. The financial crisis has left my hopes of a comfortable pension in shambles. I suddenly realise that never before have I had less to lose than in this moment. If I don't get out now, will I ever?

A little concerned about what she might have to say about my plans, I call Simone later in the evening. After some thought she doesn't hold back with the liberating answer: "Yes, let's take the plunge. I'm with you."

We had often spoken about this in the past, particularly after a few beers, that we wanted to embark on a long motorbike journey. A really long one, at least for a year or so. And then our fingers would follow along brave routes on the world map above our bed.

Our dreams have now turned into reality - well partially, at least we have progress.

To avoid chickening out and putting an early end to our plans, a process needs to be established. Firstly, inform family and friends. Reactions vary and my mom comments on the decision to leave a job, that has made me physically as well as psychologically sick for many years, with the words: "Now you're also unemployed!" Enough said about that perspective. As for myself, I feel an incredible sense of relief that the balancing act between a conservative work routine as a bank manager, whilst privately living an unconventional life, is finally over. An end to collars and long sleeves in soaring temperatures and peculiar precautions in case my extensive tattoos may cause a public scandal. No more embarrassment when sitting in meetings and suddenly realising that I have dirty hands from having to repair my motorbike on the way to work. An end to all the harassment and prejudices I have experienced with my choice of employment. Although generally based on clichés, it still wears you down and hurts. Suddenly it strikes me how long the list of "Enough with…" actually has become.

Since handing in my resignation I feel incredibly relieved and instantly healthier. Work has lost its power and with that any pressure my new employer might consider implementing. It feels as if the entire world has opened up to me, and in no time at all I will be conquering exactly that world with my sweetheart!

We will be leaving in seven months. In the remaining time leading up to our departure, we will keep on working to maximise our travel cash. Contrary to others in my industry, I will be deprived the blessings of a social contract. There will be no golden handshake to finance our adventure. It will be travelling on a shoestring for us.

Instead of immersing ourselves into detailed planning of our route and daydreaming of heroic deeds ahead, we are entirely absorbed with the demands of bureaucracy and organisational matters. Packing up and closing down our apartments and all the contents as well as selling our cars, terminating insurance policies and such, so we can keep our fixed costs at an absolute minimum. In the meantime we have to find new motorbikes for our trip, which then have to be rebuilt whilst the old motorbikes need to be prepared for storage. Equipment has to be put together, foreign health insurance papers need to be signed, visas as well as import regulations for our bikes need to be researched. Power of attorneys given, additional bank accounts and credit cards procured. And then there's the transport, which still needs to be organised. Let alone a few other things here and there.

I am lucky enough to have extensive experience in project management, which proves significantly beneficial in this environment. Having exchanged a team of "obeying" staff who loved taking orders with one sole employee, though, who to make things even worse had also her very own ideas on how to do things, could be a challenging task at times. In saying this I have to admit that compared to my professional every-day-grind this new working relationship comes with a sweet and all-important distinction, this is actually fun.

So when we finally board the plane on the 1st of May, we can barely comprehend that we've made it so far, we are "on the road" at last. A broad grin takes hold of our faces, and in the innocence of that moment there are no doubts as to whether we have made the right decision. In this very moment there is only overwhelming optimism, enhanced by a dash of bold recklessness.

A New Travel Experience

Entering Canadian ground went pretty smoothly. Having said that Simone might have to practise her credibility when being confronted by the usual cheerless interrogation officers, who are curious about her past activities in terms of criminal records. Other than that the importing of our motorbikes was terribly uneventful. Before we know it we're riding through the early springtime of the Nova Scotian countryside. Up here it is still rather cold at this time of the year, and most campsites aren't open yet. Therefore the feeling that we are doing something extraordinary grows by the minute. In addition to this I have always been a strong advocate of the motto that "I'd rather be on the road in bad weather than in the office when the sun shines".

Curiously we're listening to our hearts and are wondering if this already feels different to our former adventures. Looking at the scenery and culture, there is no doubt that we find ourselves in a different country, yet "exotic" is something different altogether. However, we notice one crucial difference: we are relaxed and more receptive towards the momentum. No high-pressure deadlines driving us day-in and day-out, and there is room for spontaneity, such as accepting an invitation to camp on the lawn of a local biker. A newfound freedom we have been missing for a long time in our lives before, simply being able to enjoy the time with others, whether it be realising dinner or overnight invitations. On past travels these encounters always seemed to deprive us of routes to be explored, places to be discovered and possibly missed due to time constraints. However, we can now finally enjoy these moments and treat ourselves to whatever our hearts desire. It isn't going to be long before we realise the difficulty of simply accepting and getting involved with others – but more to that later.

For the time being we resume being struck by the dimensions of private properties in Canada, whose large size is in stark contrast to our normal German standards. The lawn in question owned by our host measures respectable 900 x 600 yards and ends at a steep cliff, spoiling us with an exceptional view over the ocean. We're granted free residence for as long as we like – our wishes have come through!

We happily pose for snow photographs, marvel at moose, fjords and endless forests, and enjoy being the only tourists this early in the season. Despite us not having had the chance to undertake many test rides at home, we're slowly getting used to our new motorbikes. All the bits and pieces of our equipment are finding their homes whilst we're adjusting to our new rhythm "on the road".

We usually camp wild and only book into the few already opened camping grounds infrequently for the occasional shower.
Speaking of showers, we dare say that we had expected to turn into these hardened and tough individuals overnight, just to realise that the metamorphosis we had hoped for only happens at a snail's pace. As a matter of fact it is only on rare occasions that extreme character changes happen at all. One perfect example is that even after three and a half years on the road I still despise, even hate, having a shower in cold water - so much for the myth of adapting to your environment quickly (or at all). Simone on the other hand, is made of completely different stuff...

Ending in a Ditch

We're travelling along a country road at a slow pace with an extremely slow truck ahead. I move onto the opposite traffic lane to overtake when the truck suddenly decides to veer off as well – of course without using indicators or making sure that there is nobody behind him. In utter disbelief and horror I slam on the brakes, yet the rear of the truck is coming towards me at an alarming speed. The only way out of this is to the left marginal strip, let alone that I'm already struggling to keep the bike upright in gravel and strong crosswinds. The wind pushes me relentlessly towards the ditch. My deepest hopes for success within this seemingly endless moment of horror are in vain – with a last bit of momentum and in slow motion I end up in the ditch. It might be worth mentioning that I did so head first and a few yards downhill. CRASH! The bike comes to a sudden halt. My first thought is with the bike, the second with my anger over that asshole trucker! In slow motion retrospect, I inevitably wonder why I was not capable of avoiding such a tragedy. I actually often feel this way in similar situations and have difficulties understanding why they happen in the first place.

The bike is stuck. With extreme efforts we get rid of my equipment. Thanks to the help of a friendly biker the three of us drag and push the bike out of the ditch, and ten minutes later my darling finds herself again upright in standing position. At first glance it has survived the escapade unharmed and undamaged. Lucky…

Technically Simone is supposed to first take pictures and then engage in situations like these, instead she was immediately at the scene and hands-on, which is very reassuring to be on the road with somebody like that. But next time, photos first, please.

Fear of the Bear

Canadian bears were often the main topic in many documentaries we had watched at home. We read a lot about them and received countless advice on how to react when having a close encounter with a bear. Black and brown bears are very different when it comes to their skills of sprinting, running down hills, climbing and also specifically the development of their eyesight. Hence there are different tactics to be used sensibly when suddenly being confronted with a freakin' bear, such as running downhill,

climbing up a thin tree or simply turning into a pillar of salt...
The only question is that if, in the face of horror, we are actually capable of achieving the balancing act of classifying the bear in front of us and then decide accordingly on the accurate tactic to use. There is at least a consolation in the fact that one of the kinds (unfortunately I have forgotten which) quickly loses interest if you stop moving after having been bitten a few times.

Bear shit or not? Animal faeces expert Simone at work.

Sounds simple enough, although reality might look a little different. To make matters worse our travel guide pours even more oil into the fire by stating that black bears may seem of brown colour, whereas brown bears often appear Black. Remarkable advice given encompasses anything from wearing bells whilst hiking, to the use of motorbike transmitters sending unnoticeable sound frequencies for humans, yet which are highly effective in scaring off bears, or possibly infuriating them more so. Although I have to admit that I most likely might have it all mixed up by now, one thing remains certain: Before a bear has even had a chance to consider eating us, we've already spent numerous hours examining this sensitive subject from pretty much every angle, and have worried much more than required at that early stage. Our first camping experience in bear wilderness turns out to be accordingly exciting. As per standard we proceed collecting all items that might attract bears into a big pile, which happens to be taking on worrying dimensions. Apart from food this includes pretty much everything scented, such as toothpaste, shower gel and much more. Old socks, biker boots and the like as well? After thorough consideration we decide against adding the latter items as we might as well put everything onto the pile. Moving on from this first step, we roll up all the items into one piece of luggage and pull it up twelve to fifteen yards into a tree. Easier said than done: First of all you need to find a suitable tree, and then to throw, preferably in a skilful manner, a piece of rope, measuring at least 30 yards and weighted with a piece of wood at the end, over a branch to pull up the luggage. The cursed piece of wood bounces off the branches several times, invariably missing my head by inches only. When we finally manage to secure the bag in its safe location, we both agree: NEVER AGAIN!

In retrospect and after many months of experience in the land of bears, I have to admit that, yes, you should take these dangers seriously whilst not overstating them at the same time. If there are so-called bear lockers available on camping grounds, it makes sense to use them. All the other times we just placed risk items at least 30 yards away from our tent, or secured them in our bike cases. However, cracking open the latter does not pose a great challenge to a Grizzly, the main thing to remember isn't to keep anything tempting in your tent.

The true danger aren't bears itself but more the fear and risk of dying of a heart attack when crossing one. On countless occasions the dialogs in our tent went such as "Did you just hear the cracking noise?" Not to withhold our confession of those embarrassing moments, when we proceeded to banging and rattling our pots as well as singing terribly out of tune to hopefully scaring off any possible black bears or their phantoms as such. The entire forest animal habitat would have most likely had a ball witnessing the strange behaviour at hand.

Life of a Motorcycle Vagabond

There's a crackling fire beside us, and pattering rain outside. It's the beginning of June and we've been on the road for a good month now. We're often still the only visitors on the camping grounds. Today is no exception as we roll soaking wet onto the camping ground of a national park after a half an hour trip over gravel road. We refrain from setting up our tent, saving us to have to put it together wet the next morning, and take shelter in a (barbecue) hut, which is opened to one side. It is an unfamiliar luxury to have so much space and to use a warm stovetop instead of our small portable gas cooker.

Speaking of luxury, after the first month we've analysed our expenses precisely. Not adventurous at all but oh so many long-term travellers have realised long before the end of their journey that money can run faster than expected through their fingers. We're pleasantly surprised that we're lying slightly above budget. Canadian prices had startled us initially. Food is significantly more expensive than in Germany and alcohol prices even higher. Only petrol, which is our biggest

expenditure, is considerably cheaper than in Western Europe. Looking at the distances we're covering, we will still face a hefty bill in the end. Compared with our former lifestyle, we have had to tighten our belts all the same and make do with what we have. Pleasantries of past trips like restaurant visits or sleeping in a hotel at times are simply no longer possible. Rather than buying local specialities or exciting and tasty food as per usual, the rule is now: Cheap and good value for money.
Generally we buy our daily consumption at a supermarket in the morning, and much to our delight shops are conveniently open seven days a week.
We're still struggling with the fact that price tags on products don't include taxes, which again vary in kind and amount in each province, so that the final price at the checkout is always a surprise to us.

Usually, some time in the late morning or early afternoon, we enjoy a picnic in a nice spot. We're surely not getting tired of indulging in these precious moments, as this is life quality for us.

By evening, when we've found a place to camp and everything is set up, we cook a warm meal on our gas stove.

A crucial aspect for a meal to taste delicious is to check the stability of the available outdoor table and chairs before deciding to take a seat, preferably on both sides. Otherwise you may be covered in hot pasta and sauce, and anything else that might've been on the table. To make matters worse we had just washed all our clothes, and had nothing left to wear as alternative. Furthermore, to avoid attracting any bears in the middle of the night with scrumptiously smelling foods, every single piece of pasta needs to be meticulously collected from the dirt. Tapping pots might not be necessary today, as our loud cursing should've chased away any jumpy bear nearby.

Being a Motorcycle Vagabond Is a Full Time Job

Obviously, we now have more freedom than ever. Nonetheless there's always a lot to be done. Each morning the camp needs to be cleared and re-packed onto the motorbikes. With practice we become faster at this routine task, but it still takes some time to be allocated for. Particularly in bad weather this isn't a pleasurable exercise. In the evening we go through the whole procedure, just in reverse. Buying supplies, cooking, refuelling several times a day, route planning, technical service (regular check ups, when might I need which part and where can I get it from, repairs, maintenance), all this adds up. In addition there's also communication to be kept up with, such as e-mails home and with other motorbike travellers and friends we would like to visit. To take care of the aforementioned and to also undertake regular website maintenance and updates, we require an Internet connection. The many pictures we take along the way also have to be reviewed, edited and saved in various different places. An indication on how full our days are, is the fact that I generally read one book per week when travelling. I'm already stuck on the current one for five weeks now, and it might be worth a mention that I probably read most of it on the flight.

Despite all these small pains of an adventurous life, it's fantastic to ride our bikes for hours on end each day and to spend the majority of our time outdoors. We're making the most of our freedom and all it has to offer. It's our choice to decide on where to go next and when we would like to be there.

At last we have the time to get to know people we meet on our journey. It's the greatest aspect of this trip and impacts on our daily life immensely.

Fortunately there are numerous opportunities to meet people. Because of our German number plates, which prove to be an enormous magnet in terms of a communication starter, we're continually approached by others and in most cases an invitation follows shortly after. It then happens that one of the aforementioned invitations is followed by an address or directions such as the dialogue "Past the second lake to the left, you'll see two dirt roads, take the right one…" Our hosts, by the way, may follow only hours or at times even days later, which does not seem to be a problem in this country. Often doors remain unlocked or we're told where the key is hidden. Such blind confidence is difficult to understand for us and it gets us thinking. We hope to internalise such an admirable attitude.

A Life for a Motorbike

"You definitely have to visit Rudi in Edmonton" was the pushy advice by one of our hosts the other day. Instead of finding Rudi, we're actually found by Wolle, the organiser of the MRT, which is an international annual event for motorcycle travellers in Canada. We quickly let go of our original plan of riding towards the Rocky Mountains after a quick chat with Rudi, when Wolfgang states dryly "Now, you stay here for at least two days", an order which we're only too pleased to obey. The beauty of travelling this way is to actually have the freedom to spontaneously overthrow any plan, if there's one in the first place.

The encounter with Rudi is impressive, what a charismatic man. Instead of enjoying his well-earned retirement, he can be found every single day in his motorcycle shop. His credible motto is that if you were to take this from him, he would be devastated and there would be no reason to go on living. Motorcycles and travels are his everything and despite his age or physical afflictions, he still seems to be pretty fit on two wheels. Wolle confirms off the record that he has to work hard to keep up with the 79-year-old ex-motocross champion when riding in terrain.

Rocky Mountains

We leave Edmonton behind and travel West. Our next destination is the Rocky Mountains, Jasper National Park with its southern counterpart Banff.

After a few hundred miles of seemingly dull highway, which unfortunately couldn't be avoided in the process, we take a curve to suddenly be surprised with a breathtaking view of the Rocky Mountains. Hitherto our previous impressions of "grand", "fantastic" and "beautiful" fade into a sudden and trivial memory of "nice". What we have seen on our journey so far doesn't even come close to the majesty and beauty of these mountains. The following days turn into an orgy of worshipping, expressed through many "Wows", "Geez" and "Oh my goshes!"

Every few minutes we stop to enjoy another sublime and peaceful view, although peaceful has become relative here. All we see before us is just SO amazing that many other tourists probably have the same reaction.

In saying this, the influx of other visitors remains within limits by local standards as we are still within the off-season and most tracks, roads and camping grounds are still closed. We don't even want to imagine how it is in high season, where as per travel guide, the only way along the Icefields Parkway is only stop and go for hundreds of miles.

Rain, Snow and Even More Rain

It is raining when we arrive in Banff, the tourist heart of the Rockies. To escape the crowds we spend the night out of town near Lake Minnewanka, where we set up our tent in fierce hail. The water is seeping into our clothes and our hands are stiff from the cold. There are no other campers for miles and it just keeps pouring down. If we could only have some wood to make a fire, or some brandy to warm us up. After some time we're, as per usual, able to laugh about the situation and see the positives by enjoying the somewhat adventurous romantic side of it.

As it has apparently been raining here for the last 14 days, we decide on the spur of a moment to cancel our hiking plans and try our luck further south.

Kananaskis Country, the beautiful "doorstep of the Rocky Mountains" lies in front of us, but we can't see it. We're soaking wet, the visibility is poor, and it gets even worse above 6,500 feet. As our visors are covered in condensation, we have to keep them open and endure the freezing rain and snow. We later learn that we had crossed the highest pass in Canada that had only been opened two days earlier.

We're quite relieved when we finally roll into Pincher Creek in the evening, soaking wet, yet frozen solid. Despite the town seemingly being just a place where you only buy supplies and then ride on quickly, the local campsite lures us with cheap rates and most over all a small but dry recreation room. The latter might have a draft and is unheated, but we spend two funny nights with a Belgian couple, Michel and Katrien, who have already seen a lot of the world on the back of their bicycles. This proves to be one of the many great encounters with bicycle travellers throughout our journey. We've noticed again and again on our journey that there is more that unites us than separates us with this type of globetrotters. To our shame we have to admit that on many occasions we took pleasure looking at their Spartan luggage. Once again, somebody who has even less than we do, which suddenly makes you feel that you aren't that bad off.

After three days the rain finally stops and we make an escape. At first glance our unwanted stop in Pincher Creek seemed unwelcome, yet often these are the moments you will remember in detail and more vividly than the pleasant experiences, where everything is going according to plan. Have you ever experienced this? We have, many times.

With 10,000 miles behind us we reach the Pacific on the 55th day of our journey. We've achieved our first major milestone, the crossing of the second largest country of the world from East to West. The fact that we've travelled through five time zones might give you a slight impression of its dimension.

Zombie Drug Mile

Why Vancouver is considered one of the Top 5 cities worldwide with the highest quality of life becomes apparent quickly, mild climate, the mountains and the ocean right at your doorstep. It isn't surprising that several of our friends have relocated to live here. Although they aren't the only ones, who are heading for frost-resistant Vancouver, as we discover on our stroll through the city. With the strong instinct of country bumpkins, we find ourselves in East Hastings Street, the "most dangerous place in Canada" as a friendly local tells us. We've already heard of it in reports, yet we weren't prepared for its entire extent. Hundreds of fucked up crack zombies, in all shapes and forms, walking the streets, unsteady with an empty stare. Heroin junkies, desperately scanning their battered bodies on the streets, in the hope to find a clean piece of skin to re-insert the needle into. Dreadful looking shabby prostitutes, where even with an abundance of imagination you could hardly conceive what kind of pervert would be prepared to pay money for, dealers en masse on pretty much every corner. Nobody here fears the police. What we see here is the worst we've ever encountered in that regard, and throughout our downtown excursion we cross the forecourt of hell over and over again. Every time we have a funny feeling about it.

The Dopelands

We cross over to Vancouver Island by ferry, a 200-mile long and mountainous paradise for off-road lovers. In the capital of the island, we are guests at Peter's, with whom we visit the opening concert of the Victoria Ska Festival, which is the biggest in Canada. It's a great night with only one small downer to mention. As you're generally not allowed to drink in public in Canada, the festival grounds have a beer garden, which you can access by confirming that you're old enough to drink via showing your ID. As per usual, I don't have my ID on me and feel rather irritated about the fact that despite being and looking 42-years old, security denies me access to the area with alcohol. If I were a woman, I might have indulged in the indirect compliment of being considered younger than 18, yet being a man I was simply pissed off.
Let us be clear about one thing, in terms of drinking culture we Germans are head and shoulders above North Americans. Whether it be Canada or the US, it's here I realise how good we have it at home, where you can buy alcohol at fair prices in pretty much every supermarket and are allowed to drink in public, the absolute opposite of North America. No wonder the per capita Marihuana consumption in Canada is considerably higher than the Netherlands. Public consumption of weed is likely to be more tolerated than alcohol, with non-pot head ultra conservative citizens being the exception to the rule. Even smoking weed whilst driving doesn't seem to be an offence to the local police unless you show significant loss of function. Although drug

testing has become a standard in Germany, it seems to be unknown in this country.

Toad Rock Motorcycle Campground

A campsite for motorcyclists only is a novelty we look forward to. Such a concept is almost unheard of in Europe, whilst a few dozen of these can be found in North America.
We're immediately excited about the large area, it has a rustic but nonetheless excellent infrastructure. Barbecue, kitchen shed, do-it-yourself workshop and a so-called "social area", where between 30 to 60 motorcycle travellers meet each night. As alcohol can't be sold officially, beer is available by donation, which means that the amount of the donation is determined individually. The conversations with newfound friends are passionate and the barley juice is flowing in streams. One night I entertain the crowd with a slide show presentation of a journey we undertook last year. I was over excited to hold my very first presentation before an audience of strangers that I had a drink to calm my nerves. Afterwards I'm so drunk that I manage to get lost on my way home and end up at a bonfire with a group of people completely unknown to me. This is also where I delivered a grand speech in a language absolutely foreign to the people present, before I proceeded to fall over drunk as a skunk. When I am being greeted with laughter the next day, I can't remember anything scandalous and shameful. However, Mary, the campsite manager takes it upon herself to explain the escapades of the night before. Instead of being given a sermon about my behaviour though, I receive a friendly pat on the back and am then rewarded with free accommodation for the night. Mary alone, who is truly a unique and kind-hearted human being, would be the best reason to pay this exceptional place a visit.

A few weeks later we return to her Toad Rock Campground, the reason being the motorcycle travel meeting by Wolle, which turns out to be a raging success. For four days it's all about our favourite topic, and this time I even manage to hold the slide show without any embarrassing symptoms relating to excessive inebriation.
Simone is unexpectedly asked onto the stage and serenaded with a Happy Birthday by the entire horde. On the one hand it proves a strange feeling for her to be far away from her good old friends back home on this day, on the other hand there is no doubt that it feels right in that very moment to be exactly here and now. We finally live the life we

always wanted to live in a way, which previously we have only dreamt of. To be free and adventurous, only missing the "young" but we keep that at heart.

To Hell With "Long Way Round"

I can't really tell how often I've been asked specifically about "Long Way Round" by people on the road. Oh, you're travelling around the world, just like in that awesome TV Show "Long Way Round". I must say that in the meantime my response to this has become somewhat sharp, reminding them that we are actually riding without numerous accompanying vehicles and helpers. Our adventure isn't staged but real. Just the other day one of these guys actually had the audacity to address me first thing in the morning, whilst half asleep, I attempted to hurry to the loo. He had seen our motorbikes. He was there with his Harley and so it happened that their luggage for the weekend didn't fit, requiring his wife to follow in the truck. And then it happened: "What you're doing there is like in Long Way Round..." I was torn between the urge to finally making it to the toilet and my deep wish to express my opinion that the mere improper comparison is ludicrous, to say the least. Due to my pedagogical responsibility I decided for the latter. Had we have gotten a dollar for each time I had to hear these three accursed words in the years to come, we would've become so rich that we could've travelled carefree by motorbike for the rest of our lives.

On to the Arctic Circle

The Alaska Highway starts in Dawson Creek. The landscape doesn't change much in comparison to the South of Canada, but up here it becomes more isolated and wilder. Fuel stops become a strategic task, especially as the more lonesome stations tend to charge three times the price for fuel. Buildings become a true rarity and it takes us a while to get used to this deserted landscape. For more than half a day we have nothing but smoke to the left due to a gigantic fire that has broken out and can't be brought under control, we later learn that it is expected to be extinguished only by the first snow of the season. Because of this, the Stewart Cassier Highway, which is
the only alternative to the route we have taken, is only passable in a convoy with pilot vehicle. We had planned to travel along there on our way back and therefore look forward to what might await us.

Yukon Territory – sounds like a great adventure, right? From now onward it becomes incredibly lonely. There are a mere 32,000 people living in this whole province, which is a third of the population of Cologne-Ehrenfeld, a lively and popular residential area of Cologne where we used to live, with many shops, artist studios, cafes, clubs and theatres. Three quarters of the 32,000 Yukon residents live in the capital called Whitehorse, thus leaving only 8,000 people for the remaining province.
Anyone spending too much time thinking about breakdowns and defective parts he can't fix, easily risks going crazy.

On our last night in the Yukon Territory we camp wild in a prime spot. We can barely wait to make it to Alaska but consistently have to think back to last year when we camped in a similar beautiful place at Crimea, equally full of anticipation. The next day we experienced a nightmare, which ended with us being refused entry into Russia. Hence, the following morning we're riding towards the US border with mixed feelings, especially as we've heard several unfortunate stories about US border crossings recently. One particularly prominent example is the current story of a couple that were also on a motorcycle trip around the world and unfortunately admitted this when reaching the Canadian-American border. In the opinion of the border guard on duty, they obviously had given up their home and jobs, and this may be enough motivation to never want to go back home, therefore they were simply refused entry. In another incident that involved friends of ours, the border control guards interrogated them for three long hours upon entering the country and repeatedly asked why the heck they had no children. One needs good nerves to avoid any inappropriate defence of their rights to privacy, unless you'd like to lose any chances of an entry to the country.

Welcome to Alaska

But in the end, as so often, everything turns out differently than expected. Entry formalities are finalised in no time at all and, after the first sense of relief, we almost feel a bit disappointed. What did we rehearse all those fairytale-responses for? Obviously, compared to other border points, motorcycle travellers seem to be a common sight here and perhaps are considered less suspicious. Upon further enquiries on my behalf, the border guard tells me that in high season an average of one European per day comes through on his motorbike. After brief consideration he adds: "You're already pretty late for August. You're probably the last ones for this year." Hopefully this won't become a reversed Nova-Scotia-effect, where we were constantly told: "You are way too early."

Alaska – the State of Strict Conformity

The ride to Fairbanks is exactly what we were told it would be: monotonous. After three and a half months in Canada, where we were somewhat spoilt, endless forests don't seem very exciting anymore. Fairbanks itself also doesn't have much to offer. However, for us it means our first contact with civilisation in Alaska, and we already look forward to what we can buy in supermarkets here and if everything is as expensive as feared.
In the liquor store we are taught a lesson. The shop assistant would like to see BOTH our Ids. A novelty. Even in Canada, which had already been quite annoying in terms of alcohol rules, we did not have to show our IDs in a liquor store at our old age. The highlight is yet to come, though, as Simone has her passport on her, mine is, as per usual, stowed away in my motorbike case. As it so happens by law that both buyers (of this one bottle) have to show their IDs in a case as such, hence our militant hopeful shop assistant refuses us the liquor. I can't quite grasp

the situation and ask the lady if we should simply step outside so Simone can just come back in alone, prove to be the sole purchaser in this instance to then successfully receive the noble liquor. No, unfortunately this would not be possible, is her answer. She now knew that we are travelling together, which she simply could not oversee. After a moment of silence I express my verbal thanks with a gracious "Fuck You" in response to such malicious stubbornness.

Originally we had planned today to celebrate our successful entry into the US with one or two beers in a bar. A luxury we hadn't yet once indulged on our trip, so we embarked on the long walk into town. The unpleasant anecdote in the liquor store happened after a one-hour march, when the town centre and the first bar were still nowhere in sight, and we needed some provisions to continue forth on our mission. We find ourselves trudging along with dry throats, worried that all the effort might be for nothing. Had this been an exception or are all citizens of Alaska nit-pickers? Will we even be refused beer in bars? Anxiously we enter the first bar, which has a few Hells Angels Harleys parked outside, and order two pints. Naturally and without having to show any ID the two glasses of beer are placed in front of us. We are relieved, and beer has rarely tasted so good.

We're heading over the Dalton Highway that runs parallel to the Trans-Alaska Pipeline towards the Arctic Circle. However, the word "Highway" may give a slightly false impression. In Alaska everything is named Highway, even a ten-mile long back road. Then, when it comes to the road surface, they generally are far from German Autobahn standards and they often consist of gravel and dirt roads. The landscape becomes more and more tundra-like. What may seem barren at first sight, however, offers an abundance of food for humans and bears at this time of the year. I have never seen that many berries before, it's actually quite incredible. More than once in Alaska we stuff ourselves with blue-, black- and raspberries as well as currants.

I just wish we'd have a mushroom expert amongst us. I have never seen before such an array of mushrooms, ranging from tiny to gigantic. Sadly, it is of no use to us, as we have absolutely no clue, which ones are eatable or consumed before a spiritual journey or should be avoided .

We briefly flirt with Simone's theory that you don't easily die of mushroom poisoning. The prospect of explosive diarrhoea, vomiting and visions of gigantic fluoro bears in such circumstances alone is sufficient to keep our hands off those tempting mushrooms. Bummer!

A phenomenon, which needs getting used to is that the more you move from the equator towards North or South pole, the stronger the seasonal difference becomes in terms of daylight hours. Similar to the far North of Scandinavia, the sun here partially doesn't completely set in summer or rise in winter. This can be hard to cope with, and many city residents in Alaska counteract the onset of depression from the dark with prescribed drugs, un-prescribed drugs, alcohol, various breeds of mushrooms or just plain old homicidal fantasies.

However, at present we're just thrilled to be able to ride in the light until what should be night and then still have enough time to set up camp in daylight.

With the length of the travel up here, it wouldn't be possible otherwise.

My Prudhoe Bay Trauma

As so many globetrotters before and probably after us, we proudly pose at the Arctic Circle, which is clearly marked on the wooden sign. The following night we sleep north of it, and then we turn around, as the Arctic Sea can't be reached via our motorbikes on this road. The last miles are private property and can only be accessed by the tourist bus of the oil company. Why take on such an expensive and exhausting ride up there is Simone's argument. "So we can say that we have been at the northernmost point reachable by motorcycle?" is my formulated reply. Whilst still finishing these words, I realise that this is a male argument and that I could convince Simone only with something worth seeing at the end of the route. Taking on challenges for its own sake and to show off with later, is not a women thing, something I have realised in life when having similar conversations with women.
In the following years, however, I came to regret this very specific team decisions like no other. I can't remember how often we spoke with other travellers about Alaska and men especially asking me in bewilderment "You didn't ride all the way up to Prudhoe Bay? Why the heck wouldn't you do that?" My reply to this would generally be growled through clenched teeth: "Team decision! WE believed riding up to Prudhoe Bay

to be stupid." But that's how it is when you travel as a couple - you have to make compromises. Unfortunately it is unavoidable, and at times the definition "A compromise is when nobody gets what he wants" comes to mind.

The Rainiest Summer of All Times

We experience Alaska with mixed feelings. The vastness of its landscape doesn't daunt us anymore. Instead we are very pleased not to meet a single soul for hours on end. We're also particularly delighted about the Denali Highway, which doesn't see many travellers around this time of the year.
Without doubt, the landscape of this country has a lot of beauty to offer. On the other hand it isn't very different to Canada. The Southern coast with its numerous glaciers is definitely the highlight of the state, if it wouldn't be for all the rain. It seems to be constantly coming down, looks like we have hit the jackpot with the rainiest summer since weather is recorded in Alaska. Neither motorcycle travelling, nor camping are much fun in that.

The Wrong Brake Pads

"Feel free to start cooking, I'll just change the brake pads quickly." In hindsight, my optimistic announcement becomes stuck in my throat, when I compare the new and the old, very different looking pads a few minutes later. I come to realise that we're having a slight problem. We're hundreds of miles away from the next motorcycle shop and the old brake pads are down to zero. Bingo.
Again I have gained new wisdom by learning that it's advisable to double-check parts at each purchase to make sure they're the right ones. However, this new-gained wisdom doesn't help in this very moment though, but in return the long detour into civilisation has a nice side effect. As we have to wait a few days for the delivery from a Southern state of the US, we kill time on the free campsite of the Harley dealer in Anchorage, where we meet Ernesto, a motorcycle traveller from Uruguay, who also set up camp here.

With a few beers, hands and feet, pantomime and a few words of Spanish on our and microscopic amounts of English on Ernesto's behalf, we have a tireless exchange. The humorous highlight is when Ernesto tries to imitate a sheep on all four, shouting "baaa" whilst stuffing his mouth with grass and pointing at Simone. I laugh until I cry whilst the expression on Simone's face shows anything but happiness in anticipation of her possible fate as virtuous vegetarian in barbeque crazy South America.

Suitable Orgy Steam House

All roads to and from Alaska lead through Tok. We have to search a little to find the not very well signposted Thompson Eagle's Claw Motorcycle Park, but it's worth the effort. The motorcycle campsite is designed with loving attention to detail, including a fantastic cooking shelter and deluxe toilet facilities. The campsite managers are deeply committed to the cause and the reception is very warm. The absolute highlight is the steam house, which is similar to a sauna, just a tad more rustic and more 'Alaska'. This evening we have the cosy steam house all to ourselves, which can additionally be locked from the inside, as the owner tells us with a conspiratorial wink. "Oh, and..." she adds "alcohol is explicitly allowed in the steam house". We laughingly plunge into the pleasure…
The next morning the warmth of the steam house is forgotten, it's cold, and it's raining. Taking the tent down and packing the motorbikes is never fun, but it is pure agony in these conditions. We're tired of this worst Alaskan summer ever and spontaneously decide against Dawson. Especially as the "Top of the World Highway" leading up to it is in such desolate condition because of the weather that the construction workers with their "Sisyphean task" can't get on top of repairing the damage, so that the road can only be travelled twice per day in a convoy. Instead we will head into one direction for more than a year: South.

On the current leg of the tour we were told more than once by locals, how many frosty nights they have already had. Many of the already scarce campsites, service stations and other such amenities for tourists are already shut by the beginning of September. In addition, the Stewart-Cassiar Highway can only be travelled in convoy due a forest fire that has been out of control for weeks. Surely not fun for the tourism operators, who are already struggling under hard conditions anyway. Meanwhile it is merely smoking here and there, and we experience a fascinating ride through this bizarre and surreal landscape of black, dead trees.

I Hate Chains

Have I already mentioned that I hate chains with a passion? I hate the daily maintenance it requires, I hate having to tighten it constantly in its final phase of life, I hate having to assess it before every longer trip to evaluate if the fucking chain is going to make it that far or not (and also I have to note my quite frequent misjudgement of sad evaluation) and I hate having to change it. In saying this, it requires the ability of acquiring one in the first place in order to attempt all of the aforementioned. The critical point here in North America is less the chain on its own but more finding compatible sprockets.

But let's go back to our journey. In Anchorage I was again faced with the decision if the chain is going to make it to the States (lower 48), which I courageously answer with a confident "Of course!" In Whitehorse, the only city on this endless journey through Nothingness, which spans thousands of miles, I am still somewhat optimistic. As we reach the worst bit of our travel (800 miles without even the smallest town), sure enough the trouble starts, and tense days follow. 60 miles before we reach the first small town, I notice that in the meantime several of the rollers are broken and the chain is starting to slide off the pins. No wonder it has been juddering and creaking along the way. The goddamn thing is in such bad condition that we have serious doubts that night if we are going to make it into the next town at all. All the possible alternatives at hand are not tempting, and we are worried when we get started the next day in pouring rain. These weather conditions are just perfect to get stuck on the side of a lonely country road with a broken chain.

Despite the persistent death rattle from "down there" we are lucky this time and manage to make it to the first little town called Smithers. The local Harley dealer turns out to be a nice guy and finds a suitable chain from the depths of his storeroom. With this replacement we at least manage to get to Prince George, where we're expected by a friend, who we met in the ADV Motorcycle Travels forum. Luckily, he was able to organise replacement sprockets for us, a cheer to the international (online) motorcyclist solidarity. After I successfully fitted everything and treated both bikes to an oil change, the world suddenly looked much brighter.

The "Lower 48"

The border crossing to the so-called "Lower 48" (+ Alaska + Hawaii = 50 States of America) is easy, after a dozen of questions we are found to be of sound nature and no threat to national security. It was worthwhile to keep the Alaska visa, even if this means that we only have 90 days for the entire route down to Mexico, which by our standards, doesn't seem to be too much.

We continue making our way along the East Coast, heading towards South, cruising on the legendary coastal road "One-o-one (101), crossing the San Francisco Bay Bridge and collecting some of the tourist 'Must See's" of the region along the way.

In the Valley of Death

On dirt roads we explore the Death Valley National Park. One who is prepared well and possesses detailed maps can easily spend a week here on isolated dirt tracks and discover pretty much everything from dilapidated mines, ghost towns and other exciting sights. It isn't recommended, though, to underestimate the dangers of this region. It is extremely hot, and the soaring temperatures of 40°C (104°F) in the shade are very tough on us in the days to come. But where is shade to be found, we wonder, finding ourselves stuck in the blazing sun all day. We stop at the Zabriskie Point and realise how extremely hard the heat of the last five hours in this fierce furnace has physically impacted on us. Despite constantly consuming water in large amounts, we have splitting headaches and feel exhausted. Remembering our first real sunstroke in Cuba, which was accompanied by dreadful vomiting, we decide with a heavy heart to shorten our remaining program for the day drastically. All we want to do is travel through the Death Valley, head towards South and to escape the heat as quickly as possible.

Apart from cloudy skies the air temperature seems to increase further in the next miles. We feel like being roasted alive, even the airflow whilst riding is unbearably hot. And then the extraordinary happens: Rain in the Death Valley. It pours down ferociously, and within one or two minutes raging torrents, carrying rocks and mud, are crossing the road. The reputation and warnings these torrents receive everywhere, suddenly become very realistic, especially in regards to the fact that only a few minutes of rain seem to have such consequences. We have to be very careful whilst riding, as several inch thick mud layers are not for the faint-hearted. In thin pants and T-Shirts we welcome being soaked whilst riding on, as it feels wonderful after the overheating of the past hours. Unfortunately our clothes dry way too fast.

Viva Las Vegas

Since having left Halifax behind over five months ago, we have not spoilt ourselves with a hotel stay. In light of the spectacular low room rates in Las Vegas throughout the week, we book four nights in a Casino hotel. We look forward to be able to do as we like in our own four walls for the length of our stay, which is completely different to being a guest in a private home, where you have to entertain and adjust to the hosts schedule throughout the day. In addition to this we feast ourselves on all the incredibly opulent and at the same time dirt-cheap all-you-can-eat buffets available.

The consequences of the all-you-can-eat buffet paradise Las Vegas

A visit to the infamous strip is an imperative. This glamorous world has to look hard for its equals, and we also are very impressed by all the light and magic.

Our very personal Las Vegas highlight is a punkrock bar called "Double Down Saloon", which is open 24 hours and densely populated by dubious characters. That was exactly what we like, and we are especially fascinated by the colourful mix of tattooed Rockabillys and Punks, all with a good dash of Las Vegas glamour.

Two weeks later we return to the City of Sin to collect some ordered spare parts, on which occasion we are inevitably drawn to this dubious establishment of excellence at night. Unfortunately our joy is only short-lived on that occasion, as so often in life, I neglect to listen to the warning words of my girlfriend, calling after me "Don't do that!" Two minutes later I am banned from the premises, I should've have refrained from asking the square-shouldered bouncer that particular question.

Canyon Land

No matter how much time you plan for a country or region and despite the apparently relaxed timeframe of a long-term-traveller, you always move on with a feeling of having missed a lot. This feeling has rarely been as strong as in our two weeks in Canyon land, the region at the "four-state-corner", including Arizona, New Mexico, Colorado and Utah, which is our favourite landscape in the US. Narrow gorges, wild nature, bare desert-like landscapes, rocks shining in numerous colours, natural stone bridges and so much more. Countless national parks with each one being better than the other, Coral Pink Sand Dunes, Zion National Park, Grand Canyon, Vermilion Cliffs, Monument Valley, Gooseneck State Park, Valley of the Gods, Natural Bridges, Glen Canyon, Lake Powell, Burr Trail, Capitol Reef and Bryce Canyon. The list is endless and still we are certain, as already mentioned earlier, that we surely haven't seen all of the many things in this incredible landscape, where you could spend months without getting bored.

Besides nature's sensations, there is also a good chunk of Western nostalgia as per cliché. Throughout the entire day we have seen cowboys that seem to have just sprung out of the big screen into our very personal movie set. In the evening then we find out what those cowboys were doing all day, namely herding the spring calves and penning them only a few yards from our tent. Those poor little calves moo heartbreakingly their souls out in their longing for their mom. They also moo in chorus. And they moo loud. They moo tirelessly, they moo without a break throughout the entire fuckin' night. Hell, can't wait to eat the next Hamburger!

South California

Even in the Mojave Desert it hits us: Rain again. We laugh hysterically about the non-desert-like déjà-vu.

With Route 66 we're getting another American road legend behind our wheels. Although just for few and with the feeling that we're kind of spoiling the myth with a travel-Enduro, as it seems to us that a Harley alone is acceptable here.

In San Diego we're again guests at the home of a motorcycle traveller to whom we have already had numerous Internet orders delivered to. Here we bring our bikes into shape again and also use the opportunity to get a medical check-up at the local hospital. We're simply too scared in terms of the Latin American health care system, which as we realise in hindsight, was totally unfounded. After this day in the "Emergency Room", we finally understand why all long-term foreign health insurances for the States and Canada request much higher premiums than for the rest of the world. After an admittedly very professional and friendly examination, and the results of a hernia diagnosis for me and a popliteal (baker's) cyst for Simon, we hold an invoice for an impressive amount of 7,500 USD in our hands, with 2,000 USD to be settled by credit card immediately. Mind you, this is an invoice for two examinations and not for the treatment of our conditions. Those are the moments where you start reading the small print of your insurance policy. Too often I've seen how insurances try to avoid their obligations by somewhat hidden clauses in the finer details of one's policy. Regarding the payback sum at stake here, we are very nervous, it's an amount we could travel with for many months.

We Are Far from Having Enough Yet!

When we set off on our trip, we tentatively planned two years and told everybody that we could also imagine having had enough after six months without viewing it as a failure. At least we had tried. However, after being on the road for six months now and having rode over 27,000 miles, we know that we are far from having enough yet.

Although long-term travelling surely isn't to be compared with holidaying and truly has its downsides at times, we do know that the life as "Motorcycle Vagabond" is simply wonderful. Never before have we felt so much freedom and happiness, never before have we had so much time for thought.

What we miss most definite are our families and friends. All the great encounters on our trip and the interesting hosts we meet can't even slightly replace the people we have known for a long time and whom we love dearly.

When travelling you start from scratch with each and everyone and "relationships" rarely last longer than a few days. That's when you sorely miss the people you have grown fond of in the course of your life (at home).

Tomorrow we're heading towards Mexico, which geographically still belongs to the larger part of North America but whose culture, language, food and drink we view as something very new and exotic. Finally, as during our six months in Canada and the US one felt more or less in the same West European culture. When we travel (South East) Europe, we cross borders every few days, hear new languages, pay with new currencies, eat diverse cuisines, and so on. Compared to that the last six months have not been very diverse.

We are undeterred by the fact that many Canadians and Americans, who by the way have never been to Mexico themselves, look at us in a horrified manner and warn us of impending doom when we reveal where our journey is taking us to next. We also feel that the extensive press coverage is exaggerated. The impressions we gain through conversations with motorcyclists, who are either regularly in Mexico or live near the border, are very different and far removed from the scaremongering of the media. There is no doubt that it may be dangerous in the Mexican-American border area, therefore we will be crossing the border early in the morning and travel as many miles as possible towards Baja California. We also ignore the warning information of our outdated travel guide, as some of the pictures painted sound rather promising such as "… they were forced to drink large amounts of alcohol in order to reveal the PIN of their credit cards…" It is amusing to think that they would shout us drinks, even though Simone's PIN isn't even safe from her in a sober state due to her general forgetfulness.

Jokes aside, it is undisputed that Mexico should not be underestimated, but we believe that with a little healthy respect and awareness, one has a good chance to travel the country undisturbed.

Bienvenidos a México!

"Welcome to Mexico" – no way! Rather than receiving a happy reception to entering Mexico, we roar unstopped into the land of Tequila. Irritated we stop at the side of the road and consult each other. For Europeans, who are spoilt by the Schengen Agreement and can cross borders without any controls, this might not pose a problem. Fact is, though, that the rest of the world generally requires an entry stamp without which any attempt of exiting the country again could cause major concerns. It also happens quite frequently that you have to apply for a visa beforehand, which in the case of Mexico, however, has not been necessary. Let's not forget all the paperwork for the motorbike. In most countries the "vehicle" (motorbikes are classified as two-wheel motor vehicle in some registration instances) has to be imported temporarily to then be exported again later. Some states even require specific customs documents (Carnet de Passage). This is one of the few reasons why bicycle-travellers have it a little easier.

To cut a long story short, without the necessary documentation and the according stamp, trouble is bound to happen. Therefore this means for us to ride back and get the lazy, discontent official to take his eyes off the soap opera on his mini-screen for a few precious minutes to serve us. This is unfortunately a typical scenario for Latin America, which we will experience first-hand on numerous occasions in the next 15 months. Work ethic is a loose morality here, and by the end of our Central and South American leg we will hate the expression "mañana" with a passion. Literally translated it means "tomorrow", which de facto means "until the cows come home" in Latin America.

Mexico – a Feast for the Senses

We love to discover a country, and only with great effort we can focus on the road. There are just too many exciting things to see to the left and the right. We're absorbing every detail and are full to the brim with all the new impressions when we get the chance to stop somewhere and have a chat. Have you seen this? Did you realise that? That was awesome… and so on and on. In the end it came down to the luck of draw to decide who has the privilege to be the first one to inspect the range of goods in the supermarket, as one of us, no matter in which country, always stays with the packed motorbikes.

We're relieved by the prices in Mexico. It is significantly cheaper than in Europe, Canada and the US, where, despite being frugal and very disciplined when it came to expenditure, still took us above our originally set budget. To give you an example, two pounds of bananas are 23 US cents, and particularly exciting as one of our biggest cost factors, is one litre of petrol (=1/4 gallon) for 0.57 USD.

However, before we can stock up on exciting and unfamiliar groceries and liquor, we still have to get our hands on some pesos, which proves to be slightly difficult. The first four ATMs reject our credit cards and on the fifth attempt, when it seems to show mercy, it so happens that Simone forgot her PIN. Wasn't I just joking about this before?

Our first campsite costs us 4 dollar, including a premier view. We bravely take up the challenge with the local cuisine and cook a cactus ratatouille on our gas cooker. The slightly sour cactus (from the supermarket, not personally harvested) goes perfectly with the various types of chili, the zucchini, onions and tomatoes. A finely chopped chorizo sausage gives everything that special something. What a banquet, enhanced with Mexican red wine and brandy. No luxury hotel with a starred restaurant could make us happier tonight. Complementing the culinary pleasure and our upbeat mood, we are also treated to a first-class sunset. Happy and content about this being our current life, we know that we don't require anything else. It's an incredible luxury whose greatest challenge is to not overlook it.

Baja California

The 750-miles long Baja California Peninsula is very American. Many of the Mexicans here speak English and meeting Americans, who are residing here permanently, is everyday life.

We're following a rough road, which was an insider tip from our host in San Diego. The track may be a delight on a lightweight motocross bike, but for our heavy-loaded wannabe Enduros it is hard work. The conditions are consistently getting worse, however, you probably know the feeling that turning around is not an option anymore once at that point. After all you are already aware of how bad that stretch of road is going to be, furthermore this would equal to admitting failure. Hence you just keep riding, absolutely conscious of your misfortune.

Finding a spot near the water, where we can camp wild, doesn't prove to be a problem here. It is so remote that you can safely consider leaving your bathing suits behind when going for a swim. Wild donkeys and coyotes are the only ones who see us in our Adam and Eve outfits.

The daily grind continues the next day. Sweat is pouring down, and we stop every half an hour to drink water and give our motorbikes some rest in what little shade there is.

Depressing, to say the least, is that apparently a beautiful asphalt road is to be built here soon, which also means that the infamous rally Baja 1000 will then have to look for another route. Again and again we are overtaken at breakneck speed by two and four wheeled vehicles, which obviously belong to the rally occurring here in a few weeks. Besides all the dust we have to eat, we also hurt a little in the realisation that this miserable rocky piece of road can obviously be tackled in a much better way by experienced players.

Back on the Mex1 we enjoy rolling along hassle-free over an impeccable surface and soaking in the breathtaking view of the cactus landscape, which the Baja is so famous for. When the sun begins to drop, we head into the desert a few hundred yards, which is riddled with numerous different cacti types. One of the most atmospheric camping grounds we've ever been at.

Here's to the One Who Saves His Data

I just want to cry. For the last two days I desperately tried saving my netbook, which after defragmenting the hard drive, decided to come to an abrupt halt. By now I have shot all my powder and start unnervingly to search for a professional in the high-tech-desert Mexico. By the way, annoying but important, always make sure to save your data. How many times have we met people on our trip, who lamented about the loss of their entire photo collection as well as videos after their cameras were stolen or their data carrier was damaged. Old age, heat, water, vibration and many other things could cause the latter, hence you should regularly and at least once, if not rather twice, save a backup of your photos, videos and other important data. One should already develop a procedure whilst still at home, considering the data amount, as videos and hi-res images accumulate a lot of memory space, and also how you will save your date. For example uploading content to the web and such may work perfectly with a high-performance network at home, but will prove totally useless with public WiFi, or when in developing countries. PINs and passwords can easily be protected via encrypting software or at least be filed as image with an innocuous file name, so harmful programs can't find them easily or auto-select them.

Because of its complexity, I can merely touch on the subject, besides it may be far from exciting for most. Nonetheless I can't stress enough the difference a little bit of pre-dedication can make, as when disaster strikes on the road, it will become an incredibly frustrating affair. It's not a question of if disaster will strike than more when will it be.

A related topic is never to travel with one credit card alone. It is a must to have at least two, three or even four, preferably Visa as well as Mastercard. Apart from technical defects on the card, there will always be problems with some card types and banks throughout various countries. It goes without saying that ideally you should not keep all the cards in the same place in order to avoid giving thieves the chance to ruin you entirely. We have heard many a sad tale of travellers, who ended up in nasty situations and were only able to access their accounts after long and arduous efforts.

Lucha Libre

Whilst my netbook is in repair, we use the chance to join some locals at Lucha Libre. Apparently the Mexican version of wrestling has a much longer tradition than its American counterpart. It is a unique spectacle and we have great fun! The fact that the actors surely don't play in the top league, doesn't do any harm, quite to the contrary, it adds value to the entertainment. Sometimes the whole scenario comes across rather slapstick-like, and more than once the show continues in the ranks of the audience, which first and foremost delights the children attending. The top acts consist of a dwarf (it should be duly noted that you have to be considerably short to be classified a dwarf in midst all the already short Mexicans) and a skeleton, which uses every opportunity to force his enemy into anal or oral sex in an unambiguous manner. To describe it in less detail simply wouldn't suit the occasion, and I wonder all the time how some parents may have a hard time answering some of the questions their offspring may have.

Copper Canyon

We take the ferry to the Mexican mainland, and a few days later we find ourselves at the edge of Barranca del Cobre. We had already seen an amateur film about these canyons at the motorcycle meet-up in Canada, and are completely aware of what awaits us: 6,000 feet into the canyon via a narrow gravel road, all the way through endless serpentines (without guardrail, mind you). The place, thanks to a slightly intoxicated state I found myself in and newfound bravery due to that, immediately fulfilled me with great enthusiasm and became the only fixed spot in our travel plan south of the US. It seemed more like a typical men-have-to-prove-something-to-themselves-idiotic-idea to Simone. The persistent questioning of numerous people in the last months also didn't get us anywhere as reports ranged from "no problem whatsoever" to "absolutely impossible with your machines". In order to avoid a second Prudhoe Bay trauma we decide to give it a go.

Apropos, the Copper Canyon (Barranca del Cobre) is a series of 20 canyons, which together are larger than the significantly more known Grand Canyon in the US. Nine of the canyons within the Copper Canyon are even deeper than their American companion. To be accurate, it may be worth to mention that the renowned descent doesn't go into the Copper Canyon but into the Batopilas Canyon, at which end you also find the small town of the same name. We carefully heave a sigh of relief, even for a dirt road it was in reasonable condition. Nonetheless it may not be everybody's favourite discipline to slide downhill gravel roads in sharp turns. When you finally put 6,000 feet behind you, you most likely have lost some sweat over it. An extreme change of climate is the final straw, with pleasant 20°C (68°F) up top throughout the day and temperatures clearly below zero in the night, whereas the climate is subtropical in the valley.
When we finally reach the small town of Batopilas after two hours of straight riding (plus several water and photo breaks as well as the usual military checks), we are sweaty and filthy, but beam with happiness and immense pride. We have to admit that we weren't sure if we could live up to this adventure, but tackling something one initially felt unable to cope with, gives an unbelievably good feeling and an extra dash of courage for future challenges. These are the experiences we had hoped for on our travels.

Batopilas seems like a nice, peaceful little village to us, but the harsh reality looks different with six homicides in the last few years, entirely executed by drug cartels or political motivations. All those murders are unsolved, and we suppose that the local police, which is armed to the teeth, seems to be primarily busy with hanging out in front of their station, conveniently located opposite our hotel. 70% of the population live off Marihuana cultivation, and occasional prostitution amongst young Latinas seems to be no rarity. The girls are going for the boys with (drug) money and coke, which inevitably produces minors with children, who get left behind. This is one of the drawbacks of Mexico. Batopilas, however, is a friendly and peaceful place for us, where the future in form of cars and TVs lives an interesting co-existence with the past, such as cowboys on horses, cows everywhere in the streets and indigenous people in their traditional dress.

Love Motels

We have already heard about the love motels, and today we want to try one. You can see them in the outskirts of every bigger city in Mexico, and they are frequented by many young people, who generally aren't that young anymore when they finally move out of home, or for infidelity, the latter being as common in Mexico as a second or third family.

We are excited, a clean room for a fair price. And the best is that to every room on the first floor belongs a lockable garage underneath. For globetrotters it couldn't be more comfortable as you can simply leave your entire luggage on the motorcycle without having to worry.

To our surprise cold beer comes at cheap prices and is delivered via room service through a discreet chute into our private paradise, which by all means and thanks to a slightly disreputable vibe, radiates an erotic ambiance. The list of available stimulants that can be ordered conveniently by phone, range from alcohol to sex toys in various shapes and forms. Despite the reports of other motorcycle travellers, unfortunately our cable TV has no porn channels, and also the table dance pole is missing. Other than that our love motel experience couldn't have been more perfect. Maybe it was better that way, as I don't even want to imagine the wounds and back strains that could have resulted from possible pole acrobatics under the influence of alcohol.

Police Raid in Guadalajara

We criss-cross through the country and indulge in Mexico's beautiful side before heading towards Guadalajara.
Guadalajara is known, right? To be honest, we had never heard of Mexico's second-largest city before, a city with 9 Million people in the greater area, as much as in the four largest cities of Germany. Something, that we will encounter many more times on our trip around the world. Mega cities against which German metropolis seem like small villages, rivers that are significantly larger than the Rhine and the Danube, Europe's second-largest river, mountains that are much higher than the Alps, and so much more that makes you realise how little we ultimately know about our planet.
Our first impression of Guadalajara is that things are significantly different to the countryside in terms of traffic. In addition to the generally chaotic and aggressive style of driving, local interpretations regarding traffic law now also make our life more difficult, i.e. principally East-West traffic has priority to North-South traffic. To this already difficult regulation, there are numerous non-signed exceptions, which only seem to be known to the locals. It seems to us that the person, who just starts driving wholeheartedly, has priority. This is a tactic, which proves incredibly successful in the years to come, but becomes a habit very hard to break after our return home.

Former Cologne resident and now in exile, Chris, welcomes us warmly, and we spontaneously join him at a Punk concert on our first night. This turns out to be an illegal event, which doesn't seem to be unusual here. The event location is promptly stormed by heavily armed police, which indicates to all present "ID out and hands against the wall!" As per usual and due to my ever-present worry of losing or having stolen my passport, I don't have it on me. Whether because of mercy or fear of international implications, the team leader orders my immediate release after a little back and forth. I breathe a sigh of relief, a night in a Mexican prison might have been good as an anecdote but still it is an experience I can easily do without. Emerging relatively unscathed, we find the operation highly entertaining shortly after. That's world stage cinema, to say the least. Later, in a nice pub we flush down the affair with beer and spirits and review this little adventure from various perspectives.

State of Emergency

We travel at a leisurely pace and use the opportunity to look at the bigger picture. Snorkelling is fantastic, the excursions on horseback, though, are not really our thing, which is something we agree on after several attempts.

In terms of tourism, Mexico has a lot to offer, however, most of the time it seems to us exactly that, just a tad touristy. Cute little mountain towns with their small alleyways look wonderful, thanks to their one-way street regulations, they become a regular nightmare in finding accommodation via motorcycle.

In Angangueo, we experience the opposite of vertical fireworks during fiesta, when spark-spraying fireworks racks are carried through the crowd. It buzzes and hisses, smokes and bangs everywhere around us and from pretty much every imaginable direction. Our skin is scorched in countless spots and we have to squint. "Inferno-like" is the word that comes to mind spontaneously, and yet the fiesta is heaps of fun.

From there we move on to explore the Monarch Butterfly Sanctuary, where we marvel at millions of delicate butterflies, hanging in trees in large numbers. Upon returning into town, we find it deserted, which is profoundly different to the day before. All shops are closed, and there are barely any people or cars on the streets. However, the next morning everything seems to be as per usual until the guy from the tourist information catches us on the street and explains the background with a worried expression on his face. After the arrest of their leader, criminal associations had distributed flyers, announcing various campaigns. 20 people had been shot the day before and the so-called group had positioned trucks and busses as roadblocks before burning them down. The man seems genuinely worried and urges us to leave the province IMMEDIATELY. As his behaviour has shifted and is very different to the day before, when he praised every possible sight in the surrounding area, this comes across even more haunting.

We just rode a few miles when we arrive at a large-scale police check. At a road crossing a couple of dozen police officers in bulletproof vests check cars whilst policemen dug behind sandbags point their rifles at us. This feels a little more intense than the military controls which we had already gotten used to, even my body check turns out to be uncommonly rough and very thorough. A local explains the circumstances later that for ordinary citizens the provinces are the safest place to be, if the local drug lord remains untouched there. But if police and the military manage to arrest one of the heads of the crime gang, this leads to retribution as the one we have just experienced before, and a bloody internal power struggle between leading individuals flares up, often also killing civilians.

Is Mexico Dangerous?

In light of over 10,000 deaths this year alone the answer to this question may feel inclined to be YES. However, a closer look reveals that most of these are victims of gang wars or wars between criminals and the government. If not accidentally at the wrong time in the wrong place, a civilian does not have to fear much. A Mexican reassured us recently with a very vivid example: We wouldn't have to fear genuine drug smuggling gangsters as they make big bucks with their lucrative businesses and surely had better things to do than stealing old Enduro boots from two grubby motorcycle vagabonds. Makes sense!

Whereas camping wild on dirt roads and clearings could be dangerous by all means as there could be a smuggling route, which is frequented by comrades at night, who first shoot before asking any questions. We were also advised against taking souvenir photos of Marihuana plantations as these are generally guarded.
The best way is to analyse possible dangers in order to understand if these are relevant for you as a (motorcycle) traveller and if the critical region is actually located on your route. In light of this many an alert by the ministry of foreign affairs appears to be only half as bad.

Generally, when it comes to crime, a healthy dose of common sense and a certain feel for travelling, which will grow with increasing travel experience, will get you through quite well. Understandably, anyone who decides to represent his status by strutting through a Latin American city, or even the wrong district, with an expensive camera around the neck and a valuable watch on the wrist, shouldn't be surprised if his/her items of luxury find a new owner.

Moloch Mexico City

Initially we didn't want to inflict ourselves with Mexico City. This mega city with 20 million people isn't just the biggest city of the world alone, it's also renowned for its absolutely congested streets, its chaotic traffic and, due to its location, its heavy smog. These are all arguments not to go there. Nonetheless, we simply couldn't resist Garry's invitation. "Garry's Hostel" isn't really a hostel in the truest meaning of the term, he just enthusiastically accommodates motorcycle travellers on a purely private and free basis.

The word of a warm welcome and the opportunity of easily being able to stay for a few days or even for weeks had gotten around. It would surely take Garry and his wife Yvonne a while to remember all the countries from which motorcycle travellers had visited in the last few years. We stay five days and have difficulties to attach each individual name to all sons, daughters, friends, mothers-in-law, renters and dogs within this generally not very big house. Furthermore, there is a Welsh as well as a Ukrainian motorcycle traveller present, so to say that life here is lively, would be a sheer understatement.

We only dare the several hour-long-journey into the city centre by public transport, because our host patiently explains the complicated system to us, which almost seems incomprehensible to visitors. Besides sightseeing, the taking care of our shopping and to-do-list are, as per usual, also on the program. At home many things are simply easier to deal with, there you know exactly where to get things, and also to get those at good prices. In a foreign country simple sourcing literally turns into the proverbial search for a needle in a haystack at first sight. If it wouldn't be so frustrating, we could almost acquire a taste for it. We infrequently get to know entire cities by being sent from Señor A to Señora B, the latter who also doesn't have the searched for item, but is very sure in her assumption that Señor C at the other end of town would surely have it. In happy times we lovingly call it "spare parts ping pong", in frustrating moments this looks entirely different.

Including a detour to a motorcycle retailer, we accumulate 100km on the day we are leaving this so-called Molloch of city. This might not sound as much, but counts as one of the worst days in my life as a motorcycle vagabond. We make our way through the metropolitan area, traffic jam, traffic jam and more traffic jam. We ride over hundreds of "Topes", which are speed bumps to keep people driving at reduced speed. On this day we have to engage and disengage our clutches so often that we have no control over our forearms anymore, all this in an

altitude of 7,000 to 10,500 feet, and most of all including all the terrible smog.
At night we're exhausted and feel downright sick, the dry coughs will follow us for many days.

A German Pest and Mexican Hospitality

There is a campsite in Teotihuacán, a small town with pyramids of the same name. Not necessarily a rarity, but rather uncommon in Mexico. We are happy to finally find some sleep in our new home and not having to communicate with hosts for once. Our excitement proves to be too premature, we have barely started setting up our tent, when we are joined by an extremely talkative East German retiree, who's camper van is parked within a stone's throw of us. In addition to his life story, we also learn within a short period of time about anything that's shit in Mexico, and this place in particular. This long-time traveller is so negative, that we seriously have difficulties contemplating why he didn't stay home in the first place and saved himself from the efforts and burdens of travelling through the USA and Mexico. Even at dinnertime we are not safe and he bombards us with stories as well as descriptive details on his admittedly terrible medical history, which consists of awful skin rashes and bloody raw soles. Only upon us requesting repeatedly to at least let the topic go whilst we're eating, he gives it a rest. There are many types of people in the world…

The pyramids of Teotihuacán are the third largest in the world by the way, and despite the intrusive vendors, which are pestering us at every step they are definitely worth a visit.

Unfortunately we are deprived of another Mexico highlight, the street leading through Iztaccihuatl and Popocatépetl. The latter belongs to one of the most active volcanoes in the world and currently does its reputation justice, which is the reason why the road is closed indefinitely. Frustrated we just sit down at the barrier and have a picnic. A little boy brings us cheese as a gift, whilst the eight-member family belonging to him waves at us and gives us the thumbs up. In the end we take pictures of the entire family and our motorbikes. The father, who is also a motorcyclist, proudly applies our "motorcycle vagabond" sticker on his windscreen. Experiences like these lift the spirits.

Christmas under Palm Trees

We spend Christmas in a cute little village by the Pacific Ocean, which is populated by surfers, young hippies, dropouts and young backpackers. Despite getting accustomed for weeks to the bustle before Christmas, which by the way does not differ much from the craziness in Germany, Christmas under palm trees feels pretty strange.

Crossing from North to South America at the Isthmus of Tehuantepec, where both oceans are only separated by 120 miles, has no significant practical impact as such, but has high symbolic value for us personally. Instead of giving in to our elation, full attention is required. There's such a stiff breeze down here that locals recommend us to wait and only travel on over the worst leg in the less windy morning hours. It now also dawns on us why the next city is called "The Windy."

The road to Palenque is splendid, curve after curve and jungle everywhere, continually interrupted by vibrantly coloured rivers. We finally feel of having arrived in Central America, not just in a geographical sense but also scenically. The fact that this leg seems to belong to the prettiest of the countries is emphasised by more than a dozen motorcycle travellers, who cross our way within a few hours, more than we have met in the last two months in the entirety of Mexico.

On Long-Term Travel with Children

In Palenque, where we would like to camp for the next three nights, we are welcomed by a funny Swiss couple in their 60's, who have been travelling through Mexico for the last three years in their Mercedes truck with cabin on their way to South America. We also meet a family of four in their Polo station wagon with German number plates, who, as their eldest son had to start secondary school this year, took it as the opportunity to go on the road again for a year. When he apparently was at the age of the now youngest (before school age), they had already travelled with him on motorbikes. Astonished we learn that even this trip had actually been planned with two motorbikes, but one week before departure the shipping company, who had promised to ship their motorbikes from Egypt to Mexico after their East European/North African leg, had increased the costs exorbitantly, which put an end to their motorbike plans. Without further ado they reorganised the entire journey from motorbike to car within a few days, that's what I call fighting spirit. It is a shame that this fascinating family is already leaving the following morning and that we cannot talk with them a bit longer.

Speaking of, they are not the only ones doing it this way. On our trip we have already met families with school aged children several times. However, Germans are far outnumbered, although quite possibly for the reason that it is bureaucratically very difficult to home-school children in our home country. In France or Canada this proves much easier, and hence the numbers of "travelling families" of those nations is considerably higher.

Spewing into the New Year

The reason for heading towards Palenque is the historic Maya ruins, which are interesting by itself but have an even more special atmosphere with the jungle surrounding. We celebrate the New Year with Ingolf, an eccentric but very likeable motorcycle traveller, who is from Simone's region in Germany. In true love of our homeland, we already kick off with the first beer at 5pm local time, as it is midnight in our home country then. Consequently we just manage to reach the local New Year's finishing line. For a New Years morning we feel surprisingly well, actually the best ever, we feel in top shape. Somehow it still takes up to almost lunch time until we finally get going. When we then quickly stop at the supermarket to buy travel provisions, I suddenly don't feel that great anymore. Sweat flows profusely from my forehead and I feel dizzy, which I blame on the hot, humid jungle climate. When we stop an hour later to get petrol, I am so exhausted that I inform Simone "We take the next motel, even if it is only 1pm. I just can't go on any longer…" And of course Murphy's Law sets in, as ironically there's no motel in sight or even a spot, where we could set up our tent. Minutes feel like hours. At some stage I can't go on anymore and we have to stop somewhere in the middle of nowhere. I can only get off the motorbike with great effort as my sense of balance is shot, and I let myself drop on the roadside. When I still don't feel any better an hour later, Simone leaves to find accommodation somewhere. As the devil would have it, I'm finding myself on fenced private land with free-roaming cattle, which is not exactly the best spot to camp wild. During Simone's absence I feel worse and have to vomit heavily a few times. After an endless seeming one and a half hours she comes rattling back and declares to my horror that I would have to ride 15 miles to the next hotel. I don't feel capable of that at all, I'm sweating like crazy, I have temperature, a racing heart and breathing difficulties.

Those are the challenging moments on a trip, when you don't want to carry on anymore and also believe that you can't. But one has no choice and simply has to. Grit your teeth and hope for the best, which is easily said if you don't find yourself amid the mess. The 15 miles to the next hotel are the most difficult and longest I have ever ridden, and in hindsight I am glad we didn't just camp on the spot on the side of the road as I'm having a few mishaps in my feverish doze. To experience that in motorcycle pants and sleeping bag would've been a nightmare. Like this I can at least have a shower, where the world's best nurse helps with her best endeavours to clean me up in my weakened state.

After two days I am out of the woods and we continue into the direction of the Caribbean. My legs still feel like rubber and my stomach is far from being in its orderly state, but we roll again and that's the most important.

When I write a few friends about my experience, it turns out that two of them had been caught out with the same thing at exactly the same place. One had been lying in his excrements for days as he reports, which makes me realise again what an asset it is to travel as a couple. This won't be the last time that I am extremely glad about Simone's presence in such moments. More than once in the following years I would've simply fallen by the wayside without her there.

The Yucatan Peninsula

As so often happens, the search for spare parts forces us on an unpleasant detour, this time into the part of the Yucatan Peninsula, which we absolutely wanted to avoid. Playa del Carmen is the gate to the tourist zone with its most famous and notorious location Cancun. The city is almost worse than we had feared. In the last hours of daylight we arduously look for halfway affordable accommodation and finally end up in the courtyard of a hostel out of necessity, the only opportunity to camp in this city. After our tent is set up in close proximity with the other tents in the overcrowded courtyard, the originally agreed rate is blatantly increased, but it's not only us who are ripped off. What can you do, the tent is up and it is dark by now - pull down the tent again and showing them the finger? In addition to this misery, joints are circling and there is tireless chatter in close proximity throughout the entire night. I'm really getting too old and particularly intolerant to that stuff. I wishfully think back to the deserted North of Canada, where we indeed worried about bears, but those at least don't suffer from verbal diarrhoea in Italian or Hebrew. The following day we are happy to say farewell. Without problems we find a Honda dealer, who to our surprise has everything we need. Even at the hardware store I get the right aluminium seals and screws, which for Mexican standards is an incredibly swift success. Further south the Peninsula becomes bearable and we enjoy a few beautiful last days in Mexico, which we liked, but which, all in all, surely doesn't count to the most exciting motorbike travel destination for us.

Our last official act is to make laminated colour copies of our papers, which we can then hand out to (possibly corrupt) border cops in Central America. Should they try to force us into bribes as per usual scam, we will happily surrender these documents. Such a plump deceit would be unthinkable in Germany, but we have heard that this always seems to work in Central America. We'll see...

Caribbean Flair in Belize

We're already looking forward to this country, which was called British Honduras until 1981. It is a complete mystery to us how many Pan-American travellers leave it out entirely or hurry through it in only one day.
Compared with its neighbours, it is an expensive country, admittedly. But everything we have heard about Belize in the run-up sounds so

interesting that we must see it with our own eyes. For example, it is the only country in Central America that uses English as their official language, which is an unfamiliar feeling for us to be able to understand everything again.

Even the people are rather unusual for Central America, most of them are quite dark, almost black, which, especially at the coast, has a true Caribbean feel to us. Besides Latinos you also repeatedly see white men in overalls and cowboy hats and white women in dark dresses with straw hats, which are called "Mennonites", and which we have already become aware of in Canada and Mexico. Being pacifists and not willing to join the army and because they refused to pay taxes, they left The Netherlands in the sixteenth century. On their quest to find a land, where they could live by their own perceptions, they first settled in Prussia, then in Russia, Canada, Mexico, and from the 1950's onward also in Belize, where they, as everywhere else, successfully and profitably carry out agriculture. Their refusal to pay taxes makes Mennonites almost likeable, but the way they farm their lands is quite debatable. They apparently use pesticides and growth hormones at an extremely high level and farm anything that brings in money. We were at least told pretty much everywhere that they would also plant and sell Marihuana, which makes us wonder if it is truth or envy?

The intriguing mixture alone of some Latinos, Blacks, and in addition to this Mennonites and a few Chinese, who seem to own almost every supermarket, is worth a visit to Belize. Besides, the country size measures ten times the area of the European country Luxembourg but has only 300,000 inhabitants, whereas, just to compare, Luxembourg sums up to half a million after all. Belmopan, the capital city of Belize, is even the smallest capital city of the world with its 15,000 residents.

Enough now with dry facts, let's go! And in saying this we do so with a false start in terms of cash withdrawal. Simone's ATM card, which we had specifically activated from Mexico at her bank for all of Central and South America, feels out of its service area again. A call to the call centre proves to be rather difficult as the telecommunications monopolist has blocked Skype in Belize. Hence, all that is left is a normal phone call at exorbitant charges, which quickly elevates the blood pressure. The service centre agent namely gives us account over the fact that Belize, as former English colony, is now classified as EU member in their database and therefore our card activation for Central America does not cover the country we're currently in.

Welcome to Absurdistan, please take a very deep breath before you keep on talking. This is not supposed to be the last drama we have to experience with that financial institution.

Attention: Whilst on the road one can close a bank account, but no new check or credit card account can be opened, as verification of one's identity needs to be undertaken in the home country according to the Money Laundering Act. Therefore, never go travelling with one bank account only. We know cases, in which travellers, who made this mistake, suddenly found themselves in big trouble.

In Hopkins, a small town at the coast, we feel like being in the picture book impression of the Caribbean, and this not only because of the entirely black community. We enjoy this much better than the Mexican coast of the Caribbean. We camp in the shade of trees, which are five yards from the beach at most, simply wonderful. Our host is a friendly, even though eccentric ageing hippie from New York, who lives here with Elvis, her indigenous lover. The latter, however, proves to be exhausting, a "quarterly drinker" (alcoholic with recurring drinking excess) as we would call him in German slang, who is entirely wasted from morning to night in the four days we spend there. Apparently this is no rarity in this area, as we learn, and our overall impression of the male counterpart of the population is rather poor. Many seem to have a natural aversion towards honest work but more so a particular soft spot for cruel animal torture, dope and alcohol until they drop.

The second largest reef in the world, the Barrier Reef, attracts many tourists to the Caribbean nation, and the snorkelling trip with our little boat keeps us far behind our expectations of this natural wonder.

An anecdote on the side is that we make the acquaintance of a one-eyed

Israeli, a sociable fellow who doesn't leave us untouched. At one point the conversation revolves around earning money whilst travelling. When I ask him if the well-paying job in California, which he just happens to mention, was of illegal nature or actually on a tax card, he answers with a complacent smile "I had an Uzi and guarded a Marihuana field. Does this answer your question about the tax card?"

On the modest road infrastructure we explore the inland and spend a couple of nice days here and there. The final score we give the place is that Belize is definitely pretty, but not necessarily a country you have to have travelled once in a lifetime.

Guatemala – A Country Governed by Laziness

The entry into Belize still fell under the category of warm-up training, we now face the "real" Central American border. As ludicrous as it may sound I am looking forward to this challenge. Leaving Belize works just fine, you can tell that the English inheritance has a positive impact on overall procedures. However, immigration into the Guatemalan side puts a sudden end to this. The official responsible for the import of our motorcycles refuses to work as the bridge leading over the border is closed until 7pm due to construction works. And how exactly does that make any sense? Surely his shift would've ended by then and we would be forced to spend the night in no man's land, so why not process us already? It is not to be the last time that I clench my fist in my pocket at a Central American border whilst I try to motivate my opponent with the witty application of my charm to do his job. We are sent into the next town to make copies, mind you, by foot of course, as the bridge is closed. Upon my return, Señor Workshy has become sparse, but after a long search I find a friendly colleague of his, who after initial hesitation, agrees to look into our matter. The initial verdict is that we need more copies, which, against the utter attempts of make believe by the "lazy one", can actually be made around the corner without having to walk into the next town. At some stage everything is filled in properly and we hold the import certificates in our hands. Now, there are only the bridge constructions that stand in between us and Guatemala. Lo and behold, even this does not prove an issue anymore, as there is a detour that has actually been in place for the entire day. What a miserable "Baron Münchhausen" (Baron of Lies) at customs!

Despite the annoyance we are a little proud to have mastered our first test in terms of Latin American borders, and personally I enjoyed the entire affair as well. As long as something like that does not get out of control, I find it quite amusing and challenging. Besides that I secretly enjoy working myself up.

Tikal

First we head towards the attraction per se, Tikal, the most famous Maya ruins of an ancient city found in a rainforest in Guatemala. The 17 USD per person really rubs us the wrong way, as it is a horrendous amount for regional prices. In a radius of thousand miles there is no tourist attraction similarly expensive as such, but in the end we pay after all and don't regret it. If you're early, the visitor numbers keep within bearable limits. Tikal does not only fascinate with its first class architecture and pyramids but also with its vast size, the jungle setting and the lush animal life, which all top it off as a special extra.

Cave Tours for the Brave

On the Finca Ixobel we meet the four-member family again and have long discussions with these relaxed and fascinating people.
By the way, the finca follows a concept, which we have often come

across in our time in Mexico, where there is a variety of accommodation on offer, ranging from hotel rooms, cabañas (little huts) and tree houses to the opportunity to camp or simply hang up your hammock (which seems to be quite common).

The fact that an armed guard patrols here in the early evening might speak for itself, something we have never encountered in Mexico or Belize.

For an extremely fair price we join one of the best cave tours we have ever undertaken, namely one that takes us through the water most of the time. Armed with a headlamp, swim trunks and robust sandals we swim, wade and climb two long hours through the water. When stream levels are higher you even have to dive, what a fantastic experience! With all the wonder and excitement, nobody really notices the water temperature as unpleasant or whinges about all the pointy rocks. That we all carry away a few minor blemishes in the end only seems appropriate to such an adventure. The best for last, on the way in our guide places burning candles here and there, so that everything is illuminated spookily on our way back. Our tip is that you definitely have to do one of these tours, if you're in the area, it's a grand cinema experience.

Si Claro – Environmental-Friendly Disposal of Toxic Substances

In El Estor, which is located at a picturesque lake, we find a simple hotel room for 7 USD. The place is, of course, very basic and there's barely any more room than for the bed. We also haven't had warm water for a long time, so we're not really bothered by the lack of it. Anyhow, no reason for any complaints here, as these basic standards are completely sufficient for us. That the promised Internet is non-existent is annoying, but here it just often goes like that. That it is the noisiest room that we have ever had (since Mexico the measuring stick is lousily low) also isn't very tragic. For one we have got pretty used to sleeping with any kind of noise, on the other hand we will be grateful in the days to come to have a hotel room after all and not to be trapped in a tent, sick to death and with tropical steady rain.

We bath beneath hot waterfalls, paddle our canoes through gorges and are seemingly presented as guest stars by the solo entertainer on the opening ceremony of the local Honda dealer. We don't understand a word, which still doesn't keep Simone from ending up on stage.

After the free amusement program comes the obligatory work, the technical service on our motorcycles is an annoying part of everyday life on the journey. We've been looking for suitable brake fluid for our ABS brakes for weeks, and of all things we strike it rich in this dump. By good old-fashioned manual method we change the brake fluid on both bikes, a tedious task but it works.

The last act of the technical service of the day lies in the matter that Simone insists on the correct disposal of the old brake fluid. I only shake my head, but refrain from any cynical remark about the hopelessness of such an endeavour. With the help of gibberish and pantomime, Simone has the honour to drop the old brake fluid at the store, where we bought the new one, for professional and appropriate disposal. With a dumbfounded look on their face, the guys agree with a friendly "si claro", which at times and incidentally has a similar meaning as the popular double affirmation "Yes, yes" amongst wives and girlfriends. I don't have any illusions about the disposal method and am glad that they did not yet request payment for their pseudo service.

Life Endangering Radical Diet

I have been feeling worse for most of the day, and in the evening I lie flat with a fever. Even after three days I'm not feeling better. Despite extreme amounts of fluids, the dehydration symptoms are massive. On the morning of the fourth day it is so bad that I get scared. My body is burning, pain in the form of lightning bolts are exploding in my head in a cycle of seconds and alarm signals from my heart make the visit to a doctor inevitable. Without Simone's urging, I would have probably closed myself off from this insight, with most likely near fatal consequences.

To literally "go" to the doctor is unthinkable of, and Simone just barely manoeuvres me into a taxi and to a doctor she had already arranged. Thanks to a detailed description of the symptoms in the usual mix of gibberish and pantomime, he finds out in no time that I have urethritis, an inflammation of the urethra. My urologist at home would've tested my urine for that, but a missing microscope was compensated by a big dash of confidence by this good ol' man. And I have to admit that his diagnosis seemed reasonable to me. That's why I had to urinate something like 20 times a day for the last three days. And the best with the diagnosis is that a quick cure is possible via an immediate antibiotic injection, then another one a day later, and then pills for the next eight days. This means a more or less quick end to my miserable suffering and no onward transport to Guatemala City. I'd love to fling my arms around this man's neck, but it isn't quite over yet as Simone has to hurry through the rain again later to get him for a house visit, so he can give me a second injection for the pain. All I was left to do was whimper with headaches, which for the very first time gave me an insight on how migraine sufferers must feel.

Speaking of rain, whilst I was lying flat it has rained non-stop for days. The heavens opened and water was pouring down in amounts we have never witnessed before back home in Germany. It is a blessing in disguise for us as for one, the road from here onward is over dirt roads, which means we couldn't have moved on anyway, and two, thankfully the temperature dropped down to an almost bearable level. I can hardly imagine how I would've been able to endure the four days of high fever in the usual local tropical temperatures.

After the worst is over, our mood is back to its best and our wanderlust is as strong as ever. Mind you, it'll still take a few days until I'm all up and running, ready to tackle the next challenging stage of our journey. Among other things I'm facing the unusual assignment to stock up on reserves, as I have lost 14kg since embarking on our adventure. All this in this month alone due to both hefty illnesses, it might be worth a mention that the last time I was that light was when I was a teenager.

With every day I'm feeling a little better. Although I'm far from my former physical condition, the restlessness drives us on further. Firstly, we're confronted with a problem as the continuous rain of the last few days, paired with the local temperatures, has been worse to our machines in terms of rust than nonstop-usage through an entire

European Winter in Germany. Above all, both ignition switches are stuck and will no turn anymore. This is an extremely tedious issue as already before our trip around the world Simone's ignition switch repeatedly kept getting stuck, forcing us to exchange it on warranty in the end. This would prove difficult to almost impossible where we are, as local Honda dealers would most likely not be able to provide the re-programming of the engine immobiliser when installing a new ignition switch. With patience and immense amounts of WD40, both switches are moving again after some time. That we are relieved is an understatement, and it shows again that WD40 is the must have "tool" wherever you go.

The landscape on the route to Cobán is one of the finest. However, despite their tolerable road condition, half a day on gravel and dirt roads is still quite strenuous for me. In saying that, instead of boring myself to death in a hotel room, at least I'm sitting on my motorbike again, which feels great and hence proves beneficial to the convalescence.

Falls Are an Everyday Part of Life on Long Distance Motorcycle Travels

Our destination is Parque Nacional Semuc Champey, and the track leading there is in a class of its own. A few times we bring up a sweat, and on a steep bit with rough gravel it energetically knocks me off the bike. The motorcycle is facing downward, right before a curve. Simone was merely able with great efforts to stop further up and now cannot move forward or backward. Due to the steep gradient she can't even get off the bike to help me. Two other motorcycles come up the mountain and only dodge my bike in the very last minute, which, looking at the condition of the road, is truly a masterly performance, to say the least. They stop a bit further up the hill and help me to stand up my bike, which is not an easy task due to the incline. It is also not the most recommended or "right thing" in regards to my current hernia condition, but I've got no choice. Even Simone doesn't manage the passage without a fall, but she gets off lightly. One of my luggage cases has been damaged badly and is just holding.

What annoys us more than the fall in hindsight was that again it was one of those dramatically photogenic scenarios, where we even thought of taking photos before setting up the bike again. Yet we couldn't get to the camera, because it was put deeper and deeper into our cases in Guatemala for fear of possible robberies. Damn!

A few days later in the next city we go on the search for a car body repair business that could fix the case. Whereas the problem in Mexico was that garages dared to try technology they weren't able to repair by simple unjustified self-confidence, the dilemma here proves the exact opposite. Everybody declines as soon as they realise of which material the cases are made, as nobody wants to crack aluminium. Only on our fourth attempt is a garage willing to look into the matter.

The method might not be exactly material-friendly but the result is good. After 10 minutes of spirited hammer blows and the additional help of various wooden blocks and boards, the panel beater has brought the case back into a respectable condition. All the alignments are correct, the mounting brackets are in the right position, the lid fits and the buckles all lock again. Wow, that man truly understands his trade and charges just 2.3 USD for all of it.

Dirt Roads and Landslides

In terms of driving in Guatemala, it is not that bad, and it helps that we have stopped counting the landslides. A typical situation we find ourselves in, is when we ride up a steep hill around a hairpin curve and half of the road in front of us is swept away. A large truck is coming towards us from the other direction, which should actually stop and let us go through first. So much for theory, just barely we steer the bikes into the debris, slam on the brakes and thanks to the extreme gradient, together with the dirt surface, we immediately slide backwards down the slope. Fear sets in until the motorcycles come to a halt with the rear brake locked.

In another spot the roads are blocked by landslides and have become impassable. Needless to say, the detour is made up of a dirt road, a steep downward slope and hairpin curves included. My very own personal nightmare scenario is when you brake tenderly into a steep curve and the front wheel just keeps sliding on the loose surface straight ahead, let aside the fact that braking and steering safely around a curve doesn't work at the same time here. The alternative is an intense underarm perspiration experience that makes conventional tourist holidays appear as an attractive form of travelling for a short moment. Luckily, such moments of moral weakness are quickly overcome.

School Class Lessons and Small Project Office

In Guatemala, virtually every city or small town has affordable language schools, and most travellers decide for the tourist pearl and language school stronghold Antigua. However, Guatemala's second largest city Quetzaltenango, commonly called Xela, seems more attractive to us. The prices for language schools here are less, and accommodation is significantly cheaper as well. Besides that the city is less touristy, which we always prefer. At an affordable rate we book hostel accommodation by the week and Simone selects a nice language school from the perceived hundred Spanish schools in town. Five hours of one-to-one lessons daily costs an incredible 70 USD per five-day-week, and the one-to-one sessions are additionally tailored to the competence and topical requirements of each student.

When Simone comes from school her head is smoking, but she still boldly studies another two hours on top of that daily "at home". By the way, amongst other things our home has a fridge and a communal kitchen, an unusual luxury for us, which we greatly enjoy. For once perishable foods don't have to be used completely on the day of purchase and you can, for example, go to the fridge whenever you feel to grab a COLD beer, what an indulgence.

Thanks to my extreme non-talent for foreign languages it was clear straight away that I wouldn't take up the fight with the Spanish language. Instead I undertake two long weeks of online research for our further trip. How do we cross the Darien Gap between Panama and Colombia? Route-planning for South America, making contact with local motorcycle travellers, and so on. What would be a punishment for others is a lot of fun for me, to sit several hours daily in front of my notebook, research, collate information about many more topics than the aforementioned and manage these in an efficient and practical way. Furthermore it is a pleasant change to go your own ways for a few hours each day, for example deciding spontaneously and without consultation with your partner on such profane matters as breakfast time or what is to be eaten, which truly can be good for a few days.

Bandit Trails at the Lago de Atitlan

The lake and its surrounding volcanoes are truly beautiful and are the absolute highlight of the country in terms of its scenery. Circumnavigating around the lake takes several hours, and in the Southwest is a road section that is not without its challenges. Ankle-deep dust (bull-dust) and potholes in combination with the steep incline turn two rotten curves into real challenges for us, which we can only master after several attempts. As frequent armed hold-ups are common occurrences on this stretch, police escort us on this poor section of the road. Looking at how challenging it is, I can imagine well why bandits chose this spot. You have to travel extremely slow and have near to no power of resistance towards an attack, when you have your hands full in order to keep the bike in the vertical whilst climbing up the slope. On the other hand the criminal might have experienced the shock of his life, if I would've vented my frustration at him about this shit-hill and my incapability to elegantly master the track.

Ultra Low Budget

A heavily packed long-distance travel bike chugs up the mountain in front of us. This can only be our pal Nick, whom we have met with his 125cc several times in Mexico. In no time we brew a coffee on the side of the road and cheerfully chatter along, by all means the life of a motorcycle vagabond has its sunny sides. Compared to Nick we are actually travelling in exuberant style, he exclusively camps wild and has a daily budget of three dollars. You can only make do with that if you eat porridge at least once a day and consequently renounce tobacco, alcohol and a number of other essential indulgences.

His small bike's cubic capacity would probably ensure condescending contempt in Europe, North America or Down Under, but meanwhile we see the advantages instantly. On roads that cannot be mastered by us even with the greatest courage and sweat, Nick simply shrugs his shoulders and presses on. If need be the small moped can be dragged over the worst passages. What is even more appealing are the running and maintenance costs for the little bike that are much lower than for our heavy machines. Also, to the contrary of us, he can get spare parts pretty much everywhere on this continent, on which there is no motorbike over 200cc on the road.

Travelling People Meet in Antigua

In the tourist magnet Antigua the low budget travellers gather at the parking lot of the tourist police. Here you can camp safely and most overall for free, including zero stars sanitary facilities and WiFi provided by the police.

In general, Antigua and the tourist police camp in particular, are one of those bottlenecks everybody has to pass by, and so no day goes by on which we don't say a big Hello to one of our numerous globetrotter acquaintances. The nights are filled with long-distance travel conversations and information exchange, and hence accordingly cheerful.

Throughout the day there is no shortage of opportunities to become touristy. Central America has as many volcanoes as sand at the sea, and we have already done a few tours. The one we did to the Pacaya Volcano has so far been the best, wandering through fog that is constantly becoming thicker in an extraterrestrial-like lava landscape, it gets increasingly warmer as boiling hot air is surging from holes in the ground. At one spot you can even go into a cave, which feels like the thermostat in the sauna is broken, sheer hell! Later we sit in the fog soup in which you can hardly see a couple of yards ahead with roughly 50 other tourists and wait. What we are waiting for is not entirely clear to us at first, but when the sun sets, a sudden hole in the wall of fog opens up and all the grey around us abruptly disappears. The views offered to us are breathtaking, we literally stand above the clouds.

In addition to this, the descent in the twilight is also at its finest, three majestic volcanoes tower out of the cotton-cloud-sea and let us stand in awe at the view before us. Wow…

The Mother Teresa of Stray Dogs

Simone will be working in a dog shelter for the next two weeks.

Volunteer work is a real industry in Guatemala, which in most cases seems to be more about cashing up on volunteers than using their workforce. Some people fork out pretty hefty advance payments that in the worst case go to dubious agents or, in the best-case scenario, go to the individual organisation directly. Daily flat rates to be paid by the volunteer are standard, and these can either be large sums, or in Simone's case, a more or less moderate cost contribution for electricity and water (which at least corresponds to the price of a basic hostel room).

Simone's association, however, makes a serious impression to begin with, which is confirmed at a first glance when I drop her there on Monday.

When I pick her up again two weeks later, she has dark circles under her eyes and has lost weight in unhealthy measures. Typically for her, Simone threw herself into it, which, in respect to the numbers of dogs, is a Sisyphean task, or never-ending task, so to speak. Let alone her stories of two nightly barking rounds by 300 pooches and their yapping concerts every morning at 5am makes me feel a bit funny. I refuse to look at the photos of castrations, in which Simone helped actively. When it comes to such things I'm a real wimp, and just the thought alone that such acts are done to a male creation shrink my own balls to pea size. Although I have to add that it makes sense to me, and I theoretically approve of such interventions. It's not in Guatemala alone that there is no end to wild dogs, who prove a real problem and often die of starvation due to the poor conditions they live in.

Tattoo Marathon

Whilst Simone saves dogs, I get tattooed almost every second day in Antigua. It is a real torture with respect to the frequency of the sessions and the tropical temperatures, in which skin reacts differently as to back home in Germany. But the opportunity is too tempting as with a bit of luck and a careful selection process, one can get absolutely world-class standards in terms of artistic ability and technical equipment in Central and South America. And to better still, they are only at a fraction of German prices.

Our Special "A-Bit-Of-What-You-Fancy-Does-You-Good" Cash-Box

Although I only pay approximately 20% of the German equivalent for the tattoos, the entire pleasure is not cheap, compared to our general lifestyle. Nevertheless I don't have a guilty conscience about doing it.
At the beginning of our journey this looked entirely different, the fact that we had no regular income anymore and had to do with a limited budget, made us pretty nervous. Suddenly everything had a price tag and before we even realised, we stood with both feet on the cost and unfortunately also fun brake (in context of being a party-pooper, ask me).
It is indisputable that as a long-distance traveller you cannot do everything and anything, to the contrary of a two-week-holiday-maker, who can do so without hesitation. In saying this it is incredibly frustrating to deny yourself everything permanently, so the key to success is to realise what is really important to you and therefore is worth spending money on.
Let me put it simply with this example: After three days of bush camping I ask Simone if we should grant ourselves the visit to a campsite with a shower, or if we should allow ourselves a bottle of wine for our nightly picnic. The decision comes easy to both of us and is

luckily unanimous. There are a few luxuries we can forgo easily. On the other hand other things feel like pure luxury without even being costly in certain circumstances.

However, to pay too much due to laziness or ignorance is generally out of question for us, whereas we sometimes even pay excessive rates for world-class attractions, which we presumably might never be able to see again.

Surely, things of importance vary individually from person to person, the critical point for every traveller with a limited budget is to realise that and pinpoint what that is. And then you won't feel guilty if you spend money for something you truly desire.

Another helpful trick is one we implemented successfully, when we created a special "A-bit-of-what-you-fancy-does-you-good" cash box and allocate a specific amount to it. Every time something out of the ordinary comes our way that would exceed our financial framework, we take the money out of this account. We were actually surprised about the modest amounts we used in the long term. As the total expenditure is restricted through an incentive like this, you don't have to worry that you ruin your travel budget and with that the entire journey.

If the travel companions have very different preferences in terms of entertainment, two such accounts could be a good solution to avoid arguments and conflicts.

Hotspot El Salvador

We are finally on the road again! As interesting as the last weeks of our settled lifestyle in Guatemala have been for our experience, we missed our daily bike rides and the vagabond life, and are therefore relieved to be together again.

We beam with good spirits when we hit the road to El Salvador, and even the heat, which we aren't used to anymore, can't dampen that. One last night in Guatemala and in the early morning we embark on our way towards the border. We need two-and-a-half hours to tackle the border formalities and ride into the land of the Mara Salvatruchas. What sounds like an Indio-tribe is actually an extremely brutal and extraordinarily violent street gang, counting hundreds and thousands of members. It has spread into the neighbouring countries of Central America as well as far into the USA. We don't really want to cross ways with those guys, although we are interested in their large-scale tattoos.

El Salvador is home to the liberated Latin American call-to-arms. It supposedly has one of the highest crime rates in the world, which an average of ten murders per day clearly confirms. Unlike Mexico, travellers are greatly affected, as armed robberies on tourists are a common occurrence.

Incidentally the murder rate is confirmed to us via news headline on our first day in the country, January and February, 600 murder victims.

Despite statistics and warnings, the people in El Salvador are incredibly friendly and helpful. We once read that compared to other Central American states, people in Guatemala are rather introverted and reserved. Now we understand what is implied by those words, and yet we already thought of Guatemalans as very friendly. Anyhow, we are addressed in a friendly manner everywhere and are observed by many people. This might be due to us being foreigners or our tattoos, which aren't widely spread here yet in a trendy sense but rather reserved to the criminal circles. In any case the behaviour of local doesn't appear threatening, as they seem more interested. Mind you, we first have to get used to local customs, back in Germany no sales woman has ever taken me by the hand and tried to drag me into her shop against my physical resistance.

The fact that El Salvador isn't entirely harmless can also be recognised by little things here and there. In Mexico and particularly Guatemala a lot of buildings and shops were guarded by armed security, which is even more pronounced here in El Salvador. In addition to this, the entire city is generously paved with gun prohibition signs, barbed wire in several layers protects many houses and properties and the streets are noticeably deserted after dark.

Despite the unmistakable possible danger we really liked El Salvador, and since there are less tourists on the road than in the Northern

neighbours, it only made the entire country more attractive to us.
One memorable evening was spent in a bar in the red light district of Santa Ana, where we marvelled in wonder at the third-class bar girls and the tasteful interior of the establishment whilst we drank our cold Heart-Ace Pilsner beer undisturbed.

Blowflies and Border Frustration

The departure from El Salvador gives us a promising outlook to the bureaucracy bullshit that is expecting us. First of all we have to make a copy of our vehicle permit, which is a temporary import authorisation for motorbikes, before it is collected. This copy is then to be stamped and again we have to go to the copy shop to make a copy of the stamped copy. For the first time in our lives, we use the help of a border assistant for the entry to Honduras. The import procedure for the motorbike is the most comprehensive in the entire Central Americas, a process by the way that has no equal in terms of administrative agony. After every processing step of a document, we have to go back to the copy-shop, all together five or six times, whilst also having to rejoin the cue to wait each time again. Without our helper and with a few bits of Spanish on my behalf only, I most likely would've had major problems to understand the procedure. Admittedly, even he is far from understanding either, but what he may lack in knowledge, he makes up for with audacity and fraud. At least he tries to. The initially negotiated fee of 2 USD has multiplied tenfold in the end. He hits a brick wall with me there, and I'm almost tempted to give him absolutely nothing at all. Besides, his constant cock-and-bull stories, which he uses to make his value of service more palatable to me, he gets on my nerves. This experience confirms my opinion about such scum, and unless required otherwise in case of an emergency situation, I will never hire such a rascal ever again.

After over three hours the cursed entry into Honduras is finally done. Thanks to the brutal heat, the trouble with our helper, the annoyance about the incredibly cumbersome procedure and the bold fees, we are in a noticeably irritable mood. However, the day still has plenty of room for further rage potential in store for us. Honduras is renowned for its extreme amount of checkpoint runs by greedy and corrupt cops. At the first five checkpoints we manage each time to get through in the obstructed vision of trucks, at the sixth then we're due and are stopped. Contrary to the cliché the officials are super-friendly and decent. Our hands are shaken, and the only questions asked are in relation to the "where from" and "where to". We had already heard the likes from several other travellers, nonetheless the negative stories I had heard first hand from, are surely justified. Hence we are relieved when the border to Nicaragua comes in sight. Again, we are immediately attacked by "blowflies", who shower us with all sorts of lies and reassure us that the border procedure is extraordinarily complicated and could not be mastered without their help. I'm still so wound up by the bastard in the morning that I simply growl nastily at them and get to work without their assistance. And behold, it works seamlessly, after 10 minutes our passports are stamped and I have exported our motorbikes out of Honduras and imported them into Nicaragua.

Nicaragua

With a sigh of relief and in best spirits we get the first miles under our tyres in this very popular country with travellers, which also immediately lives up to its reputation as being the land of lakes and volcanoes. On a good part of the journey to Leon, we have one of the two active craters in view. We ride around the smoking volcano in a wide radius and can admire it from varying perspectives.

After managing the robber-baron-countries El Salvador and Honduras, without having even been stopped once by corrupt cops, we are a little surprised that we are already due after a short period of time in Nicaragua. One of the law enforcers tries to address the situation in a serious and threatening tone, whilst the other one of the two, despite a "dressing down" by his colleague, refuses to go along with it. He shakes my hand in a friendly manner, keeps his gun hanging casually over his shoulder and is interested in our bikes and what we think of Nicaragua. As our memories of Honduras are still quite fresh, I spontaneously give Nicaragua a double thumbs-up, which seems to come across so incredibly genuine that the passport control is ultimately abandoned and the guys explain the way to Leon instead. I have to admit that the road to Leon really can't be missed, but who would counter such friendliness by being an arrogant smart-ass? Even I can shut up tactfully now and then.

Leon is a nice little town, and as per usual we take in the atmosphere of this new country enthusiastically, whilst we also compare everything with the formerly visited countries. There are a conspicuous larger number of beggars in this country, who scrounge with the usual brazen attitude, and generally speaking the poverty rate seems to be higher here. Considering that the streets are filled with people in the evenings, which is a strong indication to us that Nicaragua is significantly safer.

Rooster Fight

Our personal highlight in Nicaragua is a cockfight tournament. For 12 dollars we are chauffeured to the location, which includes three hours of rooster fights and as much rum and beer as one can drink.

From animal welfare aspects the whole thing is not entirely kosher, but we find it exciting to have witnessed something like this once in our lives, especially as there are almost only locals present and hence the show is obviously not orchestrated for tourists. Although there is not exactly little blood flowing, it becomes apparent, not just due to our informed guide, that people in Nicaragua go to great lengths to promote relatively natural and equal fights between the opponents.

The entire circus around it is grand cinema, and the locals, who bet large amounts, go along with it all. We somehow feel reminded of glorious days on the horse race track in Cologne, Germany. It's a bit of a bummer that I'm not capable in a linguistic sense to place a fair bet and, in the unbelievable case of a win, claim it accordingly. The owners, by the way, are fully committed. Whilst rivals in Rocky movies rinse their mouths and cotton buds with dry ice are placed on the split eyebrow by their coaches, the default at rooster fights seems to be that coaches actually put the entire bloody head and throat of the rooster into their mouths and suck it to remove blood from the beak, and especially from the throat. One speaks what everybody is thinking, which is followed by prompt bursts of laughter, cocksucker!

Volcanoes, picturesque little towns, easy living, Nicaragua has a lot to offer, and yet we start to get a little bored after a few days. We miss the adventure. It is not much different in the next country, which is Costa Rica.

The Switzerland of Central America

Welcome to gringo land. No other country in Central America has more documentaries on TV than Costa Rica, which is an exemplarily state in this region in terms of political stability and safety. Moreover, the country is one of the leading worldwide when it comes to conservation-related issues and ecological tourism. There is also a lot happening in terms of action, whether it be surfing, rafting, canyoning, guided quad and motorbike tours, horse riding, zip lining, and much more. Someone visiting with the necessary means can experience a different highlight every day. The other side of the coin is that Costa Rica is not referred to as the Switzerland of Central America because of its wonderful mountains, but more because of its steep prices, thanks to the many wealthy tourists from the USA and Europe. Many a time we have tears in our eyes when it comes to paying.

At times it seems to us that every tree in Costa Rica becomes its very own National Park, for which you generally have to pay 10 USD per person if you want to enter. And self-explanatory, it all adds up.

A frustrating anecdote is the one when we have just paid again 2 x 10 USD to then realise that I have a flat tyre on my motorbike. The patches simply don't want to stick to the tube during the repair, and hence I have no other choice than to take a two-hour ride over terrible trails with Simone's bike (without GPS) in order to get a replacement in the next little town. The best part of the day is over when my motorbike is finally up on two filled to the brim tyres again, and so we decide to postpone our hike to the next day. Which then begins with more frustration, as to the contrary to many other countries we have travelled through, tickets in Costa Rica only seem to be valid on the day of purchase. Despite the fact that the cashier had watched us through our entire mishap of the day before and was sympathetic towards us, he remains firm. If we would like to enter the park, we have to pay another 20 dollars.

Although the number of sightseeing tourists seems to exceed that of wild animals, Costa Rica is definitely worth a visit for all fauna and flora enthusiasts. There is a lot to spot throughout the day and in the night. However, we are quickly annoyed by the permanent dollars-bleeding, compared to the other neighbouring states in Central America, this country is simply too expensive and too touristy for us. A positive mention is that in Costa Rica it is possible to camp more frequently than in the Northern neighbours, which we enjoyed greatly.

Tom the Baker

There's supposed to be a German bakery at Lago de Arenal, which is a traditional place to be for motorcycle travellers. We are surprised to meet our friends Andi and Susanne there. They look even more surprised than we do, especially as they fall for my April's Fool, in which I was arrested after entry to Costa Rica and deported to Nicaragua. I fear that in the future these two will belong to the not very small group of people, who don't believe a word I say on the first of April. God help me, if I were ever to need real help in the future on the first day of the fourth month of the year…
Tom is a nice guy with a big soft spot for (motorcycle) globetrotters and knows how to tell many stories about his first difficult years as immigrant in this country. We always find such first hand experiences fascinating, as the reality is something completely different than the exaggerated and sensational documentaries you see on TV. Similar to long-time travellers, the stories of dropouts, who opt out, or expats often have bright as well as downsides. Some are lucky, some are unlucky and least of all it is a question of mentality and fighting spirit that decides, how it all turns out.

Panama

Six miles after the Panamanian border frustration is called for. In a police check-up a missing stamp in our not really stamp-deprived vehicle import documents is criticised. We are frustrated about the mistake of the border guard and ride back in a grumpy mood, only to then immediately also have our luggage searched before getting hold of the accursed stamp. Unfortunately we are haunted by bad luck on that day, my back tyre bursts whilst overtaking at high speed. The tyre suddenly blows out, the wheel wobbles and jumps and I start to slide, which turns into a pure rodeo ride. In this adrenaline filled moment, I honestly believe that I will not be able to bring my motorbike to a safe halt. Nonetheless, I somehow still manage with great effort to roll off to the side, whilst partially already riding on the (wheel) rim. Crap! The tyre is so out of position that I can't push, nor ride the bike. I have no other choice than to change the tyre in brutal heat on the central reservation of a multi-lane highway, whilst cars and trucks thunder past my left and right in rather close proximity.

We visit two expats from our hometown, who run a beach bar and who tell us an extreme, but for such countries, not untypical story. As it so happened, a Colombian man was interested in the neighbouring restaurant, but instead of making a fair buying offer, he just bribed the judge, who changed the land register entry. And lo and behold, the transfer of the ownership was hence finalised, against which the legal owner practically had no legal means. In light of such stories you come to appreciate the meaning of legal certainty. By repeatedly experiencing alternatives to the "German Model" on our journey, we realise all the things that are good at home, without noticing them before. Such positive things were taken for granted or we even criticised them strongly, but our view on such aspects of life have since changed.

Panama City is again one of those bottlenecks every overlander has to pass through. Like us, many lodge at the "Panama Passage", which is specialised for motorised travellers. We exchange info and anecdotes, look after our bikes and prepare the Darien Gap crossing.

The Trip of Hell over the Darien Gap

If you look at the region on a large-scale map in your atlas, you might come to believe that it is possible to travel overland from Panama to Colombia. In reality, though, both countries are connected by practically impenetrable wetlands, which on top of everything else, is outright outlaw territory. There is no chance of getting through with normal long-distance vehicles, which is why shipping becomes necessary.

Without doubt the first choice for two-wheeled travellers is the sailing ship "Stahlratte" ("Iron Rat" in German), which is currently on a longer sailing trip. We are unfortunately bound to switch to the shady catamaran "Fritz The Cat", that is, in comparison to the other dubious alternatives, at least the better of the two. Luckily we don't know at that point that this catamaran is going to sink two years later with passengers and a motorbike on board at this exact passage. Even though the whole operation is not entirely unexciting, as the loading already is rather adventurous. The captain pockets the dough (money) and takes off quickly, despite the fact that his professional cooking skills are praised as one of the big plus of this adventure trip on their Internet page. We find out later that this is not a real loss, as the skipper who takes over the command instead, is a friendly and highly competent motorcycle world traveller. He possesses not only the nautical but also engineering skills, and with a boat in such condition, this can be worth a mint.

The first days it takes us through the picturesque landscape of the Caribbean at the San Blas Archipelago, providing us with a relaxed holiday lifestyle and fantastic snorkelling trips.

During one of our snorkelling trips I actually see a shark under water, my heart is in my mouth, to say the least. Shortly before this I tore my finger open, I am bleeding, and I'm convinced that the shark must surely smell this. Not long and it will attack me like in those popular movies of my youth. In the pointless hope this could make a difference, I freeze into absolute stillness. For whatever reason, the shark decides to reject me, which I take a little personal and truly resent him for. In any case my knees are still weak when I climb back on board. After having told the story two to three times, I feel like a freakin' hero and decide then and there that I will document this heroic moment of my life with a shark tattoo as soon as the occasion permits.

For the next 40 hours it takes us over the open sea to Cartagena in Colombia. A complete nightmare for me as, depending on the intensity of the swell, most landlubbers are caught out on this bit due to seasickness. I feel so miserable that I can barely lift my head. I bitterly regret to ever have agreed to this catamaran trip and swear to never travel via ship again, unless there is an emergency. And if I must, then at least not with such a small one, which sounds and feels like a once century storm with every wave. Each wave thunders crashing against the catamaran cabin and then rolls over the barge, groaning and creaking, as if it would burst at any moment. Through the heavily leaking hatches the water is coming down on me by the bucketful, because nobody has warned us of this, it is merely a coincidence that our camera and laptop happen to lie in one of the few dry spots of the cabin. When we dock in Cartagena on the fourth day, I'm just glad to be alive. Nevertheless I have tears in my eyes when I see what the saltwater that broke in waves against our tied motorbikes, has done to them, despite WD40 impregnation. Rust wherever you look, let alone the consequences it would have for the electrics, which one most likely will have to pay for much later. A few worrisome minutes pass until we can revive our loyal bikes with a lot of persuasion and trusty WD40.
So my entirely subjective judgement to this ship passage, despite the grand first part, never ever again!

One Year "On the Road"

The crossing of the Darien Gap wasn't a milestone for us geographically solely, but South America also means the start of our second year on the road. Never before have we been as happy as in this first year, and since we're managing the life of a motorcycle vagabond that well, the initial plan of visiting the Americas has become more ambitious. We would like to ride home on our own tyres. In other words, the motto from now onward is travelling "around the world."

Mr. Machete or How a Swiss-German-Speaking Salsa Instructor Tattooed my Heroic Deeds

We're strolling happy and relaxed through the picturesque Cartagena, when a tattoo shop called "Mr. Machete" is luring us in. The artist doesn't just look like the prototype of a salsa instructor, although he doubles as one, which he explains in the thickest Swiss-German, leaving us amazed with an open mouth. The chemistry is right with Mr. Machete and we use the opportunity to add a few more pieces of his finest skin artistry, clearly documenting our heroic deeds of the last few days.

Loco Traffic

The Colombians have the worst traffic behaviour that we have experienced on our trip so far. They constantly overtake in an inconsiderate and absolutely absurd manner. Busses and trucks often pull out at the most incredible spots behind us to then only squeeze back in seconds later with brutal force between the two of us. The overtaking manoeuvres are doomed to failure right from the start and only work out, because we make way with grinding teeth and out of sheer fear for our safety. In my home country I would take this as an affront against me personally and the situation would most likely escalate. On travels in developing countries other rules apply. The motto is to make it through in one piece, and as you never know if these idiots wouldn't run you over intentionally or if they have guns in the case of a conflict, you better shut up, keep the finger in your pocket and just move on. And all frustration and anger aside, this traffic anarchy is also fun and part of the adventure.

Extravagances at Discount Price

In Taganga Simone refreshes her slightly rusty diving skills. The opportunity is irresistible, with it being the cheapest place to dive in the world and numerous PADI accredited diving schools enticing customers. Simone pays 45 USD for two dives with a German instructor, and is not only very happy with the price but also the quality of the dive.

Although not always easy to follow, the golden rule for long-term travellers is to spoil oneself where it is affordable. Mountaineering, cave tours, wild-water rafting, horse riding, diving, hang-gliding and much more, we have indulged in many extravagances on our journey, though preferably in places where they were extremely cheap. If you can wait for your chance, it will be offered sooner or later, and you save a lot of money in the process. However, it is often very difficult to say "No" to tempting offers in adrenaline strongholds, which are in the high three-digit dollar range, especially to have the discipline and hope for a discount chance in another country. By experience these opportunities will come up over and over again though, and then you can strike without remorse even as a low budget traveller. Just as here in Colombia with diving and tattooing.

Latina-Crush or Pride Comes before a Fall

Whilst Simone enjoys herself as a mermaid underwater, I hang around at the beach and am surrounded by half a dozen of teenage schoolgirls. When I reveal that I can barely speak Spanish and proceed in English, they break into cheers, which perplexes me. It becomes clear that they're doing field exercises for their English class and are supposed to interview a tourist, before bringing them to their teacher. I find the situation incredibly amusing, and not only due to the fact that I have never been swarmed by that many beautiful Latinas before. After having arrived at the not less racy teacher, the students have to report in English what they found out. When the flow of words quickly dries up, the teacher digs deeper "Tell me, how is he personally?" One student spontaneously replies to this with the shattering term "old". My rooster-in-the-hen-house-grin freezes on my face and a long embarrassed silence follows. Ouch, that hit home. It's going to take some time to get over this emotional Waterloo, and to the benefit of my battered ego as well as out of precaution, I intend to keep clear of Latina teenies for the time being.

Venezuela - The Land with the most Beauty Queens and the Cheapest Petrol

In light of the desolate safety situation and the overall political climate, we took a long time deciding whether we should do a trip to Venezuela or not. Whereas the situation in the neighbouring country Colombia has improved drastically, it went downhill to the same extent in Venezuela. Yet we couldn't resist the temptation to visit the country that apparently has brought forth more beauty queens than anywhere else.

The border guards are uncommonly friendly and helpful, and with countless rusty car-wrecks we soon chug along the poor roads.

The technical condition of the old American cars is appalling and even tops Cuba, which so far always held special status in our eyes. Many Cadillacs are driven around at walking pace, and we assume missing brakes as the real reason for this. Nobody needs to save petrol in this country by an economical driving style, which becomes clear on our first fuel stop. The litre costs incredible 0.7 cents, so we pay for filling up twice less than 24 US cents. No wonder that the gas station attendant refused to serve us at all initially.

In the evening we camp wild on the bank of the Lago de Maracaibo that offers a ghostly sight with its hundreds of oil shaft towers on the water surface. The local curiosity, known as Catatumbo Lightning, a weather phenomenon that regularly produces more lightning than any other place on the planet, only enhances the atmosphere. The sight is covered in nightly lightning without thunder, which makes it even spookier.

Rain Season = Landslides

The problems start in the mountains. It is rain season now in the Northern Andes (Venezuela, Colombia and Ecuador), and the known weather phenomenon „La Niña" has struck with unusual virulence this year. In Colombia we already had reports of over 50 landslides in one week alone. Up to a few days ago all major roads were blocked by landslides, erosion and all sorts of rain-caused havoc.

Even here in Venezuela, there are often bits and pieces of the road missing.

Over and over again we struggle through water and mud passages, until at one point we cannot go any further. We have to backtrack and arduously look for an alternative route that apparently is traversable. The half-life of such statements in the Andes in rain season is admittedly very short.

We continually see the consequence of „La Niña", with roofs protruding out of water, flooded fields, and in regards to the latter entire fields that have come down the hillsides. It is obvious that oh so many existences have been destroyed. And as per usual it is predominantly the poorest that have to suffer.

For the Brave – Salmon and Beer Ice-Cream

The reward for all the hard work is a world-renowned ice-cream parlour in Merida, which is called Heladeria Coromoto. The diversity of varieties is astounding and strange at times. With a few friends we bravely take on the culinary challenge, and it is agreed on that everybody has to choose at least one scoop of the rather daunting varieties. Our facial expressions and the sounds that we make whilst tasting cannot be described in words. Some of our test findings are that the varieties "Beer" and "Cheese" are surprisingly delicious. There are widely different opinions on "Tomato" and "Mushroom with Wine", whereas the flavours "Salmon" and "Hamburger" receive a collective "thumbs down", including furtive glances into the direction of the trash-bin and toilet.

Colombia's Answer to the Mad Sunday

Back in Colombia we're glad that the only road far and wide that had been closed for weeks due to the landslides, is opened briefly. Nonetheless, the ride turns into a horror trip, thanks to the Columbian bus and truck driver way of driving, who pull out recklessly, even whilst overtaking. What follows next, and this more than once, are super-hairy moments, and what makes it even worse is the blind overtaking over long distances. The highlight in terms of Russian roulette is a transporter of hazardous goods that needs a good dozen of blind corners to make it past a marginally slower driving truck. If there would've been any oncoming traffic, we would've all been dead on the spot. If Mad Sunday, one of the world's deadliest races on the Isle of Man, is too lame for you, a day on East-Colombian highways in the Andes, for a real adrenaline kick, could be recommended instead.

With increased training the skills of a "motorcycle traveller" naturally improve. For example, scanning the surrounding traffic situation accurately, to anticipate the potential misconduct of other road users and then react appropriately in a fraction of seconds. However, there is always a big portion of luck required not to fall under the wheels of a crazed South American driver.

Something James, an Irish motorcycle friend, obviously had run out of. On the road, which we complained about, he cops it as we learn a few days later over the bush radio. Despite the indisputable fault of the blind overtaking truck, the truck driver is not penalised. In the end, our seriously injured mate is simply glad to escape the cops without having to pay a fine on top of it all, let aside the fact that he was the victim in the first place.

Ghetto Party

Rather coincidentally, we end up at a Heavy Metal festival in Bogota. Although the event is hard on our ears, we still always feel more comfortable in such subcultures. It doesn't take long to engage in a conversation, and the evening becomes more amusing with each beer and friend we make. When the closing time is reached at 3am, everybody is pouring out. A couple invites us to join them at their suburb and keep on partying on the street. Others warn us of the suburb in general, and specifically of the two. But we trust our intuition and knowledge of human nature and say "Yes" to the adventure, led by curiosity. The taxi drive doesn't seem to end and the urban landscape changes significantly, had we been too reckless after all? When we get out at the destination, we are scared shitless: We're in pure ghetto. A dozen or so shady characters party on the street, and the level of noise is quite high. This is definitely not an area you go to on your own as a foreigner without asking for trouble. Our hosts, however, vouch for us and also make clear to the others straight away that we are off limits, being their guests. It's been light for a while when we make our way back, which is ensured as safe passage by the entire gang until we reach the taxi. A cool experience and a super night, which we will most likely still speak of for decades down the track. Once again it has shown that certain rules and behaviours operate beyond language and (sub) culture barriers. He, who behaves respectfully and reaches out to others, manages even situations well that may look dangerous at first sight. Conversely we have observed many times that arrogant and ignorant demeanour leads directly to your ruin. Similar to the formerly mentioned, and by daily practice improved traffic skills, also social skills increase positively with the length of your travel time. We find it progressively easier to judge situations, to adapt to people and strike the right note intuitively.

No Power to Cocaine

On the festival we had seen many young people taking cocaine openly. When addressing this with our conversation partners, we learn surprisingly that many of them are categorically against the consumption of cocaine. Not because they generally have something against the white powder, but because it has brought a lot of misery over their country. Large sections of the population seem to have the conviction that only through a personal boycott of the drug something can change. No drug money to the Colombian mafia. If it is due to this opinion borne by the people or due to government measures we don't know, but Colombia has transformed in the last years from a by de facto drug mafia controlled state to a, for regional conditions, safe country which can be travelled by globetrotters without fear, with the exception of the

FARC rebel controlled areas. Venezuela on the other hand is travelling into the opposite direction for other reasons, and has unfortunately and more or less become a no-go meanwhile.

Colombian Floods

We like Colombia quite a bit, gorgeous landscapes, a lot worth seeing as well as exciting things to discover, and an interesting urban life, including a distinct tattoo scene. Unfortunately we're here at the wrong time, which can't always be avoided, despite good planning of such a trip. The twice per year occurring rain season and with its landslides and floods spoil our fun in hindsight, so that we heavy-heartedly skip a few tempting routes and attractions in the end and run further south.

80's Pedestrian Zone Feeling

Our first impression of Ecuador is great. The Panamericana is in immaculate condition, and in terms of traffic we feel as if being in a different world, compared to Colombia. With the border crossing something else has fundamentally changed, here in Ecuador you see a large majority of indigenous people, which is a huge difference to the formerly visited countries. Only Guatemala had a similar high ratio of Indios. We like this as the country appears more exotic and more exciting to us. Well, with one reservation I have to note. The first time we heard the traditional music, we suddenly feel catapulted back into our youth and any of the German pedestrian zones, where at that time you couldn't even walk a hundred yards without seeing, but most over all hearing pan flute compilations from the Andes.

Beyond the Equator Everything Will be Different

For the very first time in our lives we ride over the equator. This is a truly sublime moment and we preposterously feel like grand explorers, who accomplished whatever.

With the equator crossing some things change. From one moment to the next we formally don't have summer but winter. And from now on daylight hours will vary progressively with the seasons. Close to the equator the days are always of the same length through the entire year. Sunrise is around 6am and sunset around 6pm. We had already experienced the other extreme in Alaska, and when navigating with the sun, which we do frequently, one has to be careful. It still comes up in the East and goes down in the West, but to the contrary of Europe and North America, the sun now takes its course over the North and not the South. As easy as the theory may sound, in practice it proves way more difficult to switch deeply rooted habits.

Opposite to a few other countries of which we had a clear idea, we practically know nothing about Ecuador. Apart from the equator our list is empty, except for one other item. Simone has arranged a visit to one of the enormous flower farms, from whom she used to get roses from whilst working as a florist in Cologne, and an exciting insight awaits her on-site.

Yapping Mutts

Roaming creatures give us, especially here in Ecuador, a hard time. Cows that jump out in front of our motorcycles with unexpected suddenness and agility, chickens, donkeys, sheep, lamas and pigs are, in best-case scenario, tied up at the roadside to feed there. So it happens that they cannot defend themselves against Simone's caresses or are fed with treats that are growing out of their reach by the Mother Teresa of all animals. The worst yet are the dogs that permanently attack us, and I have to admit that even in Anatolia and Kurdistan it wasn't as bad as here. Although we haven't been bitten yet, it is extremely annoying that these mutts constantly come out of nowhere, and that you have to either slam on your brakes because of it, or that you have to accelerate more than one would like on terrible curvy roads to escape these yapping beasts. To indicate the extent of this plague, it has to be noted that even the extremely animal-loving Simone now always keeps stones handy to let the four-legged bastards have it.

13,000 Feet in Two Hours

In temperatures around freezing point we sleep at the Lago Quilotoa, and it is a first tentative taste of what is to expect us in the coming month. The next morning it still goes a bit uphill and then for a short period of time it goes downhill with speed, almost 13,000 feet in two hours. This should really only be possible in very few places in the world. Such a quick change of air pressure has drastic impact on our organisms as well as water bottles. Everything is compressed by an almost iron fist, and not only the sunscreen bottle explodes literally in our faces. What a mess.

Good and Bad Times with Latin-American Motorcycle Mechanics

A piece broke off Simone's handbrake, and hence the functionality is considerably impaired. No usual roadside fix is possible, and with a bit of bad luck the entire piece has to be replaced, which is why we need to find a Honda dealer who could hopefully order the part. However, we are very fortunate when we arrive in the garage as the two mechanics turn out to be really friendly and committed. Of course it could be welded, they would immediately get to it and we could pick up the motorbike tomorrow morning. Although relieved, we are sceptical. Our opinion on the often absolutely unrealistic self-perception of the skills-set of Latin American motorbike mechanics, is simply too bad. It is needless to say that the next morning the motorcycle is not ready, as promised. We shrug it off, after now seven months in Latin America we are used to the non-binding nature of deadlines. An hour later they are done, perfect work at first sight, although I still have my doubts regarding the long-term durability. Nonetheless, when it comes to perfection, in situations like these one has to lower his expectations in favour of momentary practicality, as this is the only way you can keep going.

The invoice that follows then is something I love this region for, the entire jobs costs 15 USD all together for the welding in a professional workshop and estimated three hours work at Honda. Any authorised dealer at home would have only offered one solution, which is replacing the casting body, naturally only available with all small parts, such as hand brake pump, springs and seals for a trifling over 340 USD, plus three work hours for at least 80 USD per hour. With that the Ecuadorian version is roughly 580 USD cheaper, let's hope it's also long lasting and professional.

Drunk Border Guards and the Most Corrupt Cops on the Continent

The biggest challenge when crossing the border from Ecuador to Peru is the boarder guard, who is renowned in traveller circles to be constantly wasted and who, because of exactly that, enjoys a certain popularity. Whilst Simone attempts bravely to keep the good old man from falling asleep, so that he can keep on processing our documents, an Ecuadorian man enlightens me with his wisdom about his Peruvian neighbours. He strongly advises to avoid side roads, as we will be mugged on those for sure, if not worse. The next big city is the most notorious in Peru, and he substantiates his claim with a drastic anecdote. I listen politely, deduct in such situations something like 90% and come to the conclusion that Peru is no bit more dangerous than its neighbouring states. However, what touches me most are the warnings by an Australian motorcycle globetrotter couple of the previous night, who tell me that they have never been checked as often by cops as in Peru. In no other country these two tried to hold up their hands as often as there, and I might have to add that both were totally pissed off.

Thus I suspect bad things, when we're already stopped by cops for the first time after only five minutes in. To our utter surprise the officer doesn't ask to see our documents, but shakes our hands and welcomes us warm-heartedly to Peru. Wow, we hadn't expected this at all.

Then again we find his enquiry into whether we'd have a camera strange. As it turns out he doesn't want to dispossess it but rather take a photo with each of us, which we may kindly send to this e-mail-address. Is this because this guy currently has an internal corruption case pending and now tries with these pictures to prove his tourist fondness to his superiors? As I'm still giving my imagination free reign in harvesting sarcastic thoughts, a second police officer brings us two cups of water. In the end each of us also have to take a packet of biscuits, just in case we might get hungry on the way to the next town. To top it all off, Simone is even bid farewell with a kiss on her cheek, almost as we would be friends who now unfortunately have to move on.

At the next checkpoint the cop already raises his arm from far away. Hang on, he doesn't want to stop us, he holds a mobile phone in his hand and just tries to take a picture of us. To complement the nice trio, the next day a police officer saluted us when we ride past him. So much for the apparently most corrupt cops of the continent.

Bitterly Poor Country

The Ecuadorian man at the border is at least right in one case: Peru seems to be bitterly poor. Many dwellings along the Panamericana are wooden shacks and not much bigger than one square yard. Initially we thought of them as livestock barns, but obviously there are people living here. Later we see entire residential areas, where the "houses" merely consist of plaited mat walls, often with no roof and so tiny that it makes me question if I could lie down fully outstretched at all. Totally nuts.

Let's Give Salmonella a Chance

We stop at a Cevicheria, which serves the Peruvian national dish: Raw fish with lots of lemon juice. We are far away from the ocean and the chances of getting freshly caught and salmonella-free fish is rather meagre. But as it so often happens, the curiosity wins. Let alone that the nice landlady leaves us no choice with the complimentary tasting plate of Ceviche. "Delicious" is our verdict, and in terms of digestibility we also can't complain. Ceviche and other local treats are rather an exception for us for various reasons. Our daily routine is as follows, in the late morning or around lunchtime we have breakfast. Here in Peru we get our preferred ingredients for that without problems, they are of very good quality and come on top of everything else at prices that are fun. Two pounds of tomatoes are 30 Cent, a pound of extraordinary yummy cheese for 1.40 USD and ten little bread rolls, that are crunchy and not soft cardboard as so often in Central America, come at 0.30 USD. All that is sufficient for both of us, and it is easily enough for two meals. Oh, and before I forget, this cheap and very delicious meal is commonly enjoyed by having a picnic with a priceless view. At night, when the tent is up and all other tasks are ticked off, we generally sizzle a simple meal on the gas cooker and drink one or the other end-of-work drop.

Kuelap - The small Sister of Machu Picchu

The several-days ride into the remote Kuelap is beautiful, tiring and here and there more exciting than anticipated due to the lack of petrol stations along the way. But the ride would've been worth it for the magnificent view alone. The facility, which can be traced back to the pre-Inca-period, lies at 10,000 feet height on a mountain ridge. Contrary to its big brother Machu Picchu, only a few alternative travellers have lost their way here, increasing its charm additionally. The fact that we camp on the grass directly in front of the entrance doesn't seem to bother anybody here. We're joined by a Swiss couple, who are, as so many other European retirees, travelling this continent on four wheels. With red wine and nibbles we chirp away with interesting and entertaining yarns about travelling, that aside there are not many reservations between bicycle, motorbike and four or more wheeled travellers down here. In this area superficial points of differences are rather less important than the things you share or have in common. This is probably also due to the fact that you meet long-distance travellers rather rarely in northern South America, and therefore the solidarity is stronger than in top destinations, where one is literally swamped by globetrotters, no matter what means of transportation.

The Panamericana Myth

Whether it be books, slideshows, travel blogs, magazine articles and many more, they all decorate themselves with the popular phrase "Panamericana". After all, everybody who is interested in travelling knows this street presumably. Although it might have to be stated that the concept of experiencing the Americas on the Panamericana is roughly as smart as an foreigner who wants to get to know Europe exclusively via Autobahn. Peru is the perfect example, the Pan-Am runs as an impeccable two-lane tarred road dead straight through the desert, more desert and even more desert. The view, which one will find rather boring than interesting after a short period of time, is merely interrupted by countless large, stinking poultry farms. All the natural and cultural highlights that are numerous and on a world-class level in Peru, are pretty much missed, if you follow the oh-so famous Panamericana dutifully. As there are many a North-American Panamericana travellers with a pretty tight timetable on the road, they have no time to leave the "Autobahn" anyway and to really experience the country and its people.

Cañón del Pato

We turn off the Panamericana lightheartedly, our destination is the much praised Cañón del Pato. The narrow canyon casts its spell on us promptly, and you could almost halt every few yards for yet another photo-shoot. This road has apparently almost 40 tunnels, and many of them are several hundred yards long. All are unlit, have a single lane and consist of crooked gravel and potholes, which you can't notice in dusty dim light.
Unfortunately time is running for us, it is again late afternoon and we can already determine that there is no way we could make it to the next town in daylight. And because we do not want to rush through this world-class-stretch of road at any price, we start to look for a spot to camp wild. Not an easy task in such a narrow canyon, but we are lucky and find a spot that is only located a few yards from the road, but protected by stonewall. At nightfall this place unfolds unimaginable

attractions. It is full moon, and the scene under the sparkling night sky in the moonlight lit narrow canyon is a wonder in its own right. After dinner we lie merry with red wine on the humpy bedrock and can't get enough of the view of the sky and this romantic place. We fall into a happy slumber and wake up some time later with a stiff neck and an aching back. Ouch, we know that we will feel like this for days, and crawl half-asleep with aching muscles into our tent.

What we get to see the next morning on our onward journey is a living firework for all the senses. This is one of the best routes that I have ever travelled.

Besides that there is also lots to marvel at away from the main road, a cemetery, which alone would be worth a visit. Grave robbers have burst open the tombs and the mortal remains lie carelessly thrown down in front of it. Creepy... Instinctively you look over your shoulder and are tempted to quickly jump your bike and ride on. Again and again we pass primitive coalmines, where with minimal staff and mostly manpower only, the coal is broken and loaded onto truck. At times the track tapers off scarily and we are glad to get through comparatively easy with our single-lane modes of transport. To have oncoming traffic in those moments surely wouldn't be fun. The same would have to be said about a tempting gaze into the abyss, which is not recommended, as you would easily become dizzy. On the other hand you have rock overhangs and vertically towering rock walls, it's almost like 1001 Nights in Peru – magical. It is a constant change from narrow passages, in which the rock walls of the two moutain ranges are sometimes only 14 yards apart from another. There are also other wide sections, that aren't less appealing.

We keep going along the Rio Santo, which is often down a precariously steep slope on the unpaved roadside. Despite all the fascination, it is a hot and dusty ride, and when we arrive at the first small town, it is time for another culinary Peru experience. I boldly buy a local refreshment, an "Inka Kola", which has the colour of toilet cleaner and tastes like a bottle of liquid German gummy bears. For the one who finds Red Bull delicious, he will surely love Inka Kola.

Cordillera Blanca

The Cordillera Blanca is a mountain region at world-class level. Over 600 glaciers and 21 summits of over 20,000 feet alone make for a panorama that almost seems too beautiful to be true at times.

We camp at a gorgeous mountain lake at roughly 11,500 feet altitude. On our gas cooker we fry delicious cheese, which is a stunner in Peru, no matter if served hot or cold. As beautiful the atmosphere, as delicious the dinner, as tasty the wine at such an amazing spot might be, at nightfall it gets cold incredibly quick and we flee into our tent, where we cuddle up with a book. Thanks to wine, a full stomach and cosy temperatures in our double sleeping bag, we again fall asleep way too early. As a result of this, we wake up too early the next morning, and as everything is covered in ice and stiff with cold, an instantaneous departure is unthinkable.

The Usual Repairs

Something is always up and the to-do-list of a globetrotter is never empty, which can be a real burden now and then. Today we're searching for brake pads once again, because in the meantime even our reserve sets are approaching their end.

Upon endless enquiring we find a professional workshop for brake pad renewal. No, we won't buy new brake pads there, as we would do at home, we submit the old and run down pads instead and have them renewed as per custom in such countries. In order to do this, the remaining old brake lining (if there is some left in the first place) is sanded down and a new friction surface, coming from any scrap metal, is riveted onto that. And I literally mean "any" scrap metal. There were old clutch disks and whatever else lying around. The new friction surfaces are hardly thicker than stud heads, but the professional ensures us that the latter are super soft and wouldn't damage the brake disk. We'll see how good this method, which almost everybody uses here, really is and which, as much as I have heard from other motorcycle travellers, is also widely spread in the Middle East and in Asia.

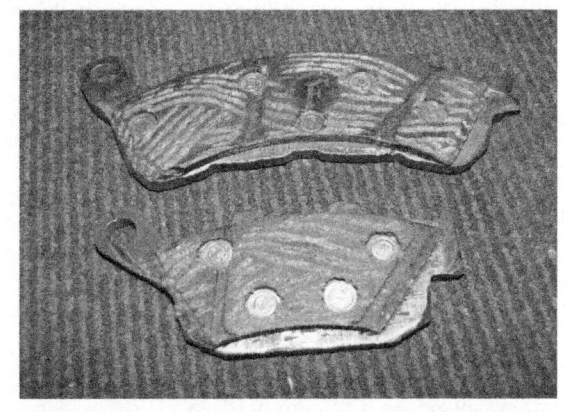

The last item on our to-do-list is to have our pants repaired. Not the first time, but on this occasion it doesn't work out that well. After the usual questioning odyssey we find a tailor. However, when we come back the next day at the time agreed on, the pants aren't finished, which is typical for South America. Two hours later the master of the swift needle has the nerve to present me with my brand new pants, sporting a huge burn hole on the pockets. Upon this, my justified complaint is viewed as a hindrance, and at times it is really hard not to fly off the handle when faced with the Latin American mentality.

Peruvian Specialities - Grilled Guinea Pig

Work before pleasure, but today a Peruvian specialty, which I have been looking forward to a while, is waiting for me, guinea pig, respectively called "Cuy" in the local language. As it is with things you have been looking forward to for a very long time, they often don't turn out as great and exciting as you dreamt. To be a bit more specific, my quarter of a guinea pig has the consistency of tough rubber and it has no more meat than a malnourished quail, to say the least. Who cares, there are experiences that you need to make yourself, as you will otherwise regret your entire life to have missed out on them. And you should also not be deterred by an angry look of reproach by your girlfriend, who considers it an act of barbarism to consume such a small cute rodent. At least I now know how guinea pig tastes and can easily announce that something like that won't make it onto my plate a second time.

Altitude Record in Bush Camping

These days I am fascinated by the altitude-reading on my GPS. 16,000 feet is our current record, which we will most likely beat in the coming weeks. Our personal record in bush camping is logged at 13,700 feet.

The symptoms of altitude sickness can no longer be denied, they start at 8,000 feet. These are difficulty in breathing and headaches, whereby the individual involvement can vary significantly. Usual familiar actions during the daily camp set-up require much more energy up here, and strenuous tasks become a challenge. Even our gas cooker struggles with the altitude, and despite boiling point the pasta takes an eternity. In return they taste absolutely delicious in these bold heights and with such an amazing mountain panorama in view. Although you should generally keep your hands off alcohol in such circumstances, it does not prevent us from having a glass or two to celebrate this achievement.

The Refuelling Affair

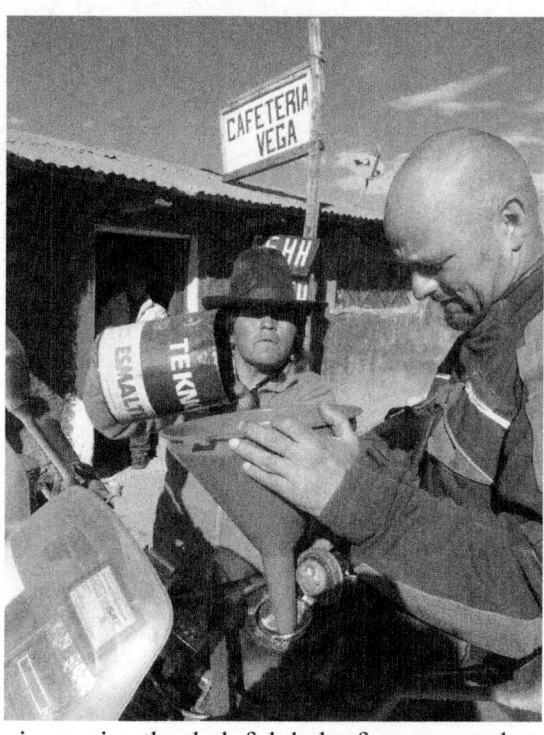

Once again some travel sorrow could have been avoided, if we would've just refilled earlier. Suddenly there was no petrol station in sight for hours and now we are forced to stock up on questionable petrol from canisters, collected from an array of small corner stores. We stop in front of one of these "petrol stations" and a mildly inebriated attendant, who can barely keep himself on his feet, comes out to meet us. Both our thoughts tell us that the likelihood of getting petrol here, is very low. Before we flee in panic, the helpful lady from next door comes rushing to our aid and rigorously takes over business. Thus my tea strainer is also finally put to good use, as I hope to at least filter the coarsest filth out of the petrol. Since it is very windy up there, a good half litre (1/8 gallon) of the precious liquid goes over the motorbikes and poor old Frank, standing there with the tea strainer in his hand. I curse so severely that even for Peruvians, who don't understand any German what so ever, my sentiments leave absolutely no doubt of their true nature. Anyway, the descent to the coast delivers another entry into our very personal Guinness Book of World Records: 13,500 feet in two hours. This is a figure, by the way, which we won't come close to in the following years.

Hard Work Instead of Never Ending Holidays

One might imagine a long-term journey as a never-ending vacation, but unfortunately the reality is far from it. Certainly we experience a lot of beauty and enjoy this vagabond life, but the lifestyle is a full time job. Something always has to be taken care of, either on the motorcycles, the equipment or in terms of the next travel stage. And as nothing can be taken care of as easily as it would be at home, the to-do-list never gets empty. When I need something at home, I generally know straight away where to get it from at a good price. I quickly hop on my motorbike, or maybe go briefly around the corner, or order it online. A short time later I have exactly what I require, well, most of the time. In a foreign country this is all significantly more difficult, and small details can turn into major challenges. That means one has to constantly ask his way and search for month for things that one takes for granted at home, such as black duct tape, silicone and WD40. In order to find these, one has to raid dozens of shops and talk to countless people. And sometimes one has to do with the less ideal. With an increasing length of a journey, the necessities grow exponentially. One who goes travelling for a few weeks, can hope with a little bit of luck that he does not have to undertake any crucial repairs, or exchange anything on the vehicle or the equipment. Even if you go on the road for a few months, one should have barely any problems, if starting off with well maintained equipment on the vehicle. In addition to this one can generally plan most of the travel route beforehand and in peace, the same goes for any formalities such as visas in relation to this. As a general rule one already leaves with anything he might need in terms of GPS, maps and travel guides in the bags, so when it comes to that, no stress should arise on the road. It is very different if one goes on tour for a few years.
Separate from and as well as the travel, time consuming tasks of everyday life are added to the formerly mentioned extraordinary things, such as set-up camps, buy and prepare food (which often takes way more time than back home), maintenance and service of the vehicles and the equipment, e-mail correspondence, homepage/blog update, view, edit and most over all save digital images and videos, plan next day's leg, and many more. Many of these daily tasks are routine, some are even fun, but everything takes a lot of time. The process of unpacking the tent and bags in the evenings alone, to set up camp and then the reverse of it all the next morning, takes, despite training, more

than an hour each day. Even if you stay in a hotel, as a general rule all the bags have to be taken off the motorbike and carried to the third floor, as it seems that every hotel has unreserved a few rooms on the upper level, and up there in the far most corner for motorcycle travellers.

A lot of flexibility is also required in regards to the specific planning of the route. This means regularly having to find an alternate route to the initially intended one due to landslides, floods, fires, earthquakes, tsunamis, strikes, elections, wars, changed entry requirements and a thousand other factors. Often this affects the next day's journey and can turn into a rough route for entire continents. To plan a trip that is spanning over several days is impossible, as too much is unforeseeable and too many things change in the meantime.

Generally I have great fun with the strategic and logistical challenges in particular. However, at times it just sucks big time. Sometimes one feels burdened that you can't take care of pressing problems ad hoc and have to carry them with you in your thoughts. Especially in my case, I am often not able to blend out the smaller and bigger sorrows in order to fully enjoy the beauty that I am experiencing in that very moment.

In the technical field in particular, you are occasionally confronted with problems you simply have no answer for. At least I feel that way from time to time. But contrary to a professional project, there is no higher authority that you could share your failure with and that will somehow find a solution with you. You are the sole entity for every seemingly unsolvable dilemma. You simply have to find a solution, as the journey would be over otherwise, even if that doesn't necessarily mean that you also have to implement it yourself. Admittedly one does not face such severe challenges on a daily basis, but depending on mentality, the psychological pressure can be enormous in such cases and may be very daunting or even be overwhelming.

In the long run one gets used to all of this to a certain degree, it just takes time.

And if it wouldn't be for all the nice people that help you along to different degrees whilst on the road, and the fantastic support team back in our home country, then all these problems would suddenly be much bigger and even unsolvable.

False Promises

If we didn't have to run so many errands in Lima, we would have not stopped there. Apart from the fact that we have to give up our altitude adjustment by having to travel down to sea level, only to then have to regain the former, is argument alone against it. But as I mentioned, we have lots to do. We need, among other things, new tyres, which costs us a week of daily efforts in Lima, despite it having been promised in the beginning. The president of the Motoviajeros Peru had invited us to give a little talk at their weekly club meeting. In Latin America small motorbikes below 200ccm are the rule. Large motorbikes as ours are seen rarely, and their owners generally belong to the wealthier. In the case of the Motoviajeros Peru the term "wealthy" would be an understatement, since the meeting takes place in a villa, where snacks and drinks are served by house staff and where we feel rather misplaced in our vagabond life marked clothes. It is very pleasant that the club members have a good grasp of the English language, thanks to an above average level of education, which is rather an exception in South America. Everybody is very friendly, and yet we don't feel amongst people like ourselves. The chatty president offers his help in the quest for tyres. "No problem at all, I'll take it into my hands", is his optimistic and whole-hearted promise. What is to follow in the coming days, is lots of hot air and no action. Time after time he shamefully leaves us high and dry. We start to think long and hard, is it because of a culturally caused communication problem, in which the Peruvian counterpart only meant to be polite and we mistakenly took the promise seriously? Or did we just cop an unreliable blithering idiot, and as a result of this our hotel bill is growing into painful dimensions? Eventually we break off the contact seriously annoyed and take care of the matter ourselves. The highlight of the entire operation is half a day at the cargo airport, where on a Sunday I struggle with the import procedure of tyres (the worst timing you could ever imagine) that had been ordered in Brazil by a local dealer.

Three Cheers to German Bureaucracy

After this de-motivating experience in terms of Latin American untrustworthiness, the application for duplicate passports at the German embassy is a feast for us due to German reliability and transparent processes. After now seven months in countries, where everything is done in „mañana"-style (tomorrow or never), we almost go into rhapsodies in the face of efficient German bureaucracy. Naturally, our rather uncommon application for a second passport is met with legitimate interest after we have briefly stated our reason why. No waving off a complicated procedure out of fear of doing something wrong (a widely spread behaviour in South America), no haggling for bribes. Instead we get a clear schedule of fees and upon our question, if it might be possible to deliver the new passports to another country where we could pick them up in a few months, the lady demonstrates the intricacy of the procedure, but ends still with "Of course this can be done, without additional costs." Three cheers to German bureaucracy.

Nazca Lines & Mummy Cemetery

Prior to our journey, we pretty much watched every documentary about South America that TV had on offer, and there is no broadcast about Peru, that does not mention the two mega-sensations Machu Picchu and the Nazca Lines. The latter are now our destination. The Nazca Lines have been "drawn" into the desert over several epochs by using various methods. 800 lines, 300 geometrical shapes and 70 phytomorphic shapes, such as animals and plants, cover an area of 200 square miles and vary in their extent and length from anything from ten yards to several miles. You can only see them properly from the air, which makes them even more mystical as that wasn't possible yet when they were created long before the birth of Christ. So why have they been created in this way? Theories are plenty, including such covering U.F.O.'s and aliens. Despite its fascinating theoretical background, the appeal of the Nazca Lines does not open up to us. For some reason the sparks won't fly for us when we look down onto them from a lookout. We can decline light-heartedly the customary flight for roughly 100 USD per person.

Instead we find a real gem close-by, which is almost free of charge. The archaeological site of Cauchilla impresses with a few dozen open graves with excellently preserved mummies sitting in them, 40 of them all in all. No glass wall or similar protects the artefacts, and if you would feel to, you could lift the red ropes and join the mummies in the pit. This is archaeology at its best, and our verdict is that one has to definitely see it.

The Apparently Most Beautiful Motorcycle Route in South America

On HUBB, one of the two international motorcycle travel forums we use, there is a discussion about the most beautiful motorcycle route in South America. None is mentioned as often as the 2-day-tour from Nasca to Cuzco, so our expectations are accordingly high. The beginning by all means is absolutely stunning. The road is winding through desert-mountains. I absolutely love such landscapes. We can see the Cerro Blanco in the distance, which is the highest sand dune in the world, standing at 6,817 feet.

The approximately 400-mile stretch is diverse and offers a variety of landscapes, whilst the desert-mountains are replaced with a high plateau. We ride for roughly two hours at approximately 15,000 feet altitude and see many lagoons as well as grazing lama herds and their wild relatives, which seem to be everywhere. It is pretty nippy and I'm definitely not dressed appropriately today with my carpenter pants, but then again too stubborn, as per usual, to stop, go through my luggage and get my warm motorcycle pants out. The cold doesn't do anything to me anyway amid such beauty. Shortly before sunset we ride down into a narrow river valley and have difficulties finding a spot where we could camp wild. On top of everything else our gas cooker breathes his last breath that night. Despite repeated dismantling and meticulous cleaning, the flame remains totally insufficient, and so we crawl into our sleeping bags frustrated and hungry.

The second day we still follow the beautiful river valley for a long time. Afterwards we again make up our way higher and higher over curves, curves and even more curves until the fun comes to an end in Cuzco.

Cuzco – Tourism Pure

Cuzco is the biggest city close to the Sacred Valley and the most renowned tourist attraction in entire South America: Machu Picchu. The average number of tourists that visit the ruins per day lies around 2,500 people. As it is also high season now, one can image how many more there are, and most of them come to Cuzco at one stage or another. It could well be 10,000 tourists that are here at the same time, and in accordance with that the whole city is aimed at that, absolutely mega tourism. Including the most hated effect of not being able to take a step without being approached by merchants, who want to sell you a tour, a restaurant, a free massage, drugs, or whatever else. My tolerance towards these blowflies is not very high and my mood generally drops significantly because of that.

The Jackpot of Squirts

We are pretty unfortunate in terms of the weather conditions, as it's coming down nonstop. Camping above the city at 12,000 feet, where it is freezing cold, I am initially not surprised that I shiver. At some stage fever also sets in and I start having the runs badly. Fuck, not now, not here! It always seems to be the same thoughts that you have in such moments. Since it is not better on the second day we decide to move into a hostel in the city. To lie in the tent in such a miserable state and have to run through the cold and rain to the campground toilet each time is not fun. However, taking down the tent and getting the motorcycles ready in my condition and in the weather, is certainly no delight either. With shaking legs I ride down into the city, and without having to search for long we're lucky to find a hostel, that is popular with motorcycle and bicycle travellers and that offers affordable rooms in the generally very expensive Cuzco. Obviously the rooms are very basic and unheated with shared amenities in the courtyard, but it is definitely an improvement to camping.

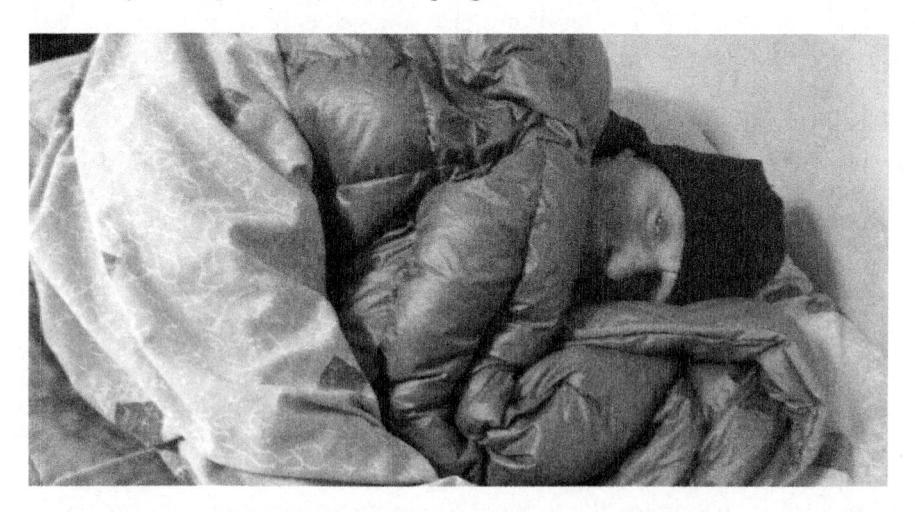

The following days I spend with fever in a frail state under a mountain of blankets and sleeping bags and am cared for by the best nurse in the entire world. In those moments I often think about friends who are travelling alone and how crap they must feel when they're sick, and nobody is there to help them.

Slowly it's going uphill with me, but the serious diarrhoea is simply not getting better. On the fifth day I go to the doctor, who diagnoses salmonella and on top of it an inflammation of the bowel after the test results. Jackpot! I have to swallow antibiotics and several other things, and for one or two weeks I have to keep a very strict diet. I'm in a very bad mood, how am I supposed to regain strength to ride my motorcycle again under these already challenging conditions? I am afraid this means adventure light for the next two weeks.

As so often Simone takes the entire situation way more relaxed than I, which may, in this very concrete case, be due to the fact that although she has to take care of a whiny patient, at least she does not have to suffer Montezuma's vengeance. Pragmatic as she is, she uses the unscheduled travel stop to do a few more days in the language school and improve her Spanish skills.

Each walk through town becomes a major gauntlet for me. The tens of thousand tourists all have to eat and drink, and hence it smells equally tempting and forbidden in every second entrance. Behind every third window I spot a bar where people drink beer without a care, which is pure hell. I try to focus on finding a new gas cooker and not to think about all these temptations, a task that turns out to be difficult in every aspect. Although there are more outdoor shops in Cuzco than in all Central America, one cannot compare those to local shops at home when it comes to their range of products. Of the 30 shops, exactly 29 have the same gas cartridge cooker, and nothing else. The 30th shop then additionally has one MSR Wispherlight left on offer, and it goes without saying that this one comes at import prices. But one who has no choice has no difficulties making a decision. I haggle down the price a little, and then we are owners of a new gas cooker, which is the third on our journey. This is a far cry of what I had expected before our trip, as for one I had believed that the gas cooker would last forever, on the other hand we had specifically bought a MSR, because we thought that we would be able to get spare parts for it all over the world. Nothing of the sort, for the second time we had to buy a new gas cooker, because we could not get spare parts anywhere. And a gas cooker is simply an indispensable piece of equipment, especially when you camp wild as we often do in Peru, and nothing works without one.

The Sacred Valley

Although it will take a while until I'm completely up and running again, we have ants in our pants. After almost two weeks of forced settlement, we finally would like to take up our motorcycle vagabond life and long to sit in the saddles of our bikes once again.
We start off into the Sacred Valley, where we take it easy with a few daily excursions.

First we ride to the Terraces of Moray, which is an agricultural test laboratory of ancient times that has a different microclimate on each terrace level. Our second destination is the Salinas, which are far more impressive than we had expected, whether it be from the air or by foot. Over 5,000 ancient terraced ponds are fed with highly salty water from a natural spring that is directed via an intricate system of tiny channels. The water is then made to evaporate, and as per usual in South America, it's all hand-made.

Machu Picchu – The Most Touristy Mega Highlight of South America

Machu Picchu is the most famous and visited attraction of all South America. I had already mentioned it earlier that it has 2,500 visitors per day. In light of this flood of tourists one inevitably asks oneself as an independent traveller, if one really wants to do this to oneself or if the pleasure would fade with all the annoying people on the route. On one hand it makes sense that the number of tourists has been regimented in the meantime, on the other side this means additional annoyance if you don't belong to the selected ones. On top of everything else we also hesitate regarding the exorbitant charges, which are matchless on this continent. In the end we decide to do it to get our own first hand impression, this is an opportunity not offered every day after all. Instead of an overpriced train ride to Aguas Caliente, which is a small town at the foot of Machu Picchu that costs a three-figure dollar sum, depending on comfort level you seek, we decide to take the option that virtually leads through the backdoor via Santa Theresa.

The 150 miles ride there is no handicap for us but instead pure motorcycle fun, despite winter conditions on the pass, where occasionally one can get stuck in the snow at this time of the year. From the tropically located Santa Theresa it then takes us via train or Siberian death march to Aguas Caliente. On the way back we select the named walking version and experience a few scary moments in terms of tunnel crossing, after I have put my ear to the tracks, announcing confidently as per good old western movie fashion, that there was no train coming. A brilliant error of judgement that gives us a pretty high dose of adrenaline only a few moments later.

Aguas Caliente by the way is exactly like you would imagine a village that has thousands of tourists with no money worries in the world, travelling through each day. From here onward it becomes very unpleasant and also expensive for us. To top it all off, we also have to show our passports on three different occasions on this day and find all this extremely irritating.

In the end we agree, though, that all the efforts and costs have been worth it, Machu Picchu is the most impressive city of ruins that we have ever seen before. This verdict is based on the site itself, but even more on its spectacular location. In pretty much every direction it goes down steeply, which really makes the place unique. Despite my cynicism I have to say that I had expected it to be worse. The crowds of people spread surprisingly well on the area, and we had experienced worse at the Maya ruins in Mexico.

Birthday Streak of Bad Luck

Do you know the feeling when you see a heap of top spots for camping and inviting accommodation in the first half of the day, but then during the last rays of light, when you specifically look out for it, absolutely nothing else follows? That's how we feel today, and it is already dark when we finally find a run-down place to stay. To describe it as "spartan" would be a euphemism. Instead of dinner we get the first bottle of beer in 14 days, which tastes simply awesome, but it stays at that one, as tired as we are. Aside from that, the bottle in your hand gets colder and colder whilst you drink in the hotel room, hell, it's like being in an igloo. The bed by the way is a sheer nightmare for somebody, who presently struggles with severe back problems. At 5am in the morning the clay brick makers in the courtyard turn on the radio on full volume and end with it one of the worst nights we have had on the entire journey. That's how my forty-third birthday begins. Generally I never cared much about birthdays in the past, but because this is already my second one "on the road", it has a positive meaning for me. It is a symbol for finally living my life exactly how I would like to. I do not foresee in those early morning hours that this 43rd birthday is going to be the crappiest of all times. At 7am we sit on our motorbikes, and in bright sunshine and temperatures below minus we take to the road again. We solidly ride in 13,000 feet above the Altiplano, which is a steppe-like alpine plateau, stretching all the way to Bolivia. It is divided by imposing snow-covered mountains and volcano ridges. Our fingers suffer from the cold but we're in a good mood.

Then misfortune strikes, Simone's back tyre is flat. I hate changing tyres, and I hate it in particular when an abundance of people are watching me and want to give me a hand uninvited. Theoretically, I understand that it is only meant well by those people, but I simply can't stand it. Furthermore, a situation like that is also a nightmare in terms of security, as all our luggage needs to be dismounted and is piling up beside the motorcycles. Tools are lying around and I can't have an eye on all of it, because I'm busy changing that bloody tyre. Simone gives her best to keep the helpers in check to some extent and to keep an eye on our things, but in such a situation we would never stand a chance against a professional thief. When Simone's bike is finally up on two bulging wheels again, the first real hit below the belt happens, my bike is not starting anymore. I can't bloody believe it and am almost falling into despair when I realise the extent of the current problem. It doesn't help to pity oneself, because no fairy with bike mechanic training will come flying around the corner to offer me her help. There is only one, who can or respectively has to solve this issue, myself.

Hence, down from the horse, with gloves thrown to the ground energetically, not to forget the swearing accompanying it. That, to say the least, reduces my frustration a bit and helps to keep local helpers at bay for a few minutes. Unpacking the motorcycle partially again to get my tools out, all under the eyes of a sensation-seeking audience. Take a deep breath, think. And once more I start with the usual quest of troubleshooting, which today simply refuses to be successful. I am at my wit's end and wonder, if I shall call the ADAC (German automobil club) to get a tow truck sent in? Unthinkable in this region, and I have no other choice than to push the heavily loaded motorbike to the next town. With a bad back this is torture, besides it is incredibly exhausting at 13,000 feet altitude as well as under the blazing sun. Every few hundred yards I stop with trembling legs and am at the end of my powers. Fuck me, I'm physically and emotionally strung out. The sun is slowly going down, and hence the entire thing also becomes a race against the clock. In the end we swap pushing the bike, as I'm totally knackered. With the last bit of daylight we reach a workshop, where bad luck laughs into my face once again. When I attempt to demonstrate my problem to the mechanic, my motorcycle starts without any problems, arghhhh! I'm freaking out, for hours I have tried everything without any success. Then the wrenching and never ending pushing at this energy-sapping altitude, and now this beast is starting like nothing had happened. The mechanic smiles and seriously demands a fee for his "repair service", not suspecting that he is risking his life in that very moment.

Today I was totally in despair, I cursed and really had enough, but when I sit in an over-heated pizzeria that night, with a pizza in front of me, having a sip of my cold beer, looking into the eyes of my beloved Simone whilst holding her hand, I know in that very moment that despite the misfortunes and frustrations of the day, I am truly a happy man. How do they say so appropriately, a problem shared is a problem halved, which carries a lot of truth. Another adventure endured together, somehow it always goes on and on.

Smoke and Mirrors

As the zipper of my tank bag is screwed up by now, we go searching for a cobbler, which we effectively even find after a long quest. After a bit back and forth we agree that the master craftsman will replace the zip for the converted sum of 5.7 USD. He makes the solemn promise of having the tank bag ready at 10am the next morning. Following, we go searching for the motorbike workshop quarter, which is generally concentrated in one suburb in Central and South America. Unfortunately this logic doesn't work in Puno. We spend half a day to make our way from one motorcycle shop to the next by foot, none of them even lying in close proximity to one another. To make matters worse, nobody can help us in terms of a 130 tube, as local motorcycles have up to a maximum of 110 out the back. At the third shop I break off the quest for the rare spark plugs of our motorbikes. Wherever you go, the only valid measure to find out the possible compatibility of spark plugs is if the thread seems to suit by visual comparison. Heat rating in particular and the general necessity of classifications, though, I cannot impart on any South American.

To my utter surprise, my tank bag is ready at the agreed time the next morning, and I am delighted about the quality of the repair. On the way home I inspect my zip again and hesitate, with a more meticulous view I realise that the rascal has tricked me. He replaced the tab and re-coloured the old zipper. I'm seriously pissed off! I am so sick and tired of Central and South American botched jobs and fraud. After now nine months in this cultural area, I have to admit that botched jobs and fraud aren't the exception but the rule. We don't hear any different from all the Europeans and North Americans who have settled here. Furiously I storm back to the cobbler, and I remain very angry although he promises instantly to put in a new zipper. That surely wasn't an accident, obviously that pig has intentionally tried to rip me off. Apart from that 6 USD is a lot of money in Peru. For that sum even a cobbler in Germany would've put in a new tab, and to take it a bit further, even for an entirely new zipper, it is considered a gringo price locally. It is fatal for us that we are extremely tight in time, we still have to make it back to the hotel, pack our stuff and get it onto the bikes, and all of which in the next 1.5 hours. Also the cobbler would have to go to the market first to buy a zipper, have I already mentioned that I'm sick and tired of all this crap? In the end I leave with a service, where the quality doesn't meet my expectations. It probably won't take long until the next time we have to go searching for a cobbler to repair this tank bag.

Altitude Record

In unpleasant chilly temperatures, our way leads us once again over the Altiplano towards Cañon del Colca. It takes us higher and higher, where the temperature sinks deeper and deeper. Visually the landscape reflects this, it looks like we are riding through a glacier. Ice walls that are several yards high and a mountain stream that freezes on its way down the slope.

We don't feel any warmer than the water of this stream. Up on the pass, which is our new altitude record with 16,000 feet, we have to force ourselves in temperatures below zero to stop and take a picture of the bizarre army of stonemen. By the way, the 16,000 feet will remain our all-time high for South America, although there a few other places, where you can come even closer to the sky.

To keep all the altitude figures of the last chapters in perspective, the highest road in the European Alps makes it to 9,200 feet, and the highest in North America is 14,240.

Aside from the already noted challenges for the organism in high altitudes, our motorbikes are also struggling. The thinner air is particularly problematic for motorcycle carburettors. Hence we have decided consciously for fuel injection that is more able to cope with the altitude. In saying this, it still does not fail to leave its mark on our long-suffering Hondas.

Culinary Highlight

Chivay, the so-called gateway to the Colca Canyone, is a disappointment for us. We are shocked by the restaurant rates, where drinks cost double or triple as much as in Puno. However, the evening offers an unexpected culinary highlight to me, Alpaca steak with a fruit sauce from the Andes region. It is an absolute pure indulgence due to the incomparable meat and a first-class sauce.
Even though I have often reported about culinary excitements in Peru in the last chapters, Central and South America are generally a big disappointment in that regard. At least in the price category we're moving in, where warmed-up, overcooked and extremely boring food is the norm. I have never been on a continent with such bland food as here, so today's meal is a real highlight.

At Eye Level with the Giants of the Air

In Ecuador we had already admired them in a wildlife park, now we hope to catch sight of them in the wild, Condors. In the afternoon, and hence apparently too late to see the giants of the air, we set our camp a mile below the famous Cruz del Condor. Not a single person around, but instead we have up to a dozen of these imposing scavengers gracefully floating above us for the rest of the day. With their wings spanning over two yards in some cases and in close proximity, they are a truly captivating sight.

On our way back towards Chivay the next morning, endless smaller and larger buses come towards us and turn the ride into a torture dust-wise. In my head I quickly estimate a rough number of tourists that are chauffered to the Cruz del Condor for the morning session and come up with a figure of over a thousand. That's incredible, and it is surely no fun to observe a natural spectacle in such crowds. Once again we have had an enormous advantage as independent travellers, which we wouldn't want to miss for the world.

Bolivia

The two border crossings at the Titicaca Lake have a certain reputation in regards to corruption. We experience the attempt by a border guard to demand a Coke, so that he wouldn't be so tired anymore and could process our application quicker, as a rather amusing affair.

Our first double room in a very touristy seaside resort costs 4.50 USD, and Bolivian prices are quite pleasant in general. Less pleasant are the business morals in the country, which we receive a typical sample of the next morning. The hotel employee only wants to let our motorbikes leave the courtyard against a 50% surcharge, although this had not been mentioned the day before when we checked in. We remain stubborn. Unfortunately this is not to remain a one-off in this country. In the coming weeks we experience such attempted frauds and rip-offs quite often, which is why Bolivia receives one of the bottom places on our entire trip around the world when it comes to honesty and fair treatment.

After a slightly adventurous crossing of the Titicaca Lake we move on over the Altiplano, the latter having significantly lost its appeal to us due to its monotony.

The Road of Death – Myth or Reality

Camino del Muerte, the Road of Death is one of the most renowned roads in South America. We had already read a lot about it and seen numerous documentaries about this dangerous piste on TV. One thing that is often mixed up by unreliable journalists and pretentious travellers is that this road used to be extremely dangerous and used to claim many deaths on a daily basis. The greatest danger nowadays, however, is the possibility of colliding with one of the hundred mountain bikers, who, contrary to bicycle travellers, bomb down the road without rhyme or reason. The reason for this defused situation is a tarred road, which has run parallel to the notoriously famous road for several years now.

We take on this road legend with our tyres in the early hours of the day and remain alone, except for a troop of Argentinean motorcyclists. Soon they stay behind us though, because they constantly stop to film themselves riding the road in the standing position, which is in immaculate condition by the way. Amidst so much posing, we can only shake our heads. We would love to hear the accompanying text to this show-off movie.

The upper half of the Road of Death is a little more exciting than the lower half, but surely no challenge in itself. However, if you realise this used to be the main road once upon a time, with lots of traffic and trucks constantly having to pass each other, then you can actually imagine quite well, where the name of the road originated. As we have already experienced several times in Peru and Bolivia, how oncoming traffic gets wedged inside and then stuck due to sheer stupidity, we have real difficulties to imagine how this would have ever worked on this stretch of road without causing constant and hopeless stalemate situations.

Around 10.30am we reach the tarred road and only minutes later a never-ending stream of mountain bikers starts coming towards us. They overtake wildly, bomb side by side around curves and some ride no hands to be able to take photos during their ride. Just so much for the real dangers of the Road of Death. Should one of those "One-Day-Heroes" die by his own fault, the press will jump on it with great enthusiasm and use the death as evidence for the notoriety of this stretch of road, and surely not without including a few ancient stories about the myth of the road in their piece.

Petrol Station Desert

In terms of "dry petrol stations", Bolivia does not outdo Venezuela. Especially outside of larger towns many petrol stations run out of petrol regularly. As we have a bit of motorcycle travelling experience by now, we now know to refill early in such areas. Hence I had already started looking out for a petrol station when our tanks were still half full. Yet there was nothing for hours on end, at least not one that wasn't dry. In Challapata I then have to provisionally call it a day, as even here there is no petrol. There is a long cue of diesel vehicles in front of one petrol station that is supposed to get a delivery in the late afternoon. Petrol is apparently supposed to arrive the next day. We ask around if there isn't somewhere we could buy petrol from canisters, but it's a dead loss. Out of necessity we ride back into the godforsaken place that is currently on hold due to siesta. After hours of waiting we finally get a room. The landlady is a bitch, demanding extra charge for toilet paper and showers. But at least our motorbikes can park in the hallway, which is nothing unusual in Central and South America. Often it is appalling and funny, where space is created for our bikes.

A few minutes later somebody tells us where we could've bought petrol from canisters for double the price, but now it is too late. In the meantime we come to like this place. We would've never landed here if not out of necessity, but that would've also meant to miss a fine chance of experiencing the everyday and authentic side of Bolivia, with absolutely no tourists in sight. We stroll around and eat delicious empanadas for eleven Cent per piece at a street stall until we're almost exploding. The next day starts in typical Bolivian fashion with the landlady demanding a fee for the motorbikes, which hadn't been discussed the day before. My tolerance for such scams has reached zero by now, and I stand my ground by bluffing loudly that I would call the cops. That is something the witch doesn't particularly like, so she furiously coughs up the missing change. Unfortunately I had to pay with a large note today.

A helpful tip for the travellers who like to avoid a little controversy: Always keep change. The one who pays the exact amount has it much easier to prevail against unjustified demands than the one who has to fight for the correct change.

Believe it or not, the petrol station has petrol when we arrive, and being motorcyclists, we are even allowed to jump the endless queue to the very front. This had already been custom in Venezuela, and we have to admit sheepishly that we are still a bit embarrassed about it.

The Devil's Miners

Potosi had been renowned for its large amounts of silver deposits. The city used to be as big as Paris or New York once upon a time. Still to this day the word "potosi" is used as an adjective in the Spanish language, which roughly translates to "filthy rich". It is estimated that this mountain, which looks rather like a huge pile of dirt, cost the lives of approximately 8 million people, and even today thousands of miners rummage for minerals in hundreds of smaller and middle size mines. The movie "Devil's Miners" provides a good insight into the perilous work conditions in those mines. It is said that a miner only has 10 years left to live, counting from the first day he starts working underground. Hundreds of the "Devil's Miners" are children.

In Potosi there are numerous tourist information centres that offer guided visits through these still active mines. These guided tours are hardcore and in no way comparable with a mine in an industrialised country. Depending on which vendor you get, a guided tour can either be a fantastic and informative adventure or a claustrophobic and life-threatening nightmare.

A Portable Spätzle Machine

With Adi and Markus, two motorcyclists from Swabia, which we coincidentally crossed ways with a few days ago, we spend some relaxing days in Sucre, which we find to be our favourite Bolivian city. After the usual exchange of travel experiences and tips, we extensively compare our experiences with the motorcycles and our equipment. It is interesting to see how priorities lie differently with each person. They even carry non-drinking water to wash, which is an absolute waste of space and weight in our eyes. In saying this, we are thrilled by their Spätzle machine, which is largely considered a Swabian speciality. The "little sparrows" are consisting of seasoned dough poached in boiling water, and as so often in German tradition, accompany hearty meat dishes with a thick sauce or gravy. Travelling with a Spätzle machine would be the ideal means to pay back all the invites one receives whilst on the road by serving a traditional German dish. Not only the Bolivian mother of the house is delighted, we, too, savour the delicious Spätzle and the company of the two.

The Salar de Uyuni

The Salar de Uyuni is the largest salt lake in the world, situated at approximately 13,000 feet. To ride our motorbikes and camp on it for a night would be the absolute highlight of South America, which we have been looking forward to for months already.

It might be questioned if this dream will come through as oncoming travellers have been reporting for several weeks now that the Salar is still under water, which is quite unusual for this time of the year as it is the dry season. The latest news we hear aren't much better, we had been prepared for -15°C (5°F) on the Salar at night, but at the moment it is supposed to be -25°C (-13°F), with temperatures below zero even during the day. Scenically the ride to the salt lake is already a direct hit, as it is considerably more attractive than the North of the country.

As so often we camp wild, which in this case turns out to be good training for the Salar de Uyuni. Night frost with double digits below zero is no rarity in the Peruvian and Bolivian Andes, but we have never had it that cold before. Even the water bottles in our tent are frozen, brrrr! When brushing my teeth in the morning, the water drops in my beard turn into ice instantly. If not experienced it first hand myself, I would've believed this to be impossible.

The only town near the Salar is Uyuni, which is a shabby, tiny little jerkwater town. The whole place is surrounded by a waste dump, and spans over several hundred yards. Besides the salt lake, the Uyuni has another world-class highlight on offer, the train cemetery.

Roughly 200 rusting carriages and locomotives stand here in varying

states of decay. This atmospheric place, in which you can go on a discovery tour for hours, is enough to make the ride to Uyuni worth it.
The next day brings long faces and bitter understanding as the Salar is massively under water at its access points. One-foot high salt water is not on our bike to-do-list, and the memory of the damage, which the salt had caused when crossing the Darien Gap, is still too fresh. And here the concentration would be even higher. Since the motorbikes have to carry us around the world for a few more years, we heavy heartedly decide against the ride over the salt lake. This is a huge disappointment, only partly alleviated by the breathtaking view of the white shimmering and endless seeming surface.

Our onward ride along the famous Laguna Route, which would have become our biggest challenge so far, is also impossible. At 16,400 feet nothing is moving due to snow and ice at the moment. This comes at no surprise for us, because we have heard of unusually heavy snowfall and impassable passes for a while now. Once again we experience the bitter understanding that even with optimal planning, things don't always work out the way they are supposed to. In this case the change of plan is a particularly bitter pill to swallow, as we don't know if life will give us a second chance to experience this adventure (ever again).

Damn Sand, Damn Diarrhoea

The alternative route to Tupiza is in a class of its own. For the entire stretch we experience so-called corrugated roads to different degrees. Several deep sand passages take a toll on Simone, and in the end her bike is bogged in the sand three times.
With combined forces it somehow always goes on and on, even if we curse and sweat.

Tupiza is famous for its amazing rock formations, which we would like to explore on a ten-mile hike. My legs feel like lead today, and with every step it becomes more and more difficult for me to walk in the blazing sun. After an hour I ask Simone to turn around, and I fear that the diarrhoea from the morning is more serious than expected. To be perfectly honest I was initially excited about it or as excited as one can be about diarrhoea, as it seemed to have been the far better result to the terrible constipation I have been suffering since the salmonella issue three weeks ago. To sit in the morning, after a night in the tent at temperatures clearly below zero, with a bare behind in the landscape, literally freezing your bum off whilst pushing like a champion with a red and pain-stricken face at the same time, definitely isn't one of the sunny sides of a motorcycle vagabond's life. Sadly, this is already the third time in five weeks that I lie flat on my back with diarrhoea and fever. Besides the general suffering you also become victim to one or the other pessimistic thought. Although the fever only lasts for 24 hours, the diarrhoea is more stubborn. I focus on one goal only, to become fit enough again, so I can get in my saddle and make the approximately last 60 miles to Argentina. There I might consider going to the hospital to get checked, should I still have this severe diarrhoea. As Argentina is reputed to have the best infrastructure or highest level of development of all South American countries, this simply seems to be better suited than Bolivia, which has to be placed at the opposite side of the scale.

Strikes and Road Blocks

This topic has already kept us on our toes since Peru, where militant protesters blocked the road to Bolivia for weeks. Large groups of people, in particular in combination with alcohol intoxication, are a ticking time bomb, and it only takes one spark to let the whole thing explode. As a globetrotter you can be lucky and they let you through, at the same time it can end fatally for arbitrary reasons. Recently even an ambulance was refused to go through by the protesters, which ultimately cost the injured patients their lives. To a certain degree one could emphasise with the radicalism of the protesters, they're with their backs against the wall and the state power dissolves the blockades violently by walking over their dead bodies often enough.

In Bolivia such blockades are everyday life, and we prematurely joke on the last hundred miles that we haven't experienced any. But we got excited too soon, and we promptly have a bus blockade in front of us.

Small motorbikes are allowed to alternatively hop over the sleepers of a train bridge, which runs at a dizzy height. We feel nauseous just by watching them. Luckily we are spared this test of courage, the protesters open the blockade to let a police vehicle through and we quickly stick to it. The next dozen blockades until the border are no problem, we can somehow always circumnavigate with our motorbikes by driving cross-country or over sidewalks. Thankfully the protesters are easy going and grant us access, but we still feel somewhat uncomfortable doing it.

A Long Way to the Southernmost City of the World

A road sign welcomes us to Argentina and makes our faces beam, 5,121 km (3,182 miles) to Ushuaia, the most Southern city in the world. But it will still take until end November at least to get there, because we can't go down there with the motorcycles due to the weather conditions. It will then be summer in Patagonia, which means 10°C (50°F) with a bit of luck, lots of rain and extreme winds. With great anticipation, we're already looking forward to this very particular experience.

In Argentina we only manage three miles before a queue of vehicles appears before us and at the end we can see another road blockade. It appears to be more of a sit-in and we try to spontaneously sneak past it, but the police prevent us from doing so. Damn, now we also have to wait. We learn that this is nothing unusual in Argentina either. Personally I don't feel much love for this kind of political expression that unpleasantly restricts my freedom of travelling. This would be hard to imagine in Germany to have main arteries with no alternative route blocked for hours or days by unauthorised demonstrations.

Bitterly Cold Tropics

To me the tropics were simply climate zones. Only a few months ago, when we crossed the Tropic of Cancer towards South, I sensed the similarity of those terms. Lo and behold, the tropics are geographically really defined as the region between two assigned latitudes, where one is located to the North and the other is located to the South of the equator. Today we're crossing over the southern one of the two, which is the Tropic of Capricorn, and we do so several times due to the winding course of the road. However, it doesn't exactly feel like we're heading into or leaving the tropics, this has darn nothing to do with what I had imagined of the tropics until now. There is no humid air, no jungle or such, and we're still in the Andes, where although the sun shines brightly, it is still commonly chilly in the day and freezing cold in the night.

Ruta Cuarenta

Before we're hitting the road towards Paraguay and Brazil, we'd like to take a last round through the Andes. From Salta it takes us through the Quebreda de Cafayate, where you can marvel at natural attractions such as the „Garganta del Diabolo", „El Anfiteatro", „El Obelisco" and „Tres Cruces", all just a few hundreds yards off the road. The way back over the legendary "Ruta Cuarenta" (RN40) is even more beautiful. The road itself, which is not really suited as it is a gravel and sand road, doesn't arouse enthusiasm, but the landscape is fantastic. Milestone markings with figures like "4,480 km" (= 2,784 miles) witness the length of this South American dream road.
Repeatedly it goes over peaks and rounded hilltops, where new and spectacular perspectives suddenly open up.

All's Well That Ends Well

The next morning starts pretty bad. The bumpy road of the day before has largely taken its toll as the spring of my centre stand has jumped off and offers a fierce resistance to be remounted. With a sling of cable ties and one of my longest wrenches we're successful after all, as per the old wisdom that enough leverage can move anything.

The next bad news is that despite frequent checks, as per rule on such tracks, one of Simone's motorcycle flat bars with which the suitcases are tied, has come off and is somewhere behind us on the road. Hence Simone now has the mission to bring all the charm and communication skills she can master to find a fitter, who can craft us a new flat bar on a presidential-election-Sunday, which seems almost impossible. Simone is being passed on and on, chauffeured through the entire city until she finally ends up with a tattooed biker, who is ready to help us in his workshop. For once without providing a botched job or trying to rip us off, and to top it all off there is nothing to complain about with the work results he provides. I wonder if this might be the exception to the South American rule or if Argentina differs to its Northern neighbours.

Alcohol Prohibition for the President Election

By the way, the president election is driving me crazy, mainly because there is a sales ban on alcohol, even for foreigners who aren't even eligible to vote and, on the night before and on the day of the election. And in my case, where I was forced to abandon beer for a whole week due to diarrhoea, this is even worse. It is to say that the fact of having to impose such a prohibition does not reflect well on this country in my eyes.

500 Miles, Straight Ahead

There lies 500 miles of straight road ahead, obviously curves seem to be a rarity here. First it takes us through the so-called dry Chaco, which with 45°C (113°F) is apparently holding the official heat record for South America. It's not that hot yet in spring time, but the combination of drought and heat still cater for sufficient bush fires on the side of the road. That at least gives us a certain change from the monotony.

We cross the Rio Parana, which easily spans double the width of the Rhine River in Germany. To be perfectly honest, we didn't even know that this river existed.

Argentinean Hospitality & Asado, Asado, Asado

In Corientes we're invited to Ricardo's, whom we've met on an Internet forum, as with so many of the hosts on our trip around the world. We feel immediately at home with him and his family, their hospitality and kindness is moving and almost limitless. Argentineans top their Northern neighbours by far in these regards, they are significantly more open and friendlier than, for example, Bolivians or Peruvians. Not that we would have any reason to complain about unfriendly behaviour in those countries in general, Argentina is just in an entirely different league when it comes to this.

On our day of arrival there are vegetarian empanadas waiting specifically for Simone, including an introductory course on preparing them. However, that's the end of it then for the almost-vegetarian Simone, because on the next days it's all about Asado. Incidentally this is the first of many we will be invited to in the next months. What's Asado? Strictly speaking, it is practically just a usual barbecue, but still totally different to what we know. In Argentina and its neighbouring countries it is celebrated free of nonsense. Aside from exceptions to the rule, there are no marinades, no dips and sauces, no salad or any other side dishes other than white bread. It's simply an abundance of meat that tastes twice as good when you invite somebody to join in. That's how it feels at least, and we will not be short on invitations to Asado in the months to come. No occasion is too small to organise an Asado, and not infrequently we enjoy the pleasure twice in a day. For Simone, who only eats meat in exceptional situations, this proves a quite challenging test, especially with a modern concept such as vegetarianism, which is rather met with a headshake down here. The refusal of the delicious meat is seen as a rejection of their hospitality. Except in rare cases, where there is placed extra fish or cheese on the grill for Simone, this means for her that she has to grin and bear it.

Ricardo's nine-month old son has way less problems with it and teaches us a lesson in Argentinean early childhood education. With his three teeth he chews cheerfully on a chunk of grilled meat and beams with happiness. Practise makes perfect when one wants to become a true Argentinean.

On Saturdays his mates meet in Ricardo's home workshop. They play around on their motorbikes and they talk petrol-related stuff. Sentimental memories to many similar scenes with friends at home come to mind, still at the same time you feel at home amongst friends with these people, which you have just known for one or two days. The general rule is that shared hobbies and passions build bridges and break the ice. No matter if they are, as in our case, motorbikes and tattoos, or if it is riding a bicycle, fishing, being a fireman or the enthusiasm for soccer, such common ground brings you into contact with people. Eventually it doesn't matter what it is, but as a rule of thumb one could say that the lesser people indulge in a particular passion, the stronger the sense of solidarity and connection gets amongst those people with the same interests. For us mostly the motorcycles and to a lesser extent the tattoos have opened many a doors, which we have never regretted walking through.

A small tip is to show what one is enthusiastic about with stickers on the vehicle or in any other ways, as this provides easy identifiable connecting points.

Biker Event

On Saturdays we ride with the pack to a biker rally. We always have lots of fun at such events, especially to observe the similarities and the differences to events we have experienced in other countries. It is not rare that on such occasions we run around like children in a toy department and point out newest observations to one another. "Did you see him?" and "They do this just as back home in Germany…" and so on. This time, however, there is a severe novelty waiting for us. We were already treated as downright heroes in Ricardo's clique, and at this event it is no different. The mix of enthusiasm for our journey and the typical Argentinean hospitality is indescribable. Everybody wants to talk to us, and without interruption we are invited to new Asados again and again. The communication becomes easier with consumption of each additional beer (1 litre bottles = 2 pints), and the fact that I only possess a rudimentary vocabulary in Spanish and that most of the others don't speak German or English, is no obstacle anymore at the advanced hour.

Even if the whole meeting is not exactly a mega event, we had a good laugh. Furthermore, a lot is exactly as we know it from home, there are embarrassing bikes to be stared at in astonishment, exhaust notes which maltreat the hearing, the usual biker games such as tug-of-war, etc. provide entertainment, burnouts smoke up the place and strippers stir up the blood of wannabe-bikies, even if the "nurse" doesn't go bare but wears panties under her panties.

One thing that is practically non-existing in Argentina or South America is female motorcyclists. This here is a real macho continent, where women are only to be found on the passenger seat, so Simone represents an exotic exception. In saying this, no one has criticised this yet, some bikers would apparently like very much to see a woman on a motorcycle, and even one or another woman gets a sparkle in her eyes. If this is lip service only, or if the general culture and moral concept on this continent discourages women, we do not know, but perhaps the contact with us brought a little change.

The clubs shower us with stickers and t-shirts, and to top it all off, we also receive a fancy goblet made of motorcycle parts in the end. A moving gesture but an unsolvable task at the same time, as we wonder how on earth we are supposed to transport this bulky and super heavy piece? If there's one thing we have learned by now, it is that in such moments factual objections are totally inappropriate. Instead we express our gratitude, hug the donors and cheerfully clap on leather-jacket-covered shoulders. To reject such a present, just because we cannot carry it, would give the wrong signal. The entire thing with the bulky, heavy goblet is to follow us actually on the many motorcycle events, which we will be visiting in Argentina, Brazil and Chile. Similar to the hotel rooms that are reserved for motorcyclists and that are always to be found on the top floor at the very end of the corridor, we merely smile at such things now.

Anniversary for the Show-Off Pannier

In Paraguay an anniversary celebration is called for as my show-off suitcase receives his 50th country code sticker. Spontaneously I set the goal to raise this figure to 2 x 50 in the next seven years up to my 50th birthday, and only in hindsight I realise how difficult this might be. At first sight such a goal might sound easy for a traveller, but the facts are always a little different. To this day we have only crossed 17 countries in 14 months on our journey around the world, and a quick calculation for the next two to three years results in less than 20 countries on our rough route back home. Even if we would graze all the countries on future trips, which we haven't yet seen between Gibraltar and Mongolia, it would not be sufficient. As per the motto, though, that only brave visions take you further in life, I don't give up on this idea quite yet.

Paraguay – Bastion of Corruption

Paraguay has the incredibly dubious reputation of being the most corrupt country out of South America. We had already heard many negatives, and two German expats, who we would like to visit here, had warned us beforehand. By no means we were supposed to play tough with cops, but simply hand over at least a small amount of money, as the consequences in the case of refusal would otherwise be quite drastic. The system virtually forces police officers in this country to open their palms, as they apparently have to cover all expenses, even for their official car, and only receive a third of the living wage as a pay. This sounds less appealing, and from our first yards on we expect to be ransacked by these highwaymen in uniform. At least into the centre of the border city Encarnation we manage to remain unchecked. Next we have to find a Visa Plus ATM and make sure not to be observed by law enforcers when we take out money. Namely they take advantage of the

129

propitious moment at times and demand a percentage of the ATM money to support the widow and orphan fund of the police. Instead we are held up by two reporters of the local radio station, who are both super friendly and dedicated, and who offer that should we have any problems in their country, specifically with cops, we should be in touch with them, as they would be happy to help us. A big smile spreads over my face when I realise the potential of that business card. In the case that we are stopped, I will make sure to speak first and ask for the address of the radio station. I will also happily add that we are invited for an interview and are already running late. Every even dumbest cop should be able to understand such a subtle threat.

To come to the point, again our fears were totally unfounded, as we were not once asked to pay in Paraguay. From other motorised travellers, who were partially up to three months in this country, we heard the same. Of course this could've been plain and simple pure luck, their thesis, however, was that the cops hold up their palms to locals, but have the order from the very top to leave the tourists alone.

The Guard Horse That Keeps Following Me to the Privy

Our hosts earn their living with the breeding of baby chicks, and in addition to that they grant asylum to several dozen dogs, cats and horses. The purest form of Noah's Arch in which every speck of spot is taken by pets. Even in bed those four-legged-friends roam about.

One curious situation is the guard horse that patrols tirelessly the borders of the land plot and attacks every intruder. Unfortunately it is impossible to sneak past it to the privy unnoticed. No matter how much effort I put in, the nag follows me and nudges the toilet door open with his head, the former unfortunately not able to be locked form the inside. And hence I end up one more time with a horse that watches me in closest proximity whilst carrying out my nature's call, extremely irritating.

The Perils of Asking for Directions

Whilst Simone struggles with the import of our motorcycles to Brazil, I am interviewed and photographed with our bikes by a Brazilian motorcycle magazine. What I dismiss as coincidence in that very moment is a tender pre-taste to the following days. Even the principle of the grapevine that most likely brought this reporter to us that quickly, will be something we will experience more often in Brazil.

The entry is extremely arduous, which may have to do with the fact that this border crossing is probably only used occasionally by travellers due to its location. We have chosen it solely, because we want to visit a motorcycle event that is close by on the Brazilian side. A few hours earlier we had actually already been here, when a motorcyclist we know from Argentina gave us the tip not to cross the border here, as the road on the Brazilian side is extremely poor. Instead we should choose a crossing further north, which was not to be found on any of our maps.

When it comes to tips from locals, I am extremely careful. Although they are always given in absolute conviction, it has shown pretty often that locals simply don't get it for various reasons, what and where problems could arise for us. Let's take the case where we ask a man on a donkey if the dirt track, which we are finding ourselves on currently, is passable for our motorbikes for the next hundred miles. He answers, yes, no problem, but the simple fact that our motorbikes can't manage to get through whereas the donkey can, might not ring a bell with him. Or he might have just spoken for the next ten miles as he hasn't ridden any further in his life before, and that the question referred to the next hundred miles, might have not become clear with him.

In South East Europe we occasionally had problems when we showed people a map and hoped for them to give us the right directions. Just in hindsight we realised that they had never seen a map before and hence weren't able to grasp the concept rapidly, which isn't surprising really. Or we made the mistake to ask for the next big city, which was hundred miles away. The respondent had, with a bit of luck, heard of it, but he had not been there yet, and also has no clue on how to get there. But as he would like to help the stranger and also doesn't want to look stupid, one is surely pointed into a direction to follow. Unfortunately in this case, it was completely arbitrary. In the meantime we have become smarter, and instead of enquiring the direction to a specific town, we now ask so-called open questions, such as "Where does this road lead to?", which increases the value of the answers significantly.

Today the pivotal question is, if the friendly motorcyclist is sure that the recommended spot doesn't only have so-called small border traffic but also the necessary facilities, so that travellers from non-neighbouring countries can actually cross the border there. Needless to say that he is absolutely certain that we can make it over there. The same happens with a friendly car driver, who stops to ask if he could help us, and perhaps you can guess his answer already. Of course we can neither export our motorcycles there, nor can we import them on the Brazilian side of the border. Therefore we have to ride back the entire stretch to the first border crossing, with grinding teeth to say the least. As I already mentioned, I have experienced such situations repeatedly, in which a local will give us a tip by deepest conviction that then turns out to be the wrong track. Hence I have become very cautious to even believe in the slightest of it.

Butt Kicking

It's the third weekend in a row at a motorcycle rally for us, nonetheless it doesn't get boring, especially as we are in Brazil, which thereby is different again to Argentina.

The amount of attention we receive here reaches a completely new level. We actually couldn't really imagine any increase to our former experience, but here in Brazil we're truly approached and photographed nonstop. We don't get a break, hundreds of photos and just as many people to meet. These are definitely too many names and faces to even remember in the high numbers they're hitting us, inevitably turning the event into a minefield for us after a few hours. To the best of our knowledge we simply can't figure out anymore whom we should already know and whom we are just meeting to the first time. This is how rockstars must feel, and we're torn between euphoria and the wish to crawl into our tent to have a communication pause for a few minutes at least. But it's good fun nonetheless, and so we resist the temptation to hide. Then this otherwise fantastic day takes a rather unpleasant turn in the evening, when an eccentric guy freaks out, because I deny him a photo with me, one, because he gets terribly on my nerves, and two, because I additionally reject his ideology. By the time he furiously grabs my neck, I don't act intelligent but by intuition, and the martial art reflexes I had learned decades ago and thought forgotten by now, transform into automatic movements. To hell with "in a foreign country you should avoid conflict at (almost) all cost", and the brawler ends up on the floor with a bloody nose faster than he can say "beep." The situation threatens to escalate, his friends attack me from behind and the hosts, which we get along with splendidly, counteract powerfully. In the end the already renowned problematic ruffian and his gang are banned from the premises, and the apologies by the club hosting the event are never-ending as they are visibly embarrassed by this incident. Without further ado we are then accommodated by the club president to avoid any vengeance at night by that roughneck, either against us, or our tent. We have no idea at this stage that this incident will have the most dramatic implications.

Iguazu Waterfalls

The Iguazu Waterfalls are in the Top 4 of our personal South America sightseeing list. The Argentinean part of the journey has already entranced us a few days ago. On the Brazilian side we are further away from the falls, which now open up to us the true dimension of this natural wonder before our eyes. Simply fabulous!

From ever-new perspectives we stare over the raging water masses, breaking thunderously into the deep. One of our favourite spots is the Gargante del Diabolo, where you can dare a long walk at lofty heights out into the wet inferno on a jetty, provided you have the courage for it. After a few seconds already one is soaking wet, but the experience is extraordinary. Despite hefty admission fees on both sides of the falls, we recommend to indulge in both perspectives as the spectacle is worth every cent.

Another temptation now is the Itaipu Dam, which is a joint project between Brazil and Paraguay. Up until the Chinese launched their superlative campaign and outdid it with the Three Gorges Dam, the Itaipu was the number one in the world in terms of power generation.

Here are a few impressive facts:
At its highest point the retaining wall is 65 floors high.
The dam is roughly 2.5 times the size of Lake Constance, which is Central Europe's third largest freshwater lake.
The power generated here covers 90% of the Paraguayan and 20% of the Brazilian electricity requirements, which is a hell of a lot, considering the size of the country and its hunger for energy.
By the way, 100% of the electricity requirement in Paraguay is gained by hydropower, whereas it is still 75% in Brazil. Let's take Switzerland in comparison to this, which is the European prime example and just makes it to 60%. As impressive the numbers are, we thought the dam to

be rather unspectacular. The construction didn't leave a great impression on us and we regretted in hindsight of having taken the tour, which cost us close to 10 USD per person.

Crash!

Our ride across Brazil to Curitiba, where we are invited by a German in exile, starts off poorly. Another flat tyre, have I mentioned already that I hate changing tyres? Otherwise the ride is simply dull. Due to a lack of alternatives we are travelling on a mix of motorways and main roads, and the boring landscape just adds to it. Apart from the mountains in the province of Santa Caterina, Southern Brazil is entirely composed of fenced fields and grazing land, which means that no wild camping is possible.
The next morning bad luck strikes with full force. We are still on the observable national route when a motorcyclist overtakes us and in typical South American style, suddenly merges in right in front of me because he sees a speed camera. An incredibly stupid riding manoeuvre, and I have to slam on my brakes. As the devil has it, Simone glances at the map in that very moment, looks up too late and bangs with full travelling speed into the back of me. I receive a mighty shove forward and my back wheel starts to go sideways. I have my hands full to catch my motorbike, avoid a collision with the idiotic motorcyclist in front of me and not to land in the ditch. My heart is racing, when I finally get it to a halt on the shoulder. I anticipate the worst when I look at Simone, the motorbike lies on its side but she's up again already. Because of her speed, she largely slid across the road and luckily stopped at the shoulder.
The culprit responsible for the accident escaped, what a bastard! I expect serious injuries on Simone and even worse bad damage to her motorbike. Will this be the end of our journey? On this day though, Simone's guardian angel has done a sterling job, I can barely believe it, but her helmet and her protective clothes have prevented the worst. Her motorcycle pants are torn in some parts, her bike jacket has a plate size hole on her elbow and even both jackets underneath are frayed all the way through. Simone's abrasions are not that bad and she doesn't feel the bruises and concussion in that very moment yet, which I know of all too well from my own painful experience.
The damage on both motorbikes is considerable, and at first sight it looks especially dramatic on Simone's bike. However, upon closer inspection the harm turns out to be as unexceptional non-vital, and

that's what always counts on travels in the end: Fuck TÜV certification (German organisation for technical, safety and certification) and appearance, the crucial questions always is, can the motorbike still ride? Many car drivers stopped and wanted to help, they alerted the breakdown service and the ambulance that comes in surprisingly quick. As you never know in such countries, how a situation like this will develop and if you might have to pay a fine or get stuck with significant costs for professional help in the end, so we wave everybody off. The paramedics can hardly comprehend that we do not want to call on their services.

With a feeling of limitless relief I ride on, the journey is not over yet. And what is more important is the knowledge that nothing happened to my girl, hell yeah! The last 60 miles to our next host are still hard work, and it takes several hours to get through the outskirts of the big city Curitiba. I'm glad to see that Simone is struggling through bravely and rides as confident as always, many a people would have turned into hesitant and frightened riders after an accident like that.

The next morning Simone's head is throbbing and she feels nauseous. Looks like a concussion, which means a break for us. In saying this, it couldn't be better timing as Simone can easily rest at our new host's home, who by the way, can barely contain the opportunity to speak his mother tongue with fellow countrymen at last. I utilise the time to bring our motorcycles back into shape. Luckily our host, who actually doesn't even ride a bike, knows the president of a local motorcycle club, who again uses his connections to secure a VIP treatment at his mechanic. The latter embarks with me on a quest for a new or used master brake cylinder housing that could fit Simone's bike. Thanks to our connection, the price for the coolant system repair is quite fair.

On the Run

Simone should stay out of the sun and off the bike for at least three to four days, which proves hard for here. In the meantime I ride to a motorcycle club house party with the formerly mentioned president of the MC. This obviously seems to be a tougher league than the ones we got to know on events so far. Camouflage clothing, tattoos and piercings en masse as well as angry-looking tough guys dominate the scene. My introduction round is met with a varying amount of restrained love, which considering the usual exuberant hospitality in these regions is quite apparent. A few minutes later "my" president whispers excitedly into my ear not to ask any questions, go to my motorbike and follow him at all costs, no matter what may happen. As many questions as there may be preying on my mind, obviously this is not the right time for them. I'm shitting bricks and I have to force myself to walk as casually and cool as possible to my bike, to then ride through the group, which only reluctantly make room. After a few miles my companion stops and explains that there perhaps aren't too many tattooed German motorcycle travellers with matt black bikes in Brazil. Everyone on the club house party seemed to know the story of the Brazilian bikie who got his ass kicked by this German motorcycle traveller not too long ago. As my luck would have it, my opponent was the little brother of the local MC boss. I would call this quite a misfortune. We are 600 miles from the place of the event, maybe the big brother even believes that his little "hermano" had actually deserved the flogging, because again he had pissed off the wrong person, but what counts here most is honour. And honour demands satisfaction. That a hearty beating alone wouldn't be enough, was instantly and firmly made clear by my companion, they all had guns and this is the Brazilian big city. "My" MC head was in a predicament between hospitality and honour codex amongst the local MC presidents, who would demand my extradition.

Apart from us, our host is in danger by this situation as well, which we feel incredibly sorry about. We hold council and can only barely downplay our feelings of panic. We decide to wait through the night, even though we find it hard to sleep. At dawn we literally flee the site although Simone is not really fit to travel yet. The entire venture turns into a real challenge, because three club members work apparently at the national police. In Europe something like this would be unheard of. The fatal thing about it as well is that the national police are responsible for the many checkpoints on all major roads, and a police check would hence be highly dangerous for us, as our Brazilian friends tell us emphatically. In our misery we cannot count on the help of the police, more so we have to view them as enemies. And so we sneak out of the danger zone on small roads, which our satnav doesn't know, and hence we get lost numerous times.

Violence and Weapons

If you fundamentally agree or disagree with the use of violence is a philosophical question, which each individual has to decide for himself. Personally, I am no pacifist, and I consider the use of violence in certain settings, whether it be by the government or private persons in situations of self-defence or emergency as generally legitimate. Yet I would normally almost advise against it when travelling, as independently of the moral justification, a violent reaction or self-defence whilst abroad is often attached to unpredictable risks. It can happen that one quickly mutates from the victim to the villain, who is then to feel the combined anger of the local community of solidarity, all the way up to the lynch mob. Although I effectively didn't stay true to my own golden rule on the Brazilian motorcycle event, de-escalation is almost always a strategy to success in my eyes. Not only in violent situations, but also when one finds himself again powerless at the mercy of cops and border guards. The one who behaves loudly and argues will mostly likely hit a brick wall. Admittedly, there are cases in certain situations now and then, where you can advance with reinforcement or intimidation. Being a traveller you develop a sense for this, well at least most do. We have also met others.

Even clearer is my piece of advice in terms of weapons, hands off! The one, who believes he could scare off an offender or thug with the mere use of a knife, might find himself in bad to worse under certain circumstances. And whoever wants to defend himself with a weapon, will experience a new level of escalation with reasonable certainty, in which the opponent will most likely also have a weapon to present. And what happens next is not funny at all anymore. Of course there are cases, where such measurements were successful, such as the ones in a possible attack of small-town crooks. Or in the case of real tough guys defending themselves. We all have heard or read stories like that or seen movies as such before. But the question is if you're the type of guy who would use a weapon first? Or would you possibly start stabbing somebody without any verbal foreplay? The truth is that this would be required, if you are in real danger and decide to defend yourself in such manner, and I only know a few people who would have the courage and unscrupulousness to do so. To leave the first attack to your opposite is the stuff of novel or movie protagonists and has nothing to do with the sheer reality of such a situation. Hence my obvious advice is for de-escalation, and if needs be the honour might be offended but the damage to your health minimised significantly.

Recap of Brazil

The Iguazu Waterfalls are one of the top attractions of South America, and taking a several day detour in account for them is definitely a valued experience. The journey through Paraguay or North East Argentina is not worth mentioning when it comes to the scenery. Although we have only travelled through South Brazil, which is still larger than Germany, it was scenically the most boring that we have experienced on our journey, and there is nothing but fenced agricultural land. There are supposed to be a few great stretches of road in the mountains of the Santa Catarina province, which we couldn't ride due to bad weather conditions. When it comes to the term "exotic", the region travelled by us was additionally disappointing as you see less black people than back home in Germany. A considerable amount of the population is descendent from German immigrants from more rural regions overseas, who still speak the old dialects. Family names such as Metz, Gehlen and Dreher are as non-exotic as the appearance of the people, who could be living around the corner from you back in Germany. Also on the negative side of things, there are the considerably high costs for South American standards. Very high petrol prices, at times hefty toll charges, in many regions no opportunities to camp wild or camp in general and even the food costs are higher, compared to the neighbouring countries. However, despite all these disadvantages, Brazil has still been a fantastic country to visit, and the sole reason for this are the people. In terms of friendliness and openness only Argentina could keep up with it so far. The trouble with the bikies, which is to stay in our bones for a long time to come, is rather filed in the category of bad luck than a reflection of this country. The larger cities are quite dangerous and should hence only be enjoyed with caution. Other than that the Brazilians have been very hospitable and "my home is your home" is here more than an empty phrase. It's a real bummer that we couldn't accept a number of invitations by the national motorcycle club Brasil Riders due to our hasty departure.

Uruguay – The Most European Country of South America

We enjoy the ride through the wetlands in the East, where the cattle stand in water up to their chest. At this time of the year, Uruguay's coast is like Sleeping Beauty in hibernation. According to what we have heard and read, all hell will break loose at the Riviera of South America in summer time, and the capacities of campsites are often gigantic with 500 sites or more. The strange thing about this is, though, that around this time of the year they are almost all shut. It seems jinxed as the weather doesn't even seem bad. Many a North Sea seaside resort would be delighted to have a summer like that.

In the capital we visit our friend Ernesto, whom we had met in Alaska some time ago. As he knows the life "on the road" only too well from his own experience, he tries to give us as much privacy as possible, which we appreciate greatly. Being a guest frequently drains you quite a bit in a communicative sense, for example it is almost always the same topics that come up, and on the other hand the intensity of conversations is quite high. At times one talks a lot and you have to focus more than having a casual conversation with friends. In addition to this, to communicate in a foreign language, often with the support of gestures and expressions, can become a real effort in the long run.

The mixture is perfect at Ernesto's with phases where we're left to ourselves and enjoy our freedom, or where we visit friends together and he shows us the most memorable parts of Montevideo. We notice how European everything here is. In Uruguay the Indios were wiped out more rigorously than anywhere else in South America, so you see a lot less people with darker skin than in any major German city. In comparison to the neighbouring states, the behaviour of people is more reserved and somewhat European, although not unfriendly.

European politics are followed intensely, and more than once we are addressed by ordinary educated people in reference to our chancellor, who earns the "thumbs up" for her rigorous course in terms of our economic and monetary union. We are gobsmacked and also become a little pensive with these experiences, as we actually wouldn't even know the name of the head of state of our host country.

Buenos Aires – Once and Never Again!

It is early afternoon when we ride onto a charming, secluded camping ground 60 miles before Buenos Aires. The owner replies to our enquiry about the price with the counter-question if we are travellers. When we answer in the affirmative his response is "Then it will cost you nothing". Such experiences rejoice the heart of a motorcycle vagabond. Despite a promising start, the next day turns out less exciting. We pick up spare parts at Dakar Motos, which is popular with motorcycle travellers and drink a leisurely coffee with Xavier and Sandra. We decline their invitation to camp in their backyard, because the 20km train trip into the centre of town puts us off, but a few unnerved hours later we regret this missed opportunity. The search for a hotel in Buenos Aires turns out to be incredibly frustrating. We were aware well ahead that hotels in this city would be quite expensive, but unexpectedly another hurdle is added to this misery. Despite the different agreement by our favoured hostel, the place has no parking. All other parking lots in the immediate surrounding that charge fees, have motorcycles on their fee structure signposts, but they refuse to take us in with the argument that "We have never had motorcycles here before". This kind of "We-always-do-it-this-way" mentality in South America has infuriated us many times, and a significant aversion to deviate from the customary scheme is widespread here. Add to that a severe lack of entrepreneurial spirit in employees, and you can imagine our despair. Both our motorcycles take up the space of an entire car and could hence bring in more profit, but none of the parking cashiers wants to grant us parking, which is totally insane. Situations like these occur over and over again whilst travelling, the logical solution is obvious and yet your counterpart won't accept it. You almost feel the urge to force your opponent into insight. Of course this isn't possible, and therefore, as so often, you are resigned to simply smile and proceed with your friendly persuasive efforts, mostly without success. The final result and victory ceremony of our dilemma of the day is that, thanks to the intervention of our hotelier, one of the guys gives in with grinding teeth, but only after a long round of discussions. The cost for parking and accommodation for two nights accumulates to an amount that is our usual average for accommodation in an entire month in South America. Hence the Argentinean capital is definitely not going to appear on the list of favourite places we would ever like to return to. Appropriately, it pours down on the day of our departure, but with prices like these there is no way but the onward journey. The rain is so heavy that even my beloved saying "Rather be on the road with bad weather than at work with sunshine" forfeits its motivational force.

La Posta del Viajeros en Moto

"La Posta del Viajeros en Moto", the contact point for motorcycle travellers in Azul, especially its manager Jorge, who is called "Pollo" (chicken) by most, is a legend. It is definitely one of the places you must experience, and without it a motorcycle journey through South America is incomplete.

The happy soul Pollo, who is always in a good mood, runs this idealistic project for roughly two decades now. It is financed by donations of guests and a lot of engagement from Pollo. There are approximately 50 motorcycle travellers who stop here per year, and this happens mostly in season, which is from December to March. In high season there can be up to 20 tents in the garden at the same time, and it is a bummer we don't get to experience this. With it being the beginning of October, we are unusually early for two-wheeled Patagonia riders, and therefore have the entire kingdom to ourselves. One can spend hours upon hours in studying the creative footprints of motorcycle travellers, and it must be up to many hundreds that have immortalised themselves with sculptures, mural paintings and tags. We discover many a friend and others we had heard of or read about. This truly is a Mecca for motorcycle globetrotters, and I know no other place that could live up to this.

We have lost track on how often we have already been interviewed spontaneously by radio stations. This time, however, it is something very special, we are guests at Pollo's. The broadcasting studio is a tiny little room, which we can only fit into with great difficulty and by holding our breaths. The remarkable thing is that Pollo broadcasts his motorcycle radio show here for two hours each week.

We reward ourselves with a meal in the "Casa de Comida", a typical buffet-restaurant, where you pay the food on the plate by weight. Two pounds cost around 4.50 USD, so you can imagine how cheap a sumptuous meal is. That Pollo is known all over town also becomes apparent to us here. Everybody entering the restaurant quizzes us, and as soon as they hear that we're travelling by motorbike, they come to the conclusion "Oh, so you're visiting "La Posta". Even the Asian manager of the place is highly interested in our journey, and upon our departure he hands us a bag full of empanadas for the long way ahead of us. Such positive encounters are the ones that make up the quality of life.

Patagonia – Where Two-Wheeled-Travellers Reach Their Limits

Patagonia, which by the way starts more north than I ever thought, welcomes us befittingly with a stiff breeze and indefinite straightforward roads.
How many daunting stories had we read and heard about this region? And what of it is true or what is, as so often, slightly to strongly exaggerated to the benefit of the narrator?
Perpetual wind and a lot of rain as well as sideway gusts of up to 60 miles/h in combination with meter-high banks can become a fatal mix. If you're blown off the road, this is often followed by a fall. It is supposed to be cold here and deserted, and hence poor in infrastructure. In short, a country that isn't suited at all for motorbikes or bicycles and where only fools on two wheels dare to travel. And apparently there are plenty of those, particularly in the short season down there, which starts in December for two-wheeled travellers, as the seasons are opposite to the northern hemisphere. In spite of all doubts of oh so many travel stories, the fact that Patagonia is wet, cold and windy is undeniable.
For many the Horizons Unlimited Motorcycle Travellers Event in Viedma is the kick-start. On Christmas and New Year most of the motorcycle travellers are all the way down in Ushuaia, the most

southern city in the world. In a positive and negative sense, this is also where the party is going on. When it comes to us, we don't want to wait until then, as we're already crazy about finally taking on this adventurous leg, even if it means being there seven weeks earlier than everybody else. Apart from that we have to hurry "on the way up" as there is still a great deal to see and experience on this stretch, and in January we are supposed to cross over to New Zealand from somewhere in the middle of Chile. We can't do it later as winter will get in our way otherwise.

This is a typical example on restrictions a world trip is subject to. Many believe that with such an abundant time frame one would be entirely flexible when it comes to the speed of travelling. But all the things that need to be considered are actually plenty, and hence restrict you with more or less narrow limits in the end, such as seasons in general, wet seasons, storm seasons and many more. And amidst all this it means to still always keep looking ahead as far as possible with one eye open to the country's particularities and restrictions, which you will be travelling through next.

The Valdez Peninsula

Our first stop in Patagonia is the Valdez Peninsula. When we arrive at the national park's pay station to pay our fee, we both look slightly confused at the handwritten scoreboard, announcing the current date, temperature (11°C/52°F) and the notation "windless". We exchange puzzled looks, if this is windless, what then is supposed to be a real windy day in Patagonia?

In terms of its scenery, the Valdez Peninsula is definitely not worth a visit, so why come here? This question is answered immediately when you get closer to the beach. There is an abundance of maritime life, and from the lookout near Puerto Piramides you get a taste of the finest.

In New England on the East Coast of the US we did a whale watching tour a few years ago that cost us a little fortune. For five long hours I tried not to empty the contents of my stomach, but proceeded to stare intensely onto the ocean with a dozen of other idiots. The highlights were two, three sights of tiny whale body parts, and that was that for me. I had sworn myself that I will never do a whale watching tour ever again.

If you compare that experience with what you can comfortably see here from the beach without the terrible rocking, the verdict is pretty clear: this is a bomb! One can partially see half a dozen of whales at the same time in the picture, and they don't show a little bit of skin, but jump out of the water or leave their tail in the air for ages. The photos we shot from the lookout alone were already brilliant, but they can't compete with the ones Simone takes the next day on a whale tour then, where her raft comes at arm's length to the giants of the ocean.

But even the sightings on land itself on the 120 miles gravel circuit over the peninsula are inspiring, cheeky grey foxes and primeval-looking armadillos. Fantastic.

400,000 Penguins in one Spot

In Patagonia and Tierra del Fuego there are plenty of opportunities to see penguin colonies. We are not just after visiting any old one, but the largest colony on this continent. In Punta Tombo there are supposed to be up to 200,000 penguin couples, something we happily accept the 160 miles detour for. The first impression is disappointing, instead of the mass effect we realise that the caves and burrows are spread widely. I have to admit that the area it all is spreading over is actually gigantic. But a much smaller colony would've also been quite impressive. Often there are a few individual breeding burrows under shrubbery, and more rarely you can see barren spots with dozens of caves at a glance. Although one always has to remain on the marked paths of the nature reserve, you get surprisingly close to the penguins. Often all you'd have to do is to stretch out your arm to be able to touch them, which is simply amazing. Contrary to the Valdez Peninsula we have unfortunately not caught the right moment, the young only start hatching end of November/beginning of December. In return we still spot some latecomers, performing the courtship display and mating now in mid October, which looks very cute.

Across Patagonia

We camp on a pebble beach, and in the morning we are woken by the mating call of an elephant seal that hangs around in the water 50 yards from us. In terms of acoustics the bull is definitely a match for any deer in heat.

From Punta Tombo it would only be some 1,000 miles to Ushuaia, the most southern point of our journey. For months this city was still so far away and hence somewhat surreal to us. Now we could easily reach it in three days, especially as there is nothing much of interest on the way there that could tempt us to linger. Instead we prefer riding down South along the Andes on the west side of Patagonia.

In Trelow, one of the many places in this area with Welsh origin, we are invited at Juan's, who once helped an English couple when their motorcycle broke down. We had met the latter in Panama and enquired about extraordinary positive experiences, which is how we got to the e-mail-address of Juan.
And here comes the big prize question for attentive readers and Argentina lovers, what do we get on our first evening? Exactly right, Asado! We enjoy a wonderful barbecue in a circle of many nice motorcyclists, and incidentally this gang is able to hold one's drink. All together we stay three days at Juan's and every night it means "Raise your cups", the latter often long into the night or even until the next morning. After such a "triathlon" we come to realise that we aren't 18 anymore.
In Juan's workshop I can quietly undertake a few urgent and necessary maintenance repairs, and we finally have the opportunity once again to wash all our stuff, including my motorcycle pants that have meanwhile started to smell of true adventure.
A cool promotion for us and a token of friendship is our t-shirt story. Originally I just needed a replacement for my extremely ragged motorcycle vagabond sweatshirt, when the search ends in Trelow with a

friendship sweatshirt, carrying the motorcycle vagabond print on one side and "Ebrios del Asfalto" (drunk by asphalt) and the club name of Juan and his friends on the other side.

The continent is already so narrow down here, that from Trelow on the east side it is only 500 miles to the Andes on the west side. There we want to follow along the mountain towards South. However, first of all it is all about natural disasters again. Many times we had to change our route in South America due to the rain season, landslides, floods, untypical snowfall for the season and demonstrations. Now again? Allegedly the Puyehue volcano has erupted, and it now seems that ash has fallen several times throughout the night. On the last eruption a few months ago the ash fall had been so heavy that it had buried half of Patagonia. Bariloche in particular had been hit severely at the time. We can't find out anything on the Internet, and from our perspective no news is good news. Therefore we set out in Trelow and hope that no road relevant to us is closed.

Over and over again we see weak tornados in the dry bushland, other than that the leg is pretty dull. But from Los Plumas onward it becomes very beautiful, and after two months of scenic boredom this proves to be a real pleasure. The colour contrasts between the blue sky, the grey rocks and the green yellow flora are remarkable. We use one of the few non-fenced sections to ride over a terrible track to the Rio Chubut, where we find an idyllic place to camp. This is pure vagabond romance.

Snow-Covered Peaks Wherever You Look

We reach the Parque Nacional Los Alerces, where we camp on the bank of the Lago Futalaufguen. There are snow-covered peaks wherever you look, and I dare to say that the border at the Futaleufú pass may scenically be one of the most beautiful we've ever crossed. In saying this we have certainly never been searched as thorough as by Chilean customs. Pretty painful, but after everything we had heard, this seems to be standard when entering this country. Other than the usual banned things, one can also not take many fresh foods into Chile, and they are very strict about it. In the first small town, which for us will also remain the only notable place for several hundred miles, there is one bank to be found. Exactly this one bank has opening hours that are challenging the "Savings Bank Bus" of more remote regions back home in Germany, which amounts to an incredible three times per week for a few hours only. The ATM, which we have already been warned of, is apparently broken. Great, and how are we going to get our hands on Chilean pesos now? First hope glimmers when a local successfully draws money from the apparently broken ATM. Unfortunate in our case, is, though, that the machine doesn't like our VISA cards, and after numerous unsuccessful attempts with even more varied approaches, I give up and try the Mastercard. Lo and behold, the box rattles and clatters and spits out a bundle of notes. Again my tactic of carrying as many plastic cards as possible has proved successful. And mostly not just VISA cards, which by the way are easier to get free of fees back home, compared to

Mastercard and others.

We stock up on food supplies for the next days at prices that are to be expected in a touristy mountain village. The first refuel a few hours later then brings tears to our eyes, with 1.60 USD / litre fuel here costs more than double as on the other side of the border. It is lucky that we filled up our canisters with foresight in Argentina. We continue on through a picture-book mountain landscape. This here is one of the most enchanting spots on earth that we have ever had underneath our wheels. The only thing that spoils our euphoria is the looming rain clouds. But as it is so often in mountainous areas, as soon as you take a turn around the mountain, the weather is completely different again. As a ranger explains, it has become absolutely unpredictable these days up there anyway as the ash erupting from the volcano throws everything out.

Speaking of volcano, this morning we learned that another volcano has apparently erupted on our route. But how did the old saying go that one finds hard to follow at times? If you can't change it, don't worry about it. Alternative routes down here are associated with gigantic detours, therefore we carry on regardless and let it be a surprise.

Carretera Austral

The mood of the motorcycle vagabonds is "top de luxe", the sun shines and on top of that we're travelling on a South American road legend, the Carretera Austral. At some point it leads us into the sleepy town of Puyuhuapi, which is situated at a pretty fjord. A few miles later we arrive at the Parque Nacional Queulat.

From the campground one can already see and repeatedly hear the "Ventisquero Colgante" glacier thunder. We hike the few miles to it in top weather conditions.
Compared to all the rain in Alaska, the glacier treat here in Patagonia is considerably better.

Even after a few days our enthusiasm for the never-ending snow covered mountains won't wane. The Carretera Austral is big travel cinema, and it's hard to pick a spot for our daily picnic. Should we take these mountain chains for our view or rather move on to the banks of the next lake? The choice seems endless on both counts and we feel we are in a motorcyclist's heaven.
Located close to Puerto Ibanez, Cerro Castillo stands out even for local means, and in the course of walking around it half way one has many changing perspectives on offer. We set up camp in the bushes near the road and enjoy the last rays of light at the banks of a pebble river. However, at dusk heavy clouds fill the sky with rain and strong winds set in, which last the entire night. Our tent is truly challenged, but again demonstrates to be outstanding. Nonetheless it is hellishly loud in our little home due to the wind and the flapping noises, generated by our tent. We're continually awoken by the noise in the night, but what might superficially sound like an annoyance is pure romance for us. We love such situations. As per homelike standards, a storm is roaring outside, in which we don't want to be unprotected, but the fact is that we aren't. We lie in our cosy sleeping bags and can cuddle up to the person we love. What an indulgence, our life couldn't be any better. Something that doesn't strike me anymore the next morning, when it still blows and rains like hell and the call of nature cannot be ignored any longer. The next minutes surely don't belong to the best moments of a motorcycle vagabond life. Also having to pack up the tent in the rain, especially not when at some stage the tent cover comes off whilst packing it up, which forces me to somehow stuff it all into the one big bag, all our clothes included.
But a few hours later the sun is shining again, and as so often we can barely comprehend why we'd been in the doldrums just a few moments earlier.

Lago General Cabrera

The last 200 miles of the Carretera Austral to Villa O'Higgins we don't ride through, because this would be a dead end road, and instead we swerve east at the south end of the Lago General Cabrera.

Apropos Lago General Cabrera, this lake is the second-largest in South America and it beats lake Titicaca by far when it comes to panorama and most of all fun riding. On the Argentinean side it is actually called Lago Buenos Aires, and you should try at all costs, to use the relevant national name for it in the individual country. I don't know what the Chilean think of the Argentinean, but in reverse it is long not forgotten, that the Chilean have helped the British in the 80's in the Falklands War. The ride along the south bank of the Lago General Cabrera is epic. It isn't only grand panorama that follows one after the other, it honestly is a world-class view that simply doesn't end. This is complemented by a track, which is real fun. It goes up, down, to the left, right again, and it just never gets boring.

Amongst Brothers or Lucky in the Breakdown Misfortune

Many times we have experienced how an initially shitty breakdown turned into a great encounterin the end. However, whilst still stuck in the drama, one is far from such insight.

This time it is a disintegrating tyre that produces worry lines on my forehead. At some point one can already see the radial coming through, dammit! This one won't last for long anymore, although it only has clocked up a few miles. If we would've only taken seriously the warnings of other motorcyclists of not buying these Brazil manufactured tyres of a German brand. In the dump we find ourselves in, there are two tyre places, but help is not to be expected here, as they only feel responsible for car tyres. There we go again, don't dare to deviate from the "That's-how-we-always-do-it" principle. As if a motorcycle tyre would have to be repaired in such a different way. Upon my enquiry if they could order a tyre, the guys burst out in laughter. How could they, they're just responsible for car tyres! Dead end, this is not how we could possibly move on into any direction. Theoretically we could get sent a tyre from one of our South American friends, but that would mean a week at least in this unlikeable jerkwater town, so we favour the decision to ride on into the next big town. On our side of the continent there is none to be found anywhere though, therefore it means again to have to ride to the other side, all together 250 miles through dull Nothingness. The only amusing thought is that we might be the first globetrotters in an eternity here, as there truly is absolutely no reason whatsoever of why anybody would want to cross the continent here from East to West. All travellers either travel along the Andes from north to south, or vice versa, or they take the Atlantic route.

On the second half then we come into oil territory. As far as the eye can see, oil pumps extract up the black gold from the Patagonian ground.

In Comodore Rivadavia, an optically rather unattractive town, we are successful in the third shop. The "Take-it-or-buy-it-somewhere-else-if-you-think-there-might-be-another-suitable-tyre" attitude and price both bring tears to our eyes, but in the end we're glad that we were able to find a "slipper" that fits in the first place. In an auto shop we get the similar game for our headlight bulb, the light bulb costs 31 USD, oh dear! My horror must be so authentic that the manager gives me a pity discount and drops the price to 28 USD. I don't even think I was being scammed, spare parts are simply incredibly expensive in Argentina as they pay at least 50% import duty on top of the European prices.

And now to the pleasant part, we're riding to the biker bar that Juan had recommended to us. We hang around in front of it for a while until the owner finally rumbles along on his Harley and rides befittingly through the door into the taproom. Marcelino is a unique specimen in the truest sense. After we've set up our tent next to the building, we're invited to the family dinner in the bar's kitchen. For once we don't get Asado but a yummy paella.

That people go out very late in Argentina is something we had noticed in Buenos Aires and Trelow already, and in saying this I mean really late. Clubs don't open before midnight and parties are only frequented around 3am. That's at least our specific experience. These are by far no times that suit our daily rhythm whilst travelling, in which we rather live by daylight due to our continuous camping. But how do they say, one should celebrate the parties as they fall and when in Rome. And today we celebrate properly, for as we are here and are somewhat like ambassadors of the German drinking ability. When the first band climbs onto the stage at 3am, our eyes are already on half-mast. For some reason our glasses simply will not empty, Argentinean hospitality can be merciless. When we finally stumble knackered and drunk as a skunk into our tent at 6am, the band still gives its best, which is, to say the least, not really appreciated by us. We don't care about the fact that our tent is only a few yards from the stage and the purpose of the separating wall is rather a visual than acoustic statement, yet we fall into a deep sleep instantaneously.

The following Saturday we spend relaxed at the house of club members and are guided through the city by motorcycle escort. Sunday we take a 200 km excursion to the next neighbouring club together, distances in Patagonia are slightly different to ours back home.

We are already familiar with the concept of the "Moto Asado" from Brazil, and on Sundays everybody sits generally well mannered at the table in a large room and it is dished-up greatly.

This time there are beef, chicken, sheep and lamb to choose from, and as per always it comes in large amounts. Today there is even red wine included in the already fair overall price. Apropos, there's still a big difference to Europe, no matter in which country in Central or South America, binge drinking and riding aren't a legal combination anywhere here, but are still practised everywhere. It is so natural that we are looked at strangely when we refuse beer and spirits with the remark that we still have to ride later. When we then add how strictly one is checked nowadays back home for alcohol and drugs, and the consequences it has when you're caught, South Americans are unfailingly shocked and toast the relief at being so far from Germany with just another good sip of their national drink, the Fernet-Coke.

When it comes to the farewell at last, it feels like we are saying Goodbye to good old friends. Many hands are shaken, on many shoulders tapped and many a kiss given. The farewell from Marcelino is especially heartfelt, and his offer to come to our rescue wherever in Patagonia, is no empty phrase. I bet he would actually drive a thousand miles with his truck to pick us up in an emergency. In terms of hospitality and readiness to help, the Brazilians, Uruguayans and first and foremost Argentineans have put us to shame many times. Our journey has already been worth it solely for these wonderful experiences.

Mud and Rain – The Vagabond Life is Not All Bright Sunshine

Today is once again one of those days, for hours nothing but fences and zero chance of finding a resting place. And on top of everything else the weather changes and gets worse rapidly, with nasty wind, freezing temperatures and heavy rain. Within a short period of time our mood is at rock bottom. In these reduced visibility conditions it is very difficult to realise the state of the road. When suddenly gravel turns into soil, or let's say mud, due to the rain, I don't realise the change and start having bad tail motion. 300 yards later I come to a halt with a pumping heart. Simone isn't that lucky, her slippery slide ends with the bike on its side in a stable position. On my way back to her I can barely walk, because the mud is so sticky, and it is a miracle I managed it in one piece. As the proverb goes "To move the cart into the vertical in two's", my hernia is less excited at this prospect, but there is no alternative at hand, and falling as well as getting up again is part of our lives.

Around 8.30 pm we finally make it to the only village for far and wide. Two dozen houses, a petrol station that is renowned of constantly running out of gas and a hostel with camping facilities, although in the case of the latter the term "campsite" is rather a euphemism, looking at the small size of the backyard. Malicious detractors even suspect a collaboration with the notoriously dry petrol station.

Cold, wet conditions, frustrations, all these are forgotten, however, when we realise in the half-light who is parked in the yard, Weggu and Chrigge! Two of our globetrotter friends, whom we hadn't seen since Panama, but whom we are in active e-mail contact with. What a fabulous long evening that we spend in their warm camper van. Time flies with travel anecdotes and the exchange of route tips, and Weggu's question if she should open another bottle of wine is answered more than once with three eagerly nodding heads. It's a bummer that we're travelling into opposite directions and we are left with just that one evening. The opportunity to re-connect to "old" travel friends instead of daily new acquaintances is all too seldom. Therefore one is always very happy when crossing again ways every few weeks or months with a "team" you have grown fond of. Such camaraderie has no class distinction for us at any rate, no matter if bicycle, motorcycle or four-wheeled traveller, the commonalities of the life and travel style outweigh the differences. Which is not to say that you go along with everybody you meet. It's similar to normal life, where sparks fly with some but not with others. And the more remote the region, the more willing one is to approach the other and find out if you're on the same wave length.

After an abundant breakfast together in the morning, we make on our way again to find the reputation of the petrol station confirmed, no petrol. Fortunately our canisters are full.

El Chaltén

The Ruta Cuarenta is not real fun. The old gravel road doesn't exist any longer, because a new tarmac road is being built, which covers it for a greater part. Soon everything is supposed to be tarred from Perito Moreno to the southern end of the RN40, but currently it means for us to wobble on a construction site road for what looks like an eternity, parallel to the not yet finished tarmac road. Thanks to the Patagonian wind the mud is considerably dried, yet still treacherous. Full concentration is necessary, which, when done over hours, tires one out.

El Chaltén is in a super cool location, with beautiful mountains and glaciers in every direction. The Fitz Roy Massif is the top attraction, although it is normally draped in clouds. However, we are lucky that in the four days that we are here, we always have clear visibility.

Mind you, at night it is extremely windy. Although we have prudently set up our tent behind a wind screen and secured it perfectly, it flaps and bends every night alarmingly, the more so because the wind comes in the most unloved form of every two-wheel-rider, namely as heavy gust. The roaring of the wind and most over all the noise of the tent make it impossible to have a quiet and uninterrupted night rest.

The area actually belongs to the "Los Glacieres NP" and is a hiking paradise. With the required level of fitness, one can spend several weeks trekking through this world-class landscape. There's not much fitness to be found with the motorcycle vagabonds, particularly not with me, I shamefully have to admit. The necessary back and shoulder muscles for riding a motorbike are in top condition, but when it comes to hiking, I instantly start groaning and gasping.

South American Deposit Lunacy

Despite the spectacular location, we don't like El Chaltén at all. It is the epitome of a tourist mecca, food and alcohol are extremely expensive and business practises are geared for scamming. In the largest supermarket they generally refuse to return deposits on PET bottles, which is no trifle with 0.60 USD per bottle. The deposit regulations in Brazil, Uruguay and Argentina have already brought my pulse up to 180 more than once, as everybody seems to handle it to their own liking here. The deposit per bottle is between 0.60 to 0.90 USD, and return is generally only possible with a receipt in the same shop where you bought it from originally. At times, though, it is only credited to a new purchase you don't really want to undertake. The worst of all are those who refuse to sell beer if you don't return empty bottles. I would love to shake and scream at them "No, you are not allowed to be dumb! You HAVE to sell me beer!"

Once again we feel like Don Quijote in the struggle against the "That's-how-we've-always-done-it" windmills. How do these idiots think the beer trade has ever begun? If everybody would've first demanded empty bottles, no bottle would've ever been sold to this very day. Such moments can truly be bitter. The entire dusty and hot day I have been looking forward to a cool beer in the evening. We even camp deliberately on a city campsite to have the opportunity of getting hold of a Pils. And now the desired drink is at arm's length in front of me, but yet I can't have it due to a stubborn idiot. Cruel, but in the same time a typical example for how you learn to value many a things you used to take for granted back home, when you come to learn the unpleasant alternative on travels.

The extreme tourism in El Chaltén holds nonetheless something good for us in the end. It has the "Mountain Repair", a shop that can practically repair anything in terms of equipment and clothing, undertaken by a professional by the way. As far as I'm concerned, I'm happy with the price as well as the quality of the work. A new carriage for my parka zipper, a completely new and heavy zipper for my tank bag and one of my boots was sewn again.

5,500 Yards of Ice Front

On the way to El Calafate the strong wind pushes us to our limits and riding is wearisome and fatiguing. The condors don't seem to have any problems with the gusty winds, which would be classified as a medium storm back home. They seem to glide effortlessly and majestically above and beside us. Large icebergs drift on the lakes, and despite knowing better one is tempted to look out for polar bears.

The Perito Moreno Glacier can already be seen from afar, one of the other top attractions of South America. The gigantic ice front is 66 yards high and three miles wide. Its crevasses seem to glow icy blue in the afternoon light. When it comes to glaciers, the Perito Moreno is what Machu Picchu is for ancient ruins. Following that, everything else seems rather disappointing, small and inconspicuous. Even in Canada and Alaska, where there really is no shortage of glaciers, we have never seen anything comparable.

Tough Blokes Wear Vests

We are in luck, this weekend there is a big three-day festival in a stadium in El Calafate. In Patagonia almost everything revolves around horses in some form. In the afternoons we watch horse ball games, and in the evenings the fun begins with rodeo.

In Germany, men in vests don't exactly belong to the obvious tough crowd. Here in Argentina it is entirely different. Yeee haw, the gauchos give it all and have to put up with rough stuff at times. While watching my "cojones" are already hurting.

Hospitality Repay

We haven't seen a house for hours. At a crossroads then, there is a lonely petrol station in the middle of nowhere. For us such places literally are the breath of the atmosphere of a life "on the road".

As per usual, everything is covered in stickers from travellers, which we study with great enthusiasm and get excited about when we spot people we know. Lucky for us, we have had made a splendid supply of motorcycle vagabond stickers in Central America, which are worth gold, particularly here in South America. Practically every motorcyclist here is in a club, and every club has it's own sticker. To exchange these stickers is a ritual. The fact that we are from Germany and hence from far away, makes our stickers even more valuable, and the ones who are given one, are extremely proud. In addition to this we have a fantastic present to say "Thank You" with when we receive smaller or larger niceties.

We experience a lot of hospitality and readiness to help on our journey, although we had to learn first to accept it. That is even more difficult on our behalf, if the giver doesn't have much him/herself. For many it is simply a wonderful feeling to help and to do good for a stranger, they often don't even think about something in return. Notwithstanding, such is common decency, and it doesn't have to be anything materialistic. A well-meant compliment, an open ear, anecdotes from the exotic life of a traveller, political information that would usually not be available, a typical meal from our homeland, radiation of the splendour when the host shows off with his foreign friends, there are countless possibilities to say "Thank You" in a subtle but effective way. The only mistakes you can make with a genuine invitation are to refuse or to reciprocate with money.

Torres del Paine

We have stopped to count how many times we have crossed the border between Argentina and Chile by now.

In front of us rises the world famous Torres del Paine National Park, which we would count in the Top 5 attractions of the continent after everything amazing we have read about it already. The park isn't only known for its great mountain massif but also for its bad weather. In that respect we are something like half lucky, it could be much worse. But even like this, it is not really the best weather to ride a motorbike in. Temperatures of 10°C (50°F), in combination with light rain and heavy wind, feel significantly colder and don't really help the morale. Apart from that the weather changes every 2 to 5 minutes, and I have never experienced something like this before. The icebergs, which have already become a common sight, have gigantic dimensions here. Other than that the appeal of the national park remains somewhat undisclosed to us. Regardless of the weather, this seems to be more something for hiker than for motorcycle travellers, and for us as transient motorcyclists the 28 USD entrance fee really wasn't worth it. The

Torres del Paine surely doesn't make it to our Top 5 experiences of South America.

Shortly before we leave the park it is time for a canister fill-up again. The distances between petrol stations down here are simply enormous, especially when strong headwind can lead to extremely higher petrol consumption. It is crucial to have a nozzle for the canister, because if you try without one in the powerful breeze or even try to use, as per South American custom, a funnel construed from a PET bottle, there'll be a huge mess in which only a fraction of the precious petrol lands in the tank.

Murderous Wind

The last 160 miles to Punta Arenas are tough stuff. The tarred road is top de luxe, but the wind blows as brutal as ever, bloody hell! We have our hands full to stay on track, and as the wind comes in strong gusts I don't manage on two occasions. The first time it pushes me to the right, off the road, but I'm lucky as this is one of the few spots where the road doesn't end in an embankment. The second time I am not able to prevent ending up in slow motion on the opposite side of the road, but I strike it lucky again as there's no opposite traffic in that very moment.
Up to this day I thought I was confident to ride in wind, but I have to say that this self-assessment starts to have cracks on this very day. This

was beyond my control, plus riding in such circumstances is torture. One has to completely concentrate, back and shoulder as well as neck muscles are horrendously stiff due to the side wind. To hold one's head, including helmet in an upright position alone is a highly tiring affair. When we finally make it to Punta Arenas, we are absolutely knackered. Originally we had wanted to camp in the small backyard of the hostel "Indepencia", which is highly acclaimed by travellers, but the wind blows merciless even here, so that we decide spontaneously to spoil ourselves with a little luxury for once. We can't resist the double room for 18 USD that adjoins the totally overheated kitchen. Also the multifunctional shower in the impeccable bathroom and the high speed WiFi are important arguments in favour of this decision. Needless to say that through our entire stay there it is almost always calm, so let's talk about Murphy's Law. But that's the way it is here, one day there are stormlike winds and on the next there might be nothing. And the weather changes every half hour anyway.

Much further south from Punta Arenas one can't ride any further on the South American mainland. The more puzzling it is at first sight that the central geographical point of Chile is a few miles south from Punta Arenas. However, the simple explanation is that Chile is huge and takes up a big chunk of Antarctica all the way down to the South Pole.

Besides a pretty museum, a not too uninteresting cemetery and a few shipwrecks south of the city, Punta Arenas has the highest density of red light bars, which I have ever seen in a town of this size before. Perhaps this is because of the harbour or due to the many gauchos in the surrounding area?

And here comes the newest lesson in regards to bottle deposits: We make sure to buy beer bottles that are specifically marked "retornable", but the next day we are refused the deposit repayment of 1.10 USD per bottle, as apparently the notation "retornable" means merely that one doesn't have to pay another deposit for a new bottle when returning the empty one. And again I realise how well off we are in Germany.

Tierra del Fuego

We take the ferry over to Tierra del Fuego, whose name means pure adventure to us. Even a landlubber like myself knows Cape Horn and the Strait of Magellan, which we have just crossed.

The term "Tierra del Fuego" derives from the time of the early European sailors, who saw the smoke columns of fire from the indigenous people when sailing around the continent. Faithful to the motto "Where smoke is there is fire", "Tierra del Fuego" received its striking name.

Although it might look like it on larger scale maps, Tierra del Fuego does not belong to the South American mainland and therefore also not to Patagonia, it is more an island.

Meanwhile we are not off to a good start in Tierra del Fuego, as a leaking rear shock absorber causes me great concern. The deserted Tierra del Fuego is pretty much the last place on earth, where I would like to experience such a problem, and true to the saying "What one can't change, should remain ignored" we ride on and try to repress any thoughts to this unsolved dilemma.

Similar to the Atlantic side of Patagonia, the boondocks landscape reigns here. In other words, flat grasslands, unfailingly garnished with an abundance of sheep. A flat tyre on Simone's motorbike doesn't exactly enhance my mood.

And as so often this calls to get down the bags on the side of the road, take off the tyre, roll up my sleeves, grab the levers and get to work. Manual tyre changes really aren't any fun, and as the weather changes in light speed mode here, we get to know the true promise of this on top of everything else when, whilst I patch up the tyre and all tools as well

as many other things lie spread out pretty much everywhere, we get entirely drenched. I swear loud and whole-heartedly, what a pain in the arse.
Showery weather turns into continuous rain through the course of the day, and when we ride into Rio Grande, the largest city of Tierra del Fuego, we are wet, frozen solid and in a foul mood. To round it all up, the two only camping facilities are closed. What a rubbish day. Quite obvious for a city, one doesn't find a spot for wild camping on every corner, and we don't want to go back to a hotel for budget reasons. After a miserable night we embark on the search of the local Honda dealer the next day. Although he can't help us much, he offers one of his employees to help us with the local "spare part ping pong" of the day, which, as per usual, takes us back and forth through the entire city. In the end we land at the place of Motocross champion Hugo, and after his initial hesitation the pensioner agrees to repair the rear shock absorber. I am sceptical as this is truly no run-of-the-mill task. However, what I get to see in the following hours is indeed pure perfectionism. And as is so often the case, the initially hopeless seeming predicament turns into a fantastic human encounter. Hugo and his wife, who were both quite reserved in the beginning, slowly warm up to us and we end up sitting with the two in their best room, drinking mate tea. Last but not least we are even invited for dinner the next day and I am allowed to tinker on the motorbikes by myself in Hugo's sacred halls, which obviously is a rare privilege.

The End of the World

After one year, six months and 22 days, or respectively 58,178 miles, we arrive with the best weather conditions in Ushuaia, the most southern city of the world. Only 2,400 miles left to the South Pole, however, we have reached the most southern point of our journey here. It's not surprising that the Argentineans call it "Fin del Mundo", the end of the world, as from here onward you can only travel on to Antarctica by ship.
In the evening we enjoy the fabulous view, indulge in a well-earned beer and are happy to have managed to get here together. Speaking of beer, Tierra del Fuego is my most favourite province in Argentina, because you don't have to pay a bottle deposit here. Yes, even such small things can make me very happy.

At times one has an idea of places before one even arrives. My idea of

Ushuaia was rather bleak, grey and cold. I was always of the impression that everybody just goes there to be able to say that they have been in the most southern city of the world. This is far from it, as Ushuaia is beautifully located. In almost every direction one can see snow-covered peaks, which is complemented by the view over the bay, absolutely breathtaking.

For four days we enjoy the scenery and gather strength until the hour has come for us, for the first time in a very long time, to go north. A good month before the traveller masses strike down here, we get on our way. Our early trip down here wasn't easy in terms of weather, but after everything we have heard, we are glad to miss the hustle and bustle around Christmas.

Icy rain accompanies us on our return trip to Tierra del Fuego. At night we're happy to spot a small protected shack that are to be found everywhere out here in the sticks.

Their condition is often nasty, but when the wind blows heavily, one is glad to have shelter. In this hut a German named Hans Stücke has immortalised himself, a man, who has cycled incredible 340,000 miles since 1962, which is truly exceptional. Not all motorcyclists achieve such a masterly feat in their lifetime, and this man was on the road with his bicycle, which deserves the upmost respect!

The Boot Thief

Meanwhile it is end of November and we pass other travellers on two or four wheels several times a day. Usually we stop when we meet other motorcycle globetrotters and have a little chat, considering the high numbers this now seems neither practical, nor desirable.
One night we camp on a campground in the middle of large wasteland. Simone goes to bed before me, and when I follow, I notice that only one of her boots is left outside the tent, where they were placed for airing. I can't find the other one anywhere, and even with united forces the search remains unsuccessful. Eventually even the campsite manager has to help, and for over an hour we scan the dry grass in a wide radius with our flashlights to no success. The boss favours a fox, but we are certain that his young dog is the culprit. The loss of the boot would be fatal, as on this continent there are no sturdy motorcycle boots in women sizes to be found, no matter how much money one is willing to spend. The ladies only sit on the back and wear matching footwear. Fortunately the boot is found the next morning, together with a sheep's head and other treasures in the bunker of our four-legged friend, who is obviously quite aware of the fact that he has done something prohibited.

Motorcycle Traveller Legends

On the parking lot of a supermarket I make the acquaintance of a German emigrant and her teenage daughter. We chat a little, and as so often in such situations an invitation to their home follows. When she tells me her name, I'm amazed "Are you THE Claudia Metz?" I look at the probably most famous German motorcycle traveller, who has ridden 16 years around the world with her husband Klaus Schubert. Our generation has most likely not one German-speaking motorcycle globetrotter, who hasn't read her book "Abgefahren" at the time, or who wasn't inspired by their multimedia presentations.

The two turn out to be charismatic people and pleasant hosts. They live with their two children and selected guests, who are passing through, in a gorgeous spot in the mountains of the Argentinean part of Patagonia. If we would be willing to contribute and help, we are more than welcome to stay longer. A tempting offer that is only refused with a heavy heart on our behalf, but we are already short in time in regards to the New Zealand winter, where our journey is to continue shortly. And if we don't want to stay a whole year, which we lack the courage for, we are bound to move on.

In Ash Country All Cats Are Grey

After Bariloche we head west into the direction of the Puyehue volcano. The formerly mentioned has notoriously spewed ash again a few weeks ago, and it still hangs in the air and covers everything in a misty veil. The cleanup has been going on tirelessly for weeks to limit the financial damage to the established tourism industry here. The approximately eight-inch high ash layer is removed from green areas and streets with many varying techniques and pushed together into gigantic hills. The picture reminds in some ways of winter sport regions, especially on less travelled smaller tracks, where there is still a thick layer of powdery ash, that reminds us of the bull dust in Central America.

The stuff is whirled up extraordinarily high by the vehicles and remains in the air for extremely long until it settles down again. In addition to this the several inch high layer also covers the potholes in a treacherous manner, without really filling it up.
Camping in such circumstances is pretty tough but super cool at the same time. We enjoy this unreal and very unusual atmosphere by all means, even if the ash is poison for our equipment.

The Americas Gloves

We meet Tobi, a young fella, who's on the road on a small motorbike with an incredibly tight budget. When he tells us that somebody has stolen his gloves, Simone instantly gives him hers. However, these are very specific ones, as our friend Ernesto was given them in frosty Alaska by a compassionate American. When we visited him in Uruguay and he saw the state of Simone's thin gloves, he passed them on to her for the cold Patagonia leg of the journey. And now we have somebody before us, who could make good use of those particular gloves that have already travelled from Alaska to Tierra del Fuego. Before we follow our own path, we make sure to get Tobi's promise to maintain this tradition of passing on the gloves to somebody in need, and I wonder who might be wearing those gloves at this very moment.

The Siete Lagos

Typical for Argentina, there are water-filled PET bottles everywhere on the side of the road. These are no wild dumping grounds but offerings at one of the numerous shrines dedicated to the Difunta Correa, who once upon a time tragically died of thirst in the desert. Her baby, however, kept sucking at her breast and survived because of this until it was found by gauchos. That's at least how the popular legend goes.

Now and then we take some days to discover the scenery, all in all, though, the sentiment prevails that we can't explore much, because our date of shipment to Oceania looms even closer. But that's how it is pretty much always on long travels, where despite an exuberant time frame at hand, you rarely leave a country or a continent without the intense feeling that you haven't seen all it has to offer yet. And as certain as the Amen in the Church, one will some day meet other travellers, who will ask in bewilderment: "You were in that country and haven't visited this and that? You've really missed something!"

Pucon lies in the heart of the Chilean lake district, the "Siete Lagos" to be precise, with picturesque lakes and rivers, emerald green fields and forests. More than once we feel like we are riding through the familiar Black Forest or through the Alps back home. The only things you constantly can see and that remind us that we are actually in Chile, is a snow-covered volcano here and there.

There are unusually many tarmac roads in the lake district. In saying this, there is no shortage in opportunities to explore this fantastic region by track. The absolute highlight is the Parque Nacional Conguillio, where it takes us through a moon landscape of cold lava stone in brutal heat. As awful these temperatures are and as big the wish to leave this furnace behind us is, we still don't make much progress. In this surreal terrain one simply has to stop every couple of minutes to pull out the camera.

A wonderful spot for camping smiles at us on a pass in no man's land between Argentina and Chile, and a storm front capturing the entire horizon helps us with the decision not to ride on. The only problem are the armies of nasty horse flies that are intent on having us for dinner. They even turn the Mother Teresa of all animals into a merciless killer, confirming every minute the death count with a hint of satisfaction in her voice. Finally we are again to be rewarded with a first class sunset. That's how we like our motorcycle vagabond life.

The Rio Colorado forms the northern border of the Argentinean Patagonia. We conclude that in honour of sheer entertainment value, as many others before us, we also will portray our anecdotes about the struggle with wind and weather in Patagonia and Tierra del Fuego a little more hero-like than it really was, when sitting around bonfires on motorcycle events. Yes, there were a few hairy moments when the wind blew so strong that we couldn't really keep control over our motorbikes anymore. But the few bad moments fade against nature's highlights, which this rough and wonderful country has on offer en masse. One has to have seen Tierra del Fuego, and to us Patagonia belongs to one of the most fascinating regions of the world.

Backpacker Free Zone in the "Villa Kunterbunt"

We celebrate Christmas Eve with two Swiss motorcycle travellers. Due to a lack of season-typical decoration in this country and in light of mid-summery temperatures, we're not really getting into the festive spirit, turning it into just another typical beer-filled evening in the circle of like-minded people.

Two days before New Year's Eve we arrive in Valparaiso at Martina and Enzo's. For many years now the two run the Villa Kunterbunt (the German word for Villa Villekulla – the home of Pippi Longstocking), a hostel of the special kind, meaning a backpacker-free zone. Here you meet almost exclusively motorcyclists, and the two process several hundreds of motorbike shipments from and to Chile per year. Nearly everyone who uses the first class service stays overnight at Villa Villekulla for a few days upon arrival and departure, so practically it feels like a motorcycle event most of the time. From the first moment we feel at ease amongst the circle of old and new friends, and we're not surprised that the Villa is one of those "quicksand places", where you remark on a daily basis "But tomorrow we will really move on", only to find another reason again to extend your stay.

Valparaiso is renowned for its New Year's fireworks. This attraction at the end of the year draws over a million visitors into the city, and a few hundred of those seem to be punks, which we appreciate a lot.

Nevertheless we prefer to celebrate amongst our friends in the Villa. On New Year's Day we stroll through the centre of town, which looks like the final day on a punk festival. Passed-out drunks lie everywhere still in the afternoon. In many places the smell of stale beer and piss mixes with etching toxic tear gas wafts, wandering through the urban canyons whilst still bringing tears to our eyes over and over again. The cops must've countered big-time if there's still so much of the stuff in the air after so many hours. Dammit, I guess we've really missed the party!

The Devil in the Shape of a Bee

On a small excursion the next day I get stung on my temple by a bee or wasp whilst riding, which is painful but not unusual. Such things simply happen from time to time when you sit in your saddle daily.

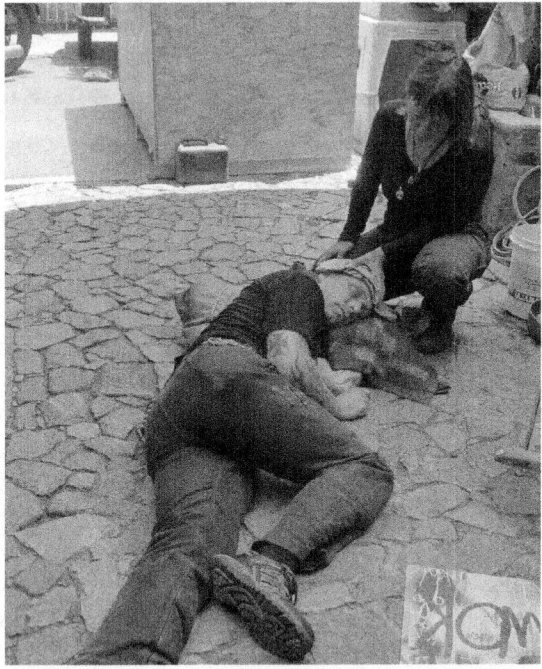

Ten minutes later we arrive at the Villa, I take off my helmet and instantly complain about severe dizziness. Smart advice for a healthier lifestyle is the only reaction by the others, which I can't blame them for, and a few seconds later I lie unconscious in the backyard after suffering an anaphylactic shock. The excitement is high. Enzo tries to call the ambulance and experiences South America in its purest form when nobody picks up the phone. In recovery position, I regain consciousness a few minutes later, lying on the ground with no recollection whatsoever on what has happened. My heart is racing, geez, this is not nice. For the following few hours I'm out of action and after that on shaky legs for the rest of the day. What remains is the worry on how to deal with this as I have obviously, at my old age, developed this annoying and also dangerous allergy for motorcyclists. If I would've fallen unconscious upon the sting at full speed, it could've most likely had life-threatening consequences. Irrespective of that, one can also die by the allergic shock itself as I found out on the Internet later.

The Pain with the Shipments

Shipment of the motorbikes by air or sea is always a difficult matter. It is incredibly expensive, measured against our normal life and travel style, and always a power struggle in terms of bureaucracy and logistics. However, on a trip around the world they are inescapable at times. On this occasion it is particularly bad. For weeks we have been trying to clarify the situation via e-mail with the few suppliers who are worth considering, which seems hopeless in this country. The only thing we know for sure is so far that shipment via sea is out of question this time as cargo happens to travel over North America, Asia and Australia from Chile to New Zealand. In the knowledge that there are always issues and partially lengthy delays to be expected when shipping via sea, one can calculate all the things that can go wrong with five harbours on the route. In saying this, it would even take too long in an ideal situation in order to make it to New Zealand before the start of winter. Hence we have to bite the "costly" bullet and send the bikes off via air cargo. To move forward, we also have no other choice than to ride into the capital to personally put a bomb under particular people's bum.

If we didn't already hate the "mañana" mentality of the South Americans, we would now at the latest saga. That our place of destination is not a common one for South American shipping agents doesn't make the situation any easier on top of everything else.

Whilst our travel budget is devilish bled by hotel prices in the capital, one day follows the other without making any progress. As it so often happens in situations like these, many a seemingly simple solution turns out to be a dead end street, and again we end up playing ping pong whilst being sent from pillar to post. After many frustrating days we finally have a candidate, who makes a reliable offer and also leaves the impression that he could deliver what he promises.

The Fat Eagle and the Lucky Swine

As it is still a few weeks until our date of shipping, we use the opportunity to have a few larger pieces added at a first class oldschool tattoo studio.

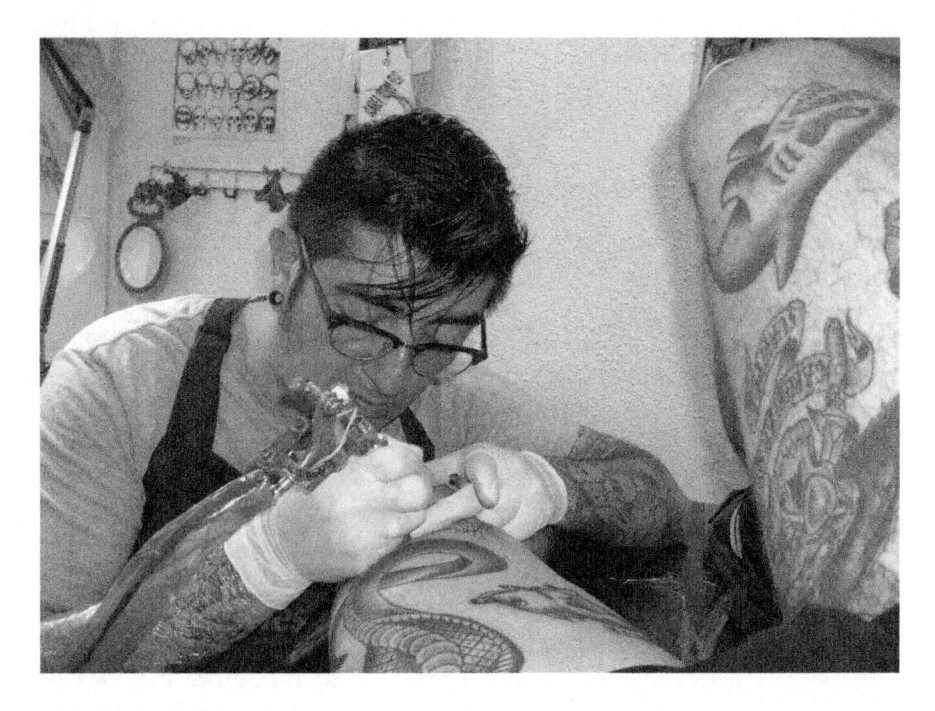

Simone indulges in an octopus, and I choose a cobra and a few killer bees for myself. Furthermore, my belly is supposed to be graced with a huge eagle in the near future. The clever idea behind my subject of choice is that should my tender tummy keep growing, I would get a free of charge and enlarged wingspan on top of it. After the first session, though, I'm not convinced by the ingenuity of my idea anymore, this was the worst tattoo torture that I ever endured. Who would've thought that of all things the tummy would be so hellishly sensitive to pain? But in for a penny, in for a pound, and so we come back a few more times in the following weeks, the last time then after a two-week holiday of my tattooist. After all our experiences with South Americans I harvest great doubts towards their reliability and in particular his commitment regarding his date of return, in which nothing can go wrong as we will be leaving shortly after. If the eagle won't be finished today, it never will. Needless to say that everything goes well in the end, and we also grant ourselves a partner tattoo. It consists of a lucky pig with the lettering "Suerte", which is the traditional farewell for travellers in South America.

Snake Visits, Frog Ragouts and Hail Storms

In between we undertake several day tours in Chile and Argentina. Both countries are interleaved geographically to such an extent that you constantly change from one into the other. At the end of our South America leg we make it to 28 stamps of those two countries alone in our passports. Perhaps it is comprehensible now why we picked up additional second passports in Peru, because in South America empty pages melt literally away like butter in the sun.

The vagabond life is quite relaxed these days. Of course there is everything possible to be repaired on the bikes and the equipment, and the to-do-list appears to be a monster at times, similar to the mythological Hydra. Each time the creature named to-do-list loses one head it is replaced with two new ones. But otherwise we go with the flow and enjoy the solitude and the plentiful wild camping.
One night we have an unexpected visit outside the tent, the first snake in many months. That our inner tent can't be closed any longer due to damaged zippers makes us suddenly pretty nervous and spurs on our imagination in an unpleasant manner. Apart from the snake, there are hundreds of frogs here that tirelessly croak us a grand concert. There are so many that you can only walk through the grass with the utmost caution at night. When taking down the tent the next morning, one promptly appears from underneath the tent. Sadly, we must've overseen another one, which must've made itself comfortable in the creases of the inner tent and which we discover when we are in setting up the tent again at night, both gagging big time. A frog that has been squashed in the process of rolling up the tent tightly and which has been warmed up in the luggage the entire day in full sun by over 40°C (104°F), is truly not an appetising thing.

Another night a storm catches us on the wrong foot, when within seconds the still wind turns into the heaviest winds we have ever experienced outdoors. In undies we plunge out of the tent and have literally our hands full to save our home in the inferno-like hailstorm. The hailstones come down on us, the wind bends our tent to unknown and most frightening extends and we have barely any hope that it will survive this test. We stoically hold on whilst the ice cold water runs down our bodies. As sudden and unexpected as the storm started, it stops again after ten minutes. Ten minutes that felt like eternity, and here we are, standing like two waterlogged rats, merely daring to take stock of the damage. Pretty much everything is muddy and soaked.

When the storm broke out, both entries to the tent were open so that the inner tent doesn't look too good either. Some things were blown away by the wind, never to be seen again. However, our tent is neither ripped, nor are any poles broken. All the same we wouldn't have thought to get off with a slap on the wrist. We laugh at each other, partially out of relief but also slightly hysterical, what a lucky escape!

The Hundred-Thousandth World Tour Kilometre

Additionally there is also a milestone due on our trip around the world that has almost gone by unnoticed. Whilst riding I raise my left fist upward and cheer loudly. Simone understands my signal, rides up beside me and we blow each other kisses! The reason for our exuberant behaviour is no other than our hundred-thousandth kilometre on our journey around the world. Who would've thought at the beginning of our trip that we would make it this far? Well, we surely weren't certain about this!

La Posta del Viajero en Moto II

On the weekends we're often on motorcycle rallies, whereas the MC Sin Fronteras, meaning "no frontiers", deserves a special mention. Henry, the president of the club, has invited us to drop by the club house, "La Posta del Viajero en Moto II", a few days earlier. The homonymous name with Pollo's meeting place in Azul is no coincidence, according to the former example, there is supposed to be set up a similar place for motorcycle travellers here, which already looks promising in its early building stage. In combination with the extraordinary level of hospitality by Henry, his wife Angelica and all the others, this is a hot tip for everybody who doesn't want to ride through the country only, but who would like to really make contact with its people.

Cleaning Marathon for New Zealand

According to my knowledge New Zealand has, aside from Australia, the strictest requirements when it comes to the cleanliness of a vehicle on entry. It is specifically requested that no plant or soil residues are stuck to the motorbike, as there will be an expensive disinfection due otherwise, or even worse as per rumours. That's bad news for me as I am a confident non-cleaner, who believes that a travel vehicle should look like an adventure. Who knows if our loyal bikes will still work if we take off all the preserving and protecting dirt? To move old cables back and forth in order to clean them, just as an example, might most likely not be a good idea either. Yet no lamenting will be of any use, because the New Zealand bio security have more pull, and after a pre-cleaning via high-pressure jet we have to, if we like it or not, try the impossible. Equipped with cloth and toothbrush we have to get a the dirt from every inaccessible corner of the bikes. For days on end we agonise in tedious work whilst motorcycle globetrotters from the Villa Kunterbunt drop by continually, emotionally fluctuating between awe and the remark "Man, am I glad I don't have to do that crap job." Some jokes would be funny if I'd be the one to make them, but instead we acknowledge the comment with unarticulated grumbling.

Our special thanks go to Bernd, who scores by constantly appearing at five o' clock sharp with a cold beer. With that our dull days have a goal at least. In the following years of our journey this becomes the running gag, as whenever we fancy a beer, we introduce it with the saying "I think it's almost five o'clock, which means that Bernd will be here soon", irrespective of what time it is.

Originally we had planned to only sand down the rusty bits and put a new layer of paint on, but a few days later it becomes apparent that matt black paint is a wonder weapon. Where toothbrush and pointy items don't get a hold of the dirt and bitumen, we paint over it without further ado. But even with this method, the bikes are still in no shape after three days of hard labour to withstand a strict check from an ill-mooded inspector. So it can only be hoped for that we catch one in a good mood. Apart from the bikes we also have to clean all our clothes, our gear and our camping equipment, and I have actually forgotten how many times we have filled Martina's washing machine. Just to pick one of the things on our to-do list, we have well over 100 Velcro fasteners on our clothing and equipment, and believe it or not, we have actually counted them, each of them has to be freed from grass and such with tweezers. New Zealand simply has to be the greatest nation on earth to visit so this grind becomes somewhat justified.

Logistically, there is also a lot to do for the jump to Oceania. Among other things we have to get together an impressive amount of money, because our agent insists on payment in cash, which is world wide quite common in regards to shipments. So we are forced to withdraw in several rounds via various credit cards the equivalent amount of 3,400 USD in pesos, and then take that fat stack of banknotes to two different money exchange offices in order to have it exchanged into dollars in the eyes of a dozen spectators. There were times I felt safer on my way home, particularly as there seems to be no shortage of dubious scum in the harbour town of Valparaiso.

Adiós América del Sur!

The delivery of our motorbikes at the freight airport is surprisingly smooth for South American standards. Thanks to airfreight, the bikes only have to be tied down on pallets after we have removed the battery and promised faithfully that the tanks are empty. In terms of dangerous goods declaration and handling I've seen the opposite side of the coin before. After roughly two hours everything is tied properly and wrapped in foil, then shock freezing, weighing, measuring and done. Done? Whilst I wait for our agent, I stroll through the warehouse facility and study the stickers on our motorbikes, when I suddenly see as destination airport MIA, which means Miami (USA) and not Auckland (AKL). My urge to kill is rising. The guys are visibly embarrassed by this mistake and rectify it as quickly as possible. Phew, lucky, that was a close call.

Thanks to a stopover in Buenos Aires that last for hours and the flight over the international dateline, we will arrive in Auckland two calendar

days after our departure.
Adiós América del Sur!

Touch Down in New Zealand

We've made it to the other end of the world, New Zealand, the land of the long white cloud, as it is known in the language of its indigenous people, the Maori. However, the long "white" cloud that covers the country before our eyes upon our approach is rather never-ending and black. It pours down when we land in Auckland, which is no surprise. The summer here had been rather rainy and from traveller friends we have only been hearing negatives in terms of the weather for weeks. Well, maybe we are fortunate and are now catching a golden autumn? To be perfectly honest, we don't really believe it.

At immigration our faces quickly brighten up again, we receive our 3-months-visa without further enquiry and without evidence of an onward ticket. Without request the female Maori officer even goes through the effort to find an empty spot on one of the pages of my passport, where she can add her stamp without wasting any space. This is where the globetrotter heart sings, and I think I like New Zealand.

Even the first contact with the bio security is relaxed, and solely our tent is put under the magnifying glass. And then we're in, in the land of the Kiwis. Apropos, the nickname of New Zealanders doesn't derive from the fruit but from their national bird, who together with the so-called silver fern, graces the New Zealand coin.

At the airfreight office then we have a culture shock. We are handed a flyer that contains the perfectly described release and import procedure for the motorbikes as well as all the according locations marked on the map. Something so efficient would've been unimaginable of in South America. In terms of a culture shock I already had that one upon my first visit at the airport. Nervously my eyes were trying to find the non-existent bucket for used toilet paper until I remembered that in industrial nations you simply throw it into the toilet. This will presumably not be the last thing we have to readjust to, but we find such things rather exciting than annoying.

The bio security inspection of the motorbikes is a sham. The lady at the counter merely asks us if we have cleaned the bikes nicely, which I confirm, but we are torn between relief and the urge to acclaim shocked "Why don't you have a look at the result of daylong freakin' cleaning!"

The left-hand traffic that will accompany us largely through Asia as well, requires a little concentration at the beginning. This will soon get better, something I know as a matter of fact from many a visits to England.

We find shelter at Sabine's, who we have met in a New Zealand motorcycle forum. She's on a motorbike trip over the weekend but the key is lying quite visible beside the door. "Just make yourself comfortable, I'll be back in a couple of days..." An attitude we had already experienced repeatedly in Canada, which is still an innocent approach that we Germans are amazed about.

In sunshine and mild temperatures we explore Auckland by foot. Everything is new to us, and there is an awful lot to discover and to comment about. The country isn't just a multicultural melting pot, some things are exotic, many familiar.

We unpack a care parcel from friends, filled to the brim with long-awaited content and moving gifts, and then pick up maps and travel guides that motorcycle friends of ours had left at a local BMW dealer. Our tent gets well-deserved new zippers sewn in at a specialist, because the old ones simply wouldn't close anymore despite pressure on the zip slider and tedious replacement of those.

We really should also undertake a current warrant of fitness (WoF) on our bikes and subsequently register them for the road (VTNZ), but such regulations for tourist vehicles are a big exception internationally. Generally the temporary import, and in some cases even a local vehicle insurance policy are sufficient, the latter, however, is not compulsory here and many locals drive around without.

Somehow South America has changed us, as we decide for the illegal variation without WoF and registration, and simply jump onto our bikes. It rains again, but who cares, we're finally "on the road" again, hell yeah.

No Camping

The North Island is a feast for friends of curves. Soft hills, narrow curves and especially for somebody, who has just arrived from the dry South American summer, everything is incredibly green.

Just in terms of wild camping things aren't that great here. Gapless fences and "No Camping" signs on pretty much every corner. Apparently the legions of caravans and camper vans are the reason why, as we learn from locals. On one hand they can be seen in abundance, on the other hand many seem to lack bush camping etiquette, forcing communities as well as private land owners to defend themselves against the pollution of the environment caused by them.

Native Amongst Bikers

A start off as per standard, the Morrinsville MC has invited us to the "Riders in the Sun Rally". Apart from a unusually high entry fee, which seems to be common for New Zealand and which we are kindly exempt from as travellers, this is a motorcycle event as we know it from back home. There are motorbikes, tents, bonfires, a small festival marquee, a truck trailer for the show at night and a mobile chip stand. The differences to South America are immediately eye-catching, with large motorcycles and 99% of the attendees being tattooed. Our foreign number plates generate interest and we meet many people, although it is to say that all this happens in a more reserved European manner and is far from the rockstar hype that was staged around us on South American meetings. We mourn it a little, but it is much less exhausting for us this way. Furthermore we can converse in English without difficulties, and it is a great pleasure to be able to finally speak the language of the country fluently again. Simone's Spanish was enough for simple conversation, whereas my hundred or two hundred words were merely enough to just make it through, but there could be no real depth in conversations. This and also the fact that rarely does anyone in Latin America speak English were part of the reason that we felt isolated at times in the last 15 months, despite all the marvellous hospitality we received.

Strippers or Porn at Arm's Length

Strippers are a fixed element on motorcycle events all around the world. Contrary to the partially quite prudish performances in South America, these three not very young (anymore) women present more naked and dated meat than tender souls appreciate. Additionally the show is full in your face, in places more porn than erotic, at arm's length from the stage and amongst the audience. Shocking.
During the prize ceremony for the dirtiest bike we both groan collectively, as that would've been ours if the New Zealand bio security hadn't forced us to scrub our bikes unnaturally clean, arrghhh.
Through the course of the weekend we take many alcoholic refreshments in the spirit of international folk communication and formed many new friendships. More than once we are told that "If you come through XXX, you definitely must visit us."
Talking about invitations, even before we arrived in New Zealand we had already received over 20 invitations through the usual channels and

particularly through the national motorcycle forum "Kiwi Biker". That's an absolute record and we don't even know how to manage it all. The chances to get an insight into the life of locals seem therefore pretty good. And that is the one thing that interests us most when abroad, besides the country's nature and riding our motorbikes. In terms of first class motorcycle routes and natural sights we already have more recommendations from motorcycle friends, forum buddies and locals than we can realise riding. We're brooding desperately over the map on how we could manage all these temptations and invitations, but it is sheer impossible. Before we even leave, it becomes clear that all these wouldn't even slightly be manageable in the two and a half months we have for New Zealand.

The Hunt for WiFi

Access to the Internet is no problem, at least not if you live in a developed country, have a home and maybe even a job with an Internet connection. Let alone with smart phones and such things. The world looks completely different when you're travelling. Obviously this subject emerges rapidly at an astounding pace everywhere in the world, but even in North America public networks are often gruesomely slow. To sign up a new contract for phone and Internet in any country we visit is a lot of work and often impossible due to the lack of a place of residence. Besides that, it costs quite a bit which again confirms the advantages of the EU, where competition lowers the prices. The aforementioned nature of competition is only existent to a limited extent in New Zealand and Australia, and consequently telecommunication pricing here is on a level as it was in Germany many years ago. To cut a long story short, low budget travellers like us are dependent on free Internet access. In North America this was often found on campsites, at McDonald's or in public libraries. In Argentina it was the petrol station outlets of a specific chain, where we ended up spending hours and days with all the required research and e-mails necessary for our onward journey. As public networks are often extremely slow, work on the laptop was regularly a very annoying question of patience. More than once "just-quickly" affairs took hours instead.
In New Zealand I find myself again in the public library, watching the Internet and how it seems to upload the newest chapter article to our homepage blog almost letter by letter, figuratively speaking. Meanwhile Simone rides into the next city to visit the botanical garden. At least this was the plan she set out with. Halfway there her bike breaks down. The

usual emergency measures fail and after 30 minutes she gives up and hitchhikes back into town. Hitchhiking doesn't sound too tempting in such a moment, right? But outside of Europe the German Automobile Club, called ADAC, is no option anymore, so who wants to go travelling abroad has to learn to become self-sufficient. Exceedingly few countries have an Automobile Club in the first place and quite often even tow trucks aren't available.

Everybody knows that motorbikes make trouble. We hardly arrive at Simone's bike, when it suddenly puts on a "I-wouldn't-start?-Nonsense-everything-is-fine-with-me!" attitude. With no conclusive findings, I simply change the spark plugs and exchange the battery. What an obvious advantage to be on the road with two identically built motorcycles.

The Cook Strait - Not for Landlubbers with a Nervous Tummy

The Cook Strait, which connects the islands of New Zealand, is renowned for being one of the world's roughest stretches of water. Allegedly the ferry service is only cancelled when the waves are higher than nine yards. Although I may sway like a sailor on shore leave at times, I cannot yet claim a robust stomach of my own. Hence I don't look forward to the crossing with much anticipation. Apart from my own wellbeing, I also worry about the motorbikes, as I have seen many fallen and damaged bikes when crossing the rough sea from France to England more than once. However, on this occasion my worries are unfounded, and we have caught a perfect day. The sun shines and the sea is glassy. There is only to hope that our return trip will run similarly smooth.

The South Island

The South Island of New Zealand welcomes us with textbook weather conditions. In brilliant sunshine we ride west on the Queen Charlotte Drive, and an endless sequence of super narrow curves offer a lot of fun. To the right we can see the windy bays and islands of the Marlborough Sounds, which we reserve for our trip back up.

We camp wild with a magnificent view of the Tasman Sea, which is the ocean between New Zealand and Australia, just to learn the following day that "Freedom Camping", at least with a tent, is generally forbidden in this district. More and more the impression dawns on us that in the last years this has become a normal practise in New Zealand. Violations are punished with a fine of 140 USD per person. While we understand the reasons for this, we're still anything but delighted about it. That's something we really dislike about this country.

Motorcycle Holiday Instead of Travelling Adventure

The West Coast of the South Island is famous for being very rainy, but as we are aware that we are not travelling in one of the best seasons here, we are content with the variable weather conditions. Besides a mood-tarnishing lack of sunshine, the New Zealand leg of our trip feels more like a holiday than an adventure. The country is beautiful but simultaneously not very exotic. The European culture and infrastructure are apparent, and in terms of the scenery it feels like a compact version of our native continent. Nature and sights, wherever you look, that invite to stay a little longer, which only emphasises the feeling of being on a holiday vacation. The one who likes it relaxed and easy-going will be very pleased with this country, whereas the one who searches for great adventure and exotic, will most likely find other more adventurous and also more affordable places to travel.

Breakdown

Vroom!, at full speed my motorbike switches off. As Simone's bike had recent problems and we exchanged batteries because of it, exactly that seems to be the major culprit to me. Another exchange brings swift clarity, my darling starts without problems and runs perfectly. The first step is taken and the problem identified, now I only have to source a motorcycle battery on the deserted West Coast. There are no notable settlements here, and the largest city on the entire coast, which we came through about 200 miles ago, if I recall accurately, has 15,000 residents. Outside the "blink-and-miss-it-town", which we rode through just before, I had seen a garage, seemingly the only one for far and wide, so that the decision is easy to make. I also have a good feeling about it, because of the stylish vintage car wreck with matching petrol pump in front of it.

Clive, who is the owner and head mechanic in personal union, has a relaxed approach. After making a lot of phone calls he sources a suitable battery on the other side of New Zealand, which should arrive the next morning. Just another situation that would've been unimaginable in South America, starting with a confident manner Clive approached the issue and promptly resolved it.

With the old battery I ride back to Simone, who waited on the side of the road for the past few hours. As expected, the bastard of battery pretends to never having been without juice. Nonetheless I am glad of not having to ride to the DOC campground that is 10 miles away, where I would have had to sweet-talk somebody into giving me a lift back to Simone with the removed and still functional battery, just so that we could bring the second bike back to the campground.

Glaciers en masse

Numerous impressive glaciers accompany our onward journey, and in the evening we land again on a DOC campground. These are campsites provided by conservation authorities, which come in varying levels of comfort and price categories, and sometimes even for free. In comparison to the not so cheap private campsites, they are often the best choice for travellers on a low budget. The one at Gillespies Beach is our favourite so far. An awesome view of snow-covered mountains with Mount Cook, the highest mountain in New Zealand, towering in the middle and an abundance of glaciers included. This panorama is on a world-class level and could easily be found in Canada, Alaska or in the Andes.

The icing on the cake is that the spot is free and even has a shelter, which is unusual for DOC camps. In between we repeatedly visit motorcycle travellers, who all prove to be very relaxed and uncomplicated hosts, and often they would love to pass us on to friends and relatives along our route. As well meant this gesture may be, we decline regularly. Apart from all the invitations, which we already had beforehand, more are to follow "on the road". We could be guests in a private home every single night and still not have been able to realise all the invitations we receive, so we make the compromise to stay a little bit wild and camp at least every second night on average.

200 Days of Rain per Year

With increasing catastrophic weather conditions we move on towards Milford Sound, which is not to be missed on a New Zealand trip. In saying this we're well on the way of becoming the great exception to this. The rain is pouring down in buckets and without intermission, and I wouldn't be surprised at all if Noah's Ark would suddenly appear on the Lake Te Anau. Not even the best clothing is adequate over long periods with such water masses, and in addition to this, ours isn't in the best condition after two years of travelling around the world. We're soaked, it's bloody cold, the view is miserable and the mood following the same path the previously mentioned. Originally we wanted to camp on one of the many DOC spots at the northern end of the lake, but that one has no shelter, where we could be protected from the infernal rain. We seriously consider to drop the highlight that is Milford Sound, but with a narrow escape our fighting spirit overtakes and we struggle on for another 12 miles to the privately run Gunn's camp. Camping would cost us 17 USD, and for 28 USD we could have a cabin with our very own coal stove. We look at each other and agree for the latter, although we had intended of never doing such a thing for the greater benefit of our travel budget. Despite the stove running like crazy all through the night, we still don't manage to have all our clothes dried by the next morning. All the same this is one of the moments, which we will perhaps cherish forever. The mix of a crap day and a rustic Happy End is simply unbeatable. A detour to the Gunn's camp is worth it for the quirky museum alone, which is free for guests and a dollar for others, an indisputable and valuable investment for this little gem. We're definitely glad that we have stopped here. The owner reports that the snowline has dropped below 2,600 feet, and the entry to the Homer Tunnel, which you come through on your way to the Milford Sound, is just over 900. Whenever the wall of fog and clouds breaks open briefly, one can see rugged hills covered with fresh snow, brrrr.

Shortly after sunrise we swing onto our motorbikes despite it being only a few degrees above the freezing point. The one-hour ride to Milford Sound, which by the way makes it to 200 days of rain per year, is great despite the icy temperatures. Wafts of fog patches are slowly dissolving and freshly fallen snow sparkles everywhere.

The Fastest Indian of the World

A visit at "E. Hayes & Sons" in Invercargill is a duty for every motorcycle fan. At first sight it seems to be a hardware shop like any other, well you might think that this one is particularly large, very well sorted and rightly prides itself with its 110-yard-tool-wall. However, the exception is the combination of a regular retail shop and a motorcycle museum. In addition to a few oldtimer cars, there are an estimated three dozen motorcycle gems to admire, and I mean real gems. These are absolute rarities from vintage darlings, rare motorcycles with car engines, legends from the racing sport to wild modifications. But the real reason why this place is so famous is a very specific motorbike, the "Fastest Indian of the World" of Burt Munro. The movie with the same title portrays the dramatic world speed record on the salt lake of Bonneville and the life of Burt Munro at the time surrounding the said attempt.

One pretty place follows the next on our onward journey along the South and East Coast, although the hundreds of camper vans with the majority of European tourists on board take the flair of being at the other end of the world. We crave solitude and New Zealanders that are not annoyed by all the tourist masses. They may rather be found inland, where many mountainous roads are closed for rented camper vans.

Unfortunately such stretches are often dead end roads, and with the onset of winter the best routes have already become impassable. Many a time we stare frustrated onto promising routes on our map, which will remain inaccessible for us at this time of the year.

The Swinger Couple with Eleven Children

Central Otago is fruit growing territory, but another reason has led us here, Keith and Kathy invited us. We had already lots to laugh in the run-up to our visit due to Keith's e-mails and forum posts, which always end with the same Bible cite "Greater love has no man than this, that a man lay down his life for his friends." Fatally I had read "wife" instead of "life", upon which Simone announces slightly irritated that we must've received an invitation from a swinger couple. In the end my error was set right, and fortunately Keith and Kathy have the right humour to be able to laugh whole-heartedly about the mishap.

Keith's nickname isn't Shrek for no reason, the resemblance to the comic hero is striking. He's the type of guy who competes pulling trucks on Euro-Sport, lifts very heavy rocks and does many other things, usually impossible to ordinary mortals. Even though he's such a nice guy if you get to know him and refrain from teasing him too much. The petite Kathy suits him well with her sunny nature, but what left us speechless is the fact that they have eleven children. Our polite enquiry whether we may be a burden is promptly met with loud laughter. Feeding two more mouths? Who cares.

With the Rescue Helicopter to the ED

In a foursome we take off to a motorcycle rally. Over remote dirt tracks, which we as non-locals would have never been able to find, we ride through picturesque meadows and creeks. Unfortunately a bad crash casts its shadow over the tour, when a young bull jumps down a slope and virtually runs over Kathy. As the track is dusty and the rear-view mirrors almost blind, it takes a while until I, as the second-last, realise that our woman at the end is missing. A few minutes later I have reached her and it becomes immediately apparent that this poor woman is going through immense pain. Due to Kathy usually being tenacious and tough, there is no doubt about the seriousness of her injuries. Bad luck adds to the misfortune, when a dead spot hinders the emergency alert. Hence Shrek has to ride back quite a long way before he can call for help. A possible hour-long transport over dirt tracks in an ambulance is out of the questions, so the solution of getting a rescue helicopter seems obvious to all locals present. We are astonished how natural the decision is made and how quickly the chopper arrives from 60 miles away in Dunedin. Despite all professionalism and efficiency it still takes roughly two hours from the time of the accident to the take-off.

The sad final outcome is that Kathy has four broken rips, a broken shoulder blade, a collapsed lung and an abundance of bruises, ouch!
After giving it some thoughts we continue our trip as a threesome, as there's nothing we can do at this stage. The motorbike will be collected by their son, and somebody from the family will be with Kathy in Dunedin.
Shrek just quickly delivers us to the rally, hangs up his hammock between two trees and rides to the hospital that is located a few hours ride away.
The guest MC welcomes us in top fashion. When we recount what a long trip to the event we have put behind us, we firstly receive a suitable liquor for reinforcement and only have to pay a third of the regular entry fee. What a fine gesture. The motorcycle event itself is not overly remarkable. It's the usual, with the one exception that there is flashlight and with that a photography ban during the one hour performance of the "Dirty Dancers". These seem to be an integral

component of every rally in New Zealand, and perhaps are even one of the main reasons for the unusual high entry fees. This is something I have never heard of in my 20 years of rally experience, and I seriously wonder if the flash would kick the local ladies out of the concept. I mean, the fact that they often miss the timing whilst "dancing" doesn't seem to bother any of the enthusiastic spectators. The true values even here are very different ones in the eyes of the audience.

Old Dunstan Road

The next day we are up for an off-road-highlight, the Old Dunstan Road. It starts close to the event, is roughly 60 miles long and consists mainly of dirt roads, leading through wonderful landscapes. It mostly takes you through grassland that is interspersed with rocks, and the northern half is particularly pretty. That this is a so-called dry weather track is not to be dismissed, and here and there you get the impression of how the track could be when it rains. However, the mud keeps within its limitations today, because it didn't rain yesterday, and even the two rides through water are trifles for New Zealand standards.

Around a dozen of times on the track you have to open the gate, ride through it, close the gate and off to the next fence. In midst cattle roam freely, needless to say also on the track, as pretty much as everywhere around the world. The familiar model in which cows, sheep and other four-legged friends are a rarity on the road, holds a curiosity level in the rest of the world. Today, to say the least, we ride past every animal with more caution than usual, as we haven't yet digested the terrible experience from the day before.

Christchurch – Marked by the Earthquake

We are invited by Warren and Lex, who live close to Christchurch. On our first day we go "disaster sightseeing". The destruction by the powerful earthquake in September 2010 was quite significant in Christchurch, and it is almost a miracle that no one died. The damage was by far not yet repaired when a second earthquake destroyed the city in February 2011. This time more than 100 lives were claimed, and since then there have been over 10,000 heavy aftershocks. Many people have left the city for good and it is unclear as to what happens next. Downtown has turned into a ghost town, and large parts are classified and have been closed due to danger of collapsing. Official notices, which prohibit access, are stuck to house entrances. Almost half of all the properties are wastelands with no buildings left, which is spooky. Once upon a time there was building on building here, now it has literally become silent. There are barely any locals to see, which is striking and oppressive.

Since California, our journey has taken us more or less through territories at risk of earthquakes and volcano eruptions, and similar to the residents of all the constantly endangered cities, such as San Francisco, and so on, we have gotten used to the dormant threat in the meantime. But it is the first time here in Christchurch that we can see the extent of the destruction with our own eyes. It doesn't take much imagination to envision the scenes of panic during the earthquake, and suddenly you find yourself unwillingly running for your life in those images. We have goose bumps.

Streetracing

The next day we move on to the Mountain Thunder in Methven. Street-racing in diverse classes has grown in popularity in the last years in New Zealand. The most intriguing is the classic bike races and the so-called "bucket class" (125), in which Neil participates. We initially don't even believe that his bike has no brakes and he only slows down by changing (down) gears, but it is actually true. There are things out there...

The Bank's Peninsula is located only a few minutes from Christchurch, and it is a paradise for motorcyclists, with plenty of dirt tracks and a fantastic panoramic asphalt road. As the peninsula is very hilly, it goes up and down, and one beautiful view chases the next.

Neil, the man without breaks from the Methven Street Thunder, is one of the founders of the race and had invited us months ago to visit him. He lives with his wife Maggie and the baby of the family, Joe, in a cute little house, which we would take for free immediately. Even the shed, holding a good dozen two-wheeled-treasures, would be sufficient for me. In the evening the oven is crackling in the room and it is so cosy that we don't really want to ride on anymore. That the entire family is barefoot has less to do with the homey living room temperatures than more with the fact that they're Kiwis. With great enthusiasm, New Zealanders love to run around barefoot in any weather condition or in the most impossible places. Wherever you look, you see them without footwear, and we've even spotted barefoot motorcyclists.

Cauliflower Ears

A trip to New Zealand wouldn't be complete without having watched the national sport of rugby at least once.

If you ask a rugby player about his opinion about American football, one generally receives a derogatory "girls' sport" for an answer. In the "man-game" rugby you don't wear cushions, pads or helmets but a headband in the best case, as apparently the most common injury is ripped or torn off ears. Although I took a good look, I couldn't see ears flying around anywhere. I also couldn't spot any one-eared players, but on the other hand it was pretty full on. Rugby is a very likeable sport with high entertainment value, even for a rules-incomprehensible-audience like us.

Concerns About Our Return Are Prohibited

In Nelson we crash befitting to our social status in the carpeted garage of a biker, side by side with our loyal motorbikes, which is pretty cool. That's roughly how we imagine our future living conditions, should we every seriously settle again, with the only thing missing being a fridge full of beer. Such moments, in which we spend thoughts on a return in the far future, are actually a rare exception. And in the case where these thoughts set in, then it is mostly on occasions like the one just mentioned. In general, we deliberately try to blend out this topic completely as for one it is still far away, and secondly the possible worries about an anything but safe future would most likely tarnish the enjoyment of the present moment.

Of course life "on the road" isn't as exciting as it used to be in the first few weeks. But despite the routine, which sets in even in a lifestyle like ours, it has still maintained most of its fascination. One thing we have definitely learned on our journey is to live life more consciously. Part of it is to bear in mind how good we have it, as this is actually exactly the case. Obviously there are dark moments, in which we are on the brink of despair, but mostly we aware of living an awesome life, which we are grateful for and which we don't want to tarnish with gloomy thoughts to a return that still lies far ahead.

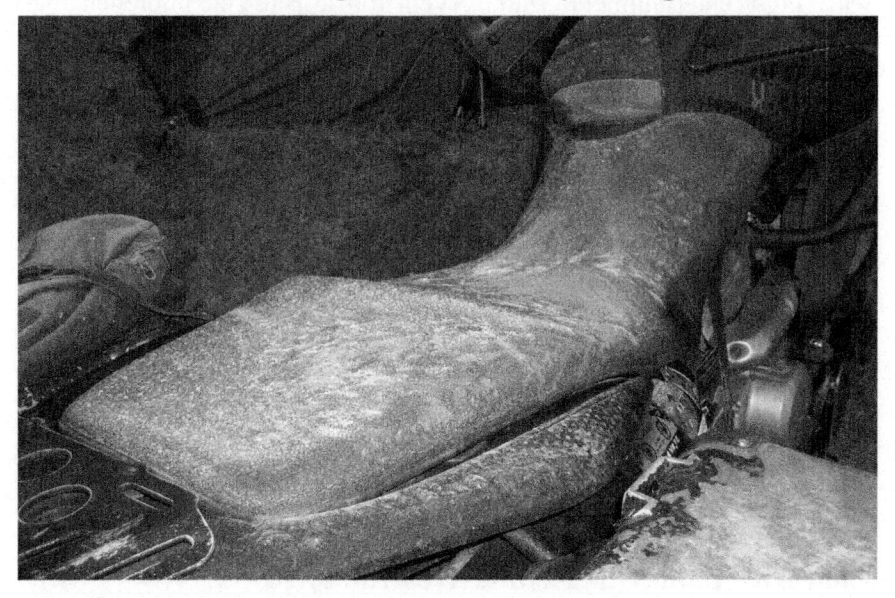

Back Pain – The Scourge of the Motorcycle Vagabonds

To have ice on the motorbike and tent becomes a familiar sight in the mornings, and the cold gives us indirectly a hard time. Especially as the sun sets shortly past six in the night, after which it becomes cold quickly. As there is generally no opportunity to make a fire, we have to retire into the tent early. In the morning, however, the sun only rises around seven, which forces us to spend roughly 12 hours per day lying in our tent. After a while this really gets to our backs. Every morning we're unfortunately not awoken by the chirping of birds but by backache, which becomes worse and more persistent with time. Thermo ointment, kidney belts and my small mobile stimulation device are in continuous operation. The mood suffers. One who has already suffered back problems knows how difficult they are to manage even in optimal conditions, like at home. Our motorcycle vagabond life with all its adversities and challenges makes the entire thing even more difficult. With every already despised flat tyre, I now break out in cold sweat. A lumbago on the side of the road in the middle of nowhere would be a mega disaster.

New Zealand at its Best – The Marlborough Sounds

On our way down we had ignored them out of tactical reason, but now the Marlborough Sounds are due! We aren't disappointed in our expectations, as this is among the best things that New Zealand has to offer in terms of motorcycle riding, never-ending curves, stunning views onto the numerous picturesque bays and little islands non-stop.

Unfortunately we have totally underestimated the time it all takes, because we need way more time than originally considered for this winding stretch and the many photo stops we take. As the devil has it, we have absolutely no leeway here of all things, because the ferry to the North Island is already booked for the next afternoon. On top of it all we are forced by technical problems to break off our god-like day tour earlier than expected. The next morning then the dense fog hangs around tenaciously, so that we are deprived of many a great view. These days something simply seems to be wrong. Nonetheless the Marlborough Sounds are a New Zealand highlight for us. Some advice on our behalf is to make sure to plan at least two days for riding your motorbike alone, well, at least. A few dozen DOC camps in great locations and a number of hiking trails are arguments to remain even longer in this region.

Again we take the Bluebridge ferry over the Cook Strait, renowned for its rough sea, which presents itself smooth as glass once again. This time I don't feel of having missed an adventure. As much as I cherish challenges on two tyres, I can gladly forego any form of excitement in the shape of high waves whilst on sea.

Motorcycle Journey VIPs in New Zealand

It is dark when we dock in Wellington and it is also significantly warmer. Something you would almost expect it being the North Island. We only start getting really warmed up on our turning manoeuvre on the ultra steep road, which leads to the house of our host. We are visibly relieved when we finally park the bikes in front of the garage of Jo and Gareth.
A good half a year ago we sat in Azul/Argentina in Pollo's famous motorcycle globetrotter asylum and studied the keepsakes and wall tags that had been left behind in the course of 20 years by countless motorcycle travellers. One in particular that took hold of me was the in text marker eternalised claim of a New Zealand couple, which stated that they had travelled all continents including Antarctica by motorbike. I had once written to them to learn more about their journeys, and now the circle is complete. Right in this moment we sit opposite Jo and Gareth, and in the course of the night we exchange many anecdotes, always revisiting maps whilst pointing at new spots on the globe. Time and time again both combine their passion for motorcycle travels with social and environmental aims. That's how the Antarctica project came to life and it is also this kind of philanthropic motivation that encourages their next motorcycle journey. They are in negotiations with the North Korean government to travel the country by motorbike and to deliver a quite large cheque from New Zealand donors in their function as UNICEF ambassadors. Which motorcycle globetrotter, I wonder, can actually decorate with such a flag?

The Travel Doctors

A few of my immunisations require some refreshment, so a visit at the Travel Doctors is called for. This organisation runs clinics specialised in travel medicine and vaccinations in many cities across New Zealand, Australia, Asia and South Africa, which is particularly practical if you need multiple vaccinations. This means one can simply travel on and collect the next shot in another city. In the obligatory basic package for roughly 68 USD, to which one has to add the individual immunisations as an extra though, a comprehensive and really competent consultation for all countries, which we will be visiting in the following year, is included. I have to admit that the doctor has provided an outstanding value for the money and she actually knew what she was talking about. It is not for nothing that, as a rule as it seems, the very comprehensive personal travel experiences of their doctors are listed as qualification on the according website of the Travel Doctors.

There are uniforms wherever your look. In every town we come trough soldiers, veterans and civilians flock to the public festivities for Anzac Day. Not only the horrendous human losses of the New Zealand and Australian troops in the battle against the Turks in the First World War are remembered, but also all the other national lives lost in more recent wars and peace missions. To us it is kind of impressive that these festivities, taking place in the entire country, aren't only celebrated by a crowd of forever yesterday's people but by a majority of the population. Frustrating memories of my time as a soldier in the 90's come to mind, when we had to be honour guards at a memorial for the fallen on Sunday in commemoration of the dead. However, quite to the contrary, demonstrators would display contempt and chant "murderer, murderer" as an appropriate response to our presence there.

A compulsory stop for tourists is the longest town name in the world, counting 85 letters all in all. Until now I always thought that this was the name of a town, but it is merely a historic site, where a Maori chief mourned for a long time for his war fallen brother. But that in no way impacts on the record setting itself, as superlative is superlative and we are in awe of this letter monster.

Going Other Ways

Several of our motorcycle globetrotter friends have highly recommended a visit at Michael's in Katikati. In the 80's and 90's he rode his XV750 ten long years around the world. Every year in Kiwifruit-season (the fruit, not the bird), he worked his butt off for two, three months to be able to continue his low budget motorcycle journey for the rest of the year. I'm delighted, finally somebody who isn't on the road with one of the typical and more or less optimal travel Enduros, but who simply does his own thing. Despite all the prophecies of doom, he has done heroic deeds in my eyes. The overall performance alone is already awe-inspiring with 260,000 miles on the odometer. When I ask about technical problems, Michael has to give the answer long consideration. This engine, which is the successor model and which I have ridden myself once for 50,000 miles, is simply indestructible. Many half faded photographs in his album are proof that you can even ride the toughest tours on a soft chopper with the right mindset. Let's talk about deep sand tracks in the Sahara, or Bhutan and Russia in winter, just to name a few, to leave you standing, mouth open, in sheer admiration.

Typically for New Zealand, as it seems, is that Michael and his wife Tracy have five children, a fact we don't find notable any more. This is already the fifth time that we are guests at New Zealand families, who have five or more children.

The Coromandel Peninsula is one of the favourite areas to ride a motorbike in New Zealand. Most are enthusiastic about the hundreds of curves on asphalt roads. But also the dirt tracks are pleasant, and I like the northern tip in particular. It's not only the motorbike riding and the beautiful views that make Coromandel so magnificent, it is particularly a fest for the eyes in terms of its fauna and flora. Everywhere one looks, one can see trees from a fairytale forests, almost expecting to spot a few gnomes or other mythical creatures. Something one can easily spot for sure, are dolphins.

Two Years "On the Road"

Today starts our third year "on the road". To mark the occasions we spoil ourselves with a feast of smoked mussels, fish and a few other goodies, all complemented with our favourite New Zealand white wine "Pinot Gris" and plenty of pseudo German beer. We reminisce fondly and play theoretically with route options ahead. Right now we're great.

The 90 Mile Beach is famous for being allowed to ride along the beach legally for miles on end. However, we are surprised, as compared to the less known Bayley's Beach, which we had almost to ourselves just before, there's lots of traffic here. In almost minute intervals cars turn onto this unusual for us, but nonetheless official sand road.

In hindsight we agree that we could've saved the last bit to the northernmost point of New Zealand. Cape Reigna is nice without a doubt, but this is true for pretty much every little spot in New Zealand. And the tick on the statistics list is not temptation enough, to be perfectly honest. As one says befittingly in the English language: been there, done that, tick it off.

Premature End

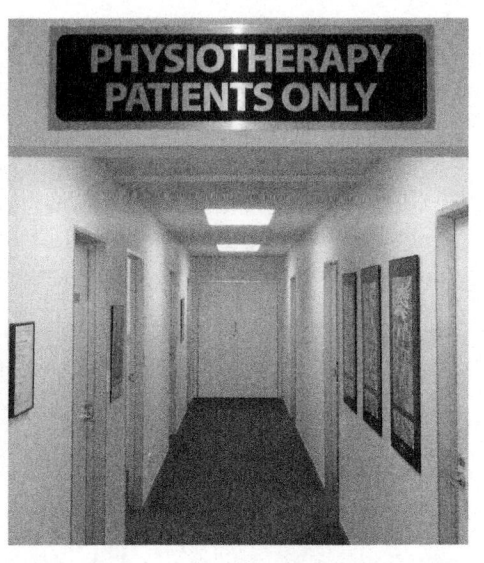

Our back pains get worse by the minute. Meanwhile, in my case, it has become so severe that I practically can't sit without intense pain. It is frustrating, and we decide to go to the hospital. The doctor, who I have to pay out of my own pocket more or less, thanks to a high supplementary contribution to our foreign travel health insurance, is not worth his money. His hasty and careless examination doesn't do a thing. The physio, who I then also have to pay myself, because something like that is also excluded from our insurance, is very helpful instead. However, even she cannot accomplish a miracle cure and therefore urges us emphatically to have more sessions. Unfortunately this is neither very compatible with our lifestyle as nomads, nor does it agree with our travel budget. I am depressed. In addition to the physical torment, new worries start wearing me down, such as the thought of what happens now with my back and also the question if this might cause a fatal problem, which may impact on our onward journey. With a heavy heart we decide to cancel all further motorcycle travel plans for New Zealand and to travel a week earlier to Auckland instead to continue the treatment. The decision hurts, especially because we had planned to visit the most popular rally in the country for the weekend to meet many of our New Zealand friends there.

Frogman in Auckland

Fortunately we can live at our friend Frogman's place in Auckland. His nickname can be found in numerous collector's items in his flat, which is a real overdose for non-frog-fans. Frogman, whose real name is Rik, has become one of our best friends we have made on our travels. Besides common passions for motorcycling and tattoos, it is also a similar path of life and his very easy-going manner that make him so likeable. It is a matter of honour for Rik, to move to his girlfriend and leave us his bed during our ten-day stay, which contributes significantly to the improvement of our back problems. Obviously the local physio is also not able to perform a miracle, but at least he has pragmatic ideas, paying tribute to our specific living conditions.

What is not very helpful is that we have to again clean the bikes meticulously for the Australian bio security. We hate it to such an extent that the task itself almost causes us physical pain. The stiff crouching and kneeling in front of the motorbike is additional poison for my maltreated back. With a lot of patience and daily exercises it slowly but steady goes upward.

Despite back torment and the hated cleaning program, the ten days at Frogman's pass in a flash. In the evenings Rik shows us the facets of his city, and our favourite is the roller derby. What fun! A bunch of fully tattooed girls push each other brutally off the roller skating rink. At least this is how you could phrase it provocatively. We loved the spectacle, and it was entertainment at its best, in which it gets tougher than we expected it to be. Contrary to the first superficial impression, it is a sport where tactics counts a lot. Watching it is entertaining and exciting at the same time. Roller derby is constantly gaining popularity worldwide, and in more and more countries teams are formed. So one definitely doesn't need to travel to the other end of the world to enjoy the fun.

The organisational part of shipping our motorcycles to Australia, including box construction, eats away many days again, but in comparison to South America everything here proceeds simply and in a structured manner.

And then it is time to take our farewell from the land of the long white cloud, where we have felt very happy and comfortable. In terms of the scenery and hospitality New Zealand was excellent. After 15 months in Latin America, we experienced the contrast as pleasant and the familiar culture as calming. However, we slowly crave more exotic destinations and adventure again, and we're already looking forward to what extent Australia has to offer.

In the Land of the Surf Crazy Maniacs

When the doors of our plane open in the early evening at Brisbane, surprisingly warm air welcomes us. In Australia we have to again unpack our tent at customs. Otherwise the entry runs pretty easy, thanks to the formerly arranged visa, which we had applied for online in the run-up. We work ourselves to death, carrying our luggage to the train, as what usually the motorcycles have to carry effortlessly, lets us work up a proper sweat. But the joy of being reunited is great, when Philip and Sonja pick us up 60 miles further south at the train station in Kirra. We haven't seen our friends from Cologne, who emigrated to Australia around a year ago, since our departure two years ago. There's a lot to tell, and despite the shockingly high beer prices we drink and laugh a lot that night.

Speaking of, there is an all dominating topic at the Gold Coast, surfing! Every company signpost has somehow integrated "surf" in its name, and the one who doesn't stand daily on a board for at least one or two hours, seems to be a real freak. Simone's first steps on the narrow board unfortunately happen in rainy conditions, which we seem to have almost the entire time we are there. However, this does not prove any reason whatsoever for all the other surfers, not to give into their almost addiction bordering passion. Shortly after Simone's preliminary exercise, the rain sadly forces me to bring our camera into safety. I would've loved documenting her surfing, characterised with a lot of euphoria and unconventional techniques.

After two weeks of waiting our motorbikes finally arrive. The release costs us a lot of nerves and money. Australia suffocates in bureaucracy, which doesn't even stop at the harbours. In addition to this, shipments via sea are generally distinctly more complicated than shipping by air. We grind our teeth when paying the fees, as we have to fork out more than the actual shipment from New Zealand has cost us. That's not a good start in this country, which has already filled us with horror in regards to its prices. To save the three digit costs for the disposal of the wooden boxes, we meticulously take them apart by hand and with the help of my body weight.

Several drives with our hired car to the far-off disposal site are required until all is gone and we are finally allowed to clear off with our motorcycles. At least the thing with the transport crates would've been much easier in South America.

The start in Down Under then also turns directly into a false start. Due to the regulations for dangerous goods, motorcycle tanks need to be almost empty for shipments via air or sea. Despite my optimistic estimation, the remaining petrol is not enough for the last few miles to the next petrol station, so that I have push a good chunk of the way along the highway. For goodness sake, if I wouldn't have already sweated enough that day!

Hundreds of Motorcycle Travellers in One Place

After roughly a month of a compulsory break, we're finally back in the saddle and are overwhelmed with a mix of relief and euphoria. It is almost a disappointment that we can only ride 20 miles on that day, as it is not any further to the event sponsored by Horizons Unlimited, one of the two big international motorcycle travel forums. Three days of photography and video presentations by motorcycle globetrotters as well as diverse workshops. Around a hundred people will share their passion from morning to night, and will not only have the topic of motorcycle travel during the official program points. In such an atmosphere we feel home. It is a question of honour that even I will give a presentation on one of our favourite topics, namely "How do you come in contact with local motorcyclists?" I fear it is not only due to the topic of my presentation that it naturally rains personal invitations for three days. Again, many more than we can even consider realising in the near future.

Particularly interesting were the presentations of two couples that are quite well known in the scene. With nine years of travel time, Lisa and Simon Thomas claim the official record of "longest motorcycle trip as a team". Initially they had planned to ride 18 months only, so obviously we truly aren't the only ones who're on the road longer than anticipated. The second celebrity couple are Peter and Kay Forwood, who both are legends. In 13 years they have travelled all countries on earth on their Harley Electra Glide, which came up to 193 countries all together. Anybody who has familiarised themselves even slightly with that topic knows just how complicated the last 20 – 25% of those visits were due to their political and security situation or the geographical location (island states). With my 55 countries I suddenly feel quite inadequate in face of that. It should be noted that meanwhile the number of countries

has increased by one, since South Sudan has declared itself independent.
Apart from the record in statistics, which I personally liked a lot, the presentation of Peter Forwood was also impressive in another aspect. Again it has shown that you can practically go travelling on any motorcycle, and that it doesn't have to be a Touratech upgraded Enduro. Those two have demonstrated impressively that you are not stuck on asphalt even with a "big fish" Harley. And more than once it wasn't only the presentation of their photographs that made the audience sigh, capturing the E-Glide on its several-day long struggle through the deepest mud in the Congo. I take my hat off to the achievements of Peter and Kay.

After three days of constant communication on the motorcycle event, we are tired and our livers yearn for a break. Unfortunately Bea and Helle, a very likeable couple from Bavaria, who have found their way down here from Asia, have proven to be extremely able to hold their liquor. In face of the hefty prices Down Under, this as well has not been very beneficial to our travel funds. But now and then you have to spoil yourself, and this was definitely worth the occasion.

The Downsides of the Motorcycle Vagabond Life

Two days later the daily life of the motorcycle vagabond shows itself from its downside, when Simone's motorbike dies at a petrol station. Nothing seems to work anymore. The troubleshooting provides a flat battery as the reason why. The question now is, if the battery itself is the problem, or if a faulty control unit or even an issue with the alternator are causing the trouble. Sadly, we can't solve this on the day anymore as this remote town folds up its sidewalks and locks the doors when night falls at 5pm, including the door of the only garage in town. Disgruntled I search for a spot we can camp at, which I find a few miles further at a rest stop. There I explain the situation to two retirees, who are travelling in a caravan, and ask them if they could keep an eye on my luggage. Both listen fascinated and are ready to save us, and their thirst for action is emphasised by a spirited gulp from their red wine glasses. Next I have to ride back to Simone, strap her luggage onto my bike, transport that to our retirees and then ride back again to pick up Simone in a third trip. Her bike remains in the yard of the petrol station. The next morning I ride back to the petrol station, where I fit my battery into Simone's bike once again. Combined with the problems we had in

New Zealand, I most likely will have mounted and removed a battery something like a couple dozen times by the end of this operation. On the other hand I am again glad that we both ride two identically constructed motorcycles, where I can quickly exchange the power supply of both.

With Simone's machine I rattle to the Monopol garage in town, where the mechanic kindly measures the old battery and the charging current of her bike for me. The power pack is officially dead, which is especially annoying, because we have bought it only two months ago. The good news is that the charging current is fine. Hence, all I have to do is to source a new battery, which in face of the enormous distances in this country, should be no trivial challenge. It would take at least three days to order one. We don't really want to wait in this sleepy nest called Gin Gin for that long, no matter if it has apparently been named the friendliest town in the state of Queensland in 2003. The next biggest city has roughly 20,000 residents and is only 30 miles away, a stone's throw for Australian standards, so to speak. To my utter surprise I'm already successful at the first motorcycle dealer, albeit only thanks to superhuman patience and great persistence. The salesman is very friendly, but incredibly incompetent. It takes an entire hour until we both find out that he has the right battery in stock. This could've been done in two minutes, I may mention. And to make matters worse, if I wasn't extremely suspicious by nature, I would've also almost driven off the yard with the wrong battery, reliving the "Alaska-Brake-Pad-Drama".

Killer Kangaroos and Other Deadly Critters

As exotic and funny kangaroos might be for us foreigners, they still represent a great danger for motorcyclists. Pretty much everybody we talk to warns us from these animals, as they always tend to run into viewing direction instead of away from danger. In most cases that means exactly into the front wheel. Even if they jump hundreds of yards parallel to the over the road gliding motorcycle, they often enough happen to suddenly jump into the way of a vehicle eventually. For two-wheeled riders this generally ends in a crash. In the course of our trip through Australia we meet more than one who had that happen. In addition to this, great care is required at dawn and dusk, because of all the other wild animals that are most active at that time of the day.

As is well known, Australia has more life-threatening animals on offer than any other country in the world. These include but are not limited to spiders, who prefer to lurk under toilet seats, freshwater crocodiles, who enjoy eating careless campers in river proximity, deadly jellyfish and sharks, who turn the experience of swimming in the ocean into Russian Roulette. In this country pretty much everything seems to be either poisonous or deadly. Now, it is to say that we have accumulated a little bit of experience in the meantime, and won't let ourselves go crazy anymore. It cannot be disregarded, however, that we think about these things in this country and take unusual precautions because of it. By no means are our boots and helmets lying openly in our awning any longer. I prefer not to have a snake in my boots and also not, as seen so often, a spider crawling from the depth of my helmet over my bald head whilst riding, on its innocent quest for freedom.

True to the motto "The one who knows the facts is only half as scared" we pay impressive 15 dollars per person for the biggest white shark museum in the world. I love this superlative, which is thrown at one almost every day when on travels. Unfortunately this white shark museum focuses predominantly around its founder and numerous collected reports about shark victims. I would call this an epic fail. Now I'm anything but assured and am definitely not planning to go for a swim anytime soon.

In Gracemere we watch the daily cattle auction. If Dieter Thomas Heck (famous German TV presenter, who possessed the ability to talk under water) would've lived in Australia, he would've been a cattle auctioneer. The incredibly fast speaking MCs take quick turns to catch a breath again, and wander with the group of cattle buyers in a 5-minute interval along the endless row of cattle yards. It is an interesting experience to watch this highly modern and computer chip based process, which on top of it all, is also free. Recommendable.

The Land of the Grey Nomads

Within a few days we see one particular street sign each time we ride through a slight dip in the road. Freely translated it means that the road can be flooded, and there are benchmarks indicating depths accompanying it. It is superdry and brutally hot, and we wonder where the heck a flood should come from here? But then we remember that we had read often about this exact scenario. Lately torrential rains seem to happen in Australia more than usual, and when rivers overflow the banks, everything stands still. Last year 70% of Queensland was under water. Both the percentage as well as the size of the absolute area, which is equal to France and Germany together, is incomprehensible. Being a motorcyclist, if you end up in a catastrophe like that, there is no escape from the ocean of brown water.

Nowadays the greatest challenge for us is the monotony of the Australian bush. Every few miles different and partially quite original funny lines on street signs warn from the dangers of falling asleep behind the wheel, with the possible result of a deadly crash. We happily follow the request each night to take a break at one of the many rest areas, if you cannot keep your eyes open any longer. For us this means free overnight stays each day. The infrastructure of these places is deluxe, compared to our usual standards, and toilets, running water, free BBQ amenities and canopied tables are the norm. At times one even has hot showers, electricity and light for free. A paradise for low budget travellers like us, and obviously for all the Australian Grey Nomads, too. The latter are four or several wheeled retirees on travels, which Australia has thousands of. Guided by special travel guides, containing a detailed list of all the free spots to stay at, we meet them everywhere. Queensland is eaten alive by these locusts, who flee their homes for a few months each year to the comparatively cooler South.

Everyday Philanthropists

In Mackay we visit Paul and Janet, who live in midst of the omnipresent sugar cane fields. On the recent event we had visited, the two had shown films about their travels through Africa and Nepal and invited us to drop by on our way up north. Apart from their absurd humour, we specifically like about the two that they always do well when travelling, and all in a well-grounded manner. As an example of such, they gave a micro loan to an African man they met on one of their last tours. The few hundred dollar they gave him enabled him to build up an existence for himself and his family, and it helps him to be self-sufficient. To us that is very powerful and sustainable. Less exciting is how we feel about do-gooders, who throw their money around without rhyme or reason in developing countries. Often enough we have witnessed how such donations end up in the wrong hands or have a counterproductive impact due to a lack of perspective. One could fill books with this topic, and a few simple questions one should ask may offer help in the

decision-making:
Do I change the behaviour of the donee with my gift, such as in the future, will he always expect a return for a favour? Would he rather choose to beg than work as he earns more through the former? Will children rather scrounge and buy drugs from the money, instead of going to school or getting an education, and so on.
Is the donee really in need? In the case of cops, border guards and many other well-earning businessmen, I would most likely deny that. Does the donation remain with the person I originally gave it to? One of the contrary examples would be the "milk-and-cookie-for-glue-scam in Nepal

The one who wants to do good to others, can do this by getting involved in a local project amongst other things. Often this is an efficient, thoughtful thing to do, and apart from other social aspects also an exciting experience.
Motorcycle or travels under a charitable banner in general are very popular. However, some projects bring up doubts in regards to their motivation and also the degree of efficiency. Generally, the donation process is not controlled. In some cases a 50/50 split between own travel costs and charitable usage is added. In other cases all that is left is speculation. Besides that it is always easier to find sponsors for a trip if it is in the service of a good cause, and there might be one or the other amongst those, who actually blatantly hope for this bonus. I definitely don't want to judge anybody but inform only. Have a close look and think about how you could best help. The one, who wants to make the world a better place, can do this either with great deeds or with simple little gestures. It can either be systematically planned or happen spontaneously, when a unique opportunity arises or when your heart tells you to do so. Most over all it doesn't always have to be materialistic by nature. Transfer of know-how, the provision of valuable information or living an ideal, such as how you treat children/women, against discrimination, saving energy, conservation to increase tourist income via eco-tourism and much more can actually set impulses, which then again generate a change.
Last but not least a few harsh words of advice. If one can't cope with injustice or hardship, it is recommended to avoid certain countries completely. Poverty and suffering are so big there that you have it in view continuously. It is impossible to save all the people and animals, and there is no chance to put a halt on the environmental devastation. Some countries, predominantly the ones that are strongly influenced by religion, to describe it rather carefully, can be tough on women in

particular. Not every woman can cope to be treated like a person of second class, with lesser rights and more constraints than a man.

The balance between moral courage and adaptation to local customs is often difficult, and the one who voices his opinions too strongly and undiplomatically, will experience often enough a lack of understanding, which can quickly lead to a lot of trouble. To keep your mouth shut and grin and bear it, however, often feels equally wrong. It's a dilemma that requires the ability to deal with sensitive issues and is frustrating in many cases.

Monoculture Monotony

Bushland is now replaced more and more by monoculture. In terms of landscape boredom this still does not mean any improvement. As it is harvest now, we see little trains with countless barred wagons riding through the fields everywhere, all filled with shredded sugar cane. Their destinations are factories with high and white smoking chimneys. The entire land is covered with a pungent, sweet smell, which reminds me of the hops odour produced in my hometown brewery. As a kid this specific smell would fill the air in the village I grew up in, given certain weather conditions. Thanks to more improved filter systems this remains a nostalgic memory only.

The travel management of the motorcycle vagabonds has set up an incredibly long list of unusual plants and animals that can only be found in Australia, and which we want to catch sight of. And it is today that Simone can tick off a real exotic species. In the Eungelle NP we spot a platypus several times, which is an exceptionally unusual creature, reminding us of a cross between a beaver with a flat tail and a duck with an equally flat but over-dimensional beak.

20 Oil Changes

My coolant system leaks and I can't get matching seal rings anywhere. It is hopeless. But luckily motorcycle travellers help each other, and hence it was a matter of honour for Mitch in Townsville, where we've been invited to for weeks already, to source some for us. Even for a local with connections, this is no easy task. Needless to say, he managed nonetheless, which is awesome. We're not only happy about the solid result but more so again about the international solidarity. After we trawled through diverse shops in our search for oil, I also use the advantages of his dry garage to make the tenth oil change on this journey. In the case of two motorcycles this amounts to the considerable amount of 20. What is no big deal at home in terms of space and oil filter procurement, proves to be difficult over and over again when abroad. And the oil change is only one of the many topics, which is actually a comparatively easy one. I think it must be roughly two dozen of tyres that we had to find on our trip around the world by now. Chain kits, brake pads, spark plugs and many more I haven't even counted. And only rarely you get any of those as quick and uncomplicated as back home.

The Wallaman Falls also come with so-called great reputation, at 880 feet it is the highest, permanent, single-drop waterfall in Australia, and that is exactly the free fall each of the drops takes on it's way down. However, once you see it in reality, it does not appear that impressive, I dare to say."

Another tourist treat tempts us in Tully, a gigantic golden gumboot. By now we can truly fill a thick coffee-table book with photos of similar over-dimensional and bizarre landmarks, which as per rule, are located in absolutely insignificant little towns.
In saying this, gumboots are generally required quite often here, because it is supposed to be the rainiest place Down Under. We're not too sad that we ride through it in absolutely untraditional bright sunshine.

Crocodiles

We are repeatedly warned of freshwater crocodiles by signs at riverbanks, but it seems that some heavily drunk guys are quite obviously not intimidated by any of the warnings. And so we watch an entertaining "manhood" drama unfold in front of us for a while, and I have to admit that I can entirely justify the urge of the young driver to prove to his friends that only pussies use the bridge but real tough guys actually drive through the river. However, as it happens, the car seems to be stuck miserably there for a few hours now, and on top of it all the engine is flooded in a literal sense. Modestly speaking, I am glad that it is not me who stands in midst of the river, looking all crestfallen.

WWOOFing

Every few minutes we wipe the sweat from our brows and for the umpteenth time half-heartedly all the green ants and spiders off our bodies. Those namely try desperately and painfully for us to prevent the destruction of their habitat, but to no avail. For hours we've been tirelessly pulling and cutting through the weeds and vines that have overgrown the fence of the kangaroo enclosure. This is hard, physical labour and in terms of creepy crawling animals, this is not for the fainthearted. On top of everything we are also not paid for this drudgery.

So, why are we doing it in the first place then? A question I am asking myself more than once, and the answer is WWOOFing.

WWOOF stands for "Willing Workers on Organic Farms" and is an organisation that brings together idiots like us, who are willing to slave away four to six hours daily, in exchange for food and accommodation with a variety of potential employers or hosts. In theory the tasks offered are supposed to be environmentally conscious, however, practically the boundaries often overlap, to put it carefully.

The cultivation of diverse vegetable and fruit varieties, livestock and the "alibi-garden" (which is formally enough to do anything WWOOF-wise) are the most common work available in Australia.

One should be careful when selecting an employer. With a little luck one can have a splendid experience and learn a lot, with a little less good luck one will be exploited as an unpaid farm slave. We have heard not only the winner stories from other travellers. Although I was quite sceptical at first, I have to say that we have had a lucky draw with David, our first host. This man captivates through a tirelessly dry humour and takes the piss well and proper. His announcement via e-mail that we wouldn't need to bring a "crocodile gun" or a "snake bite kit" to work on his fish farm, was taken seriously by us at the time, so that we promptly shat our pants. We thought it plausible by any means that snakes and most over all crocodiles would be attracted by the delicious barramundi fish he breeds. That his quotation was a joke, as we only had contact with snakes on three occasions in the end, was something we didn't know at that time yet. Besides being a funny guy, David also knows how to keep his WWOOF slaves happy by letting them play with all the many cool power tools on his farm. Who wouldn't love the opportunity to stir around wildly with a leaf blower or to cut greens with a whipper snipper? A hedge and chain saw as well as a quad bike with a trailer to remove all the biological debris also belongs to our daily toys to play with.

As a plant-lover and woman of the trade Simone is totally in her element, and her face beams happily all day long. She only seems a little tense, when she has to structure all the never-ending tasks that are required and when she has to fit unskilled labour-like components for dear Frank. I'm assigned the pleasant task to drive away all the mountains of green stuff, which Simone cuts down, saws off and thins out, with the quad bike. This is really an assignment I like to do even without pay. To reach the compost dumping ground, one has to ride far and then manoeuvre backwards around the corner along the fishpond. This is something I haven't done in a damn' long time, but thanks to solid truck training in the army, it works out again after a few awkward attempts, just as in the good old times. If my quad bike had a window on the side, I would boastfully and casually hang out my left elbow and turn up the truck stop music.
However, despite all these fine work tools, sweat shoots from all our pores, we're in the tropics after all. Especially such strenuous actions like the one mentioned earlier with the battle against the weed vines.

Whilst cleaning up, two other WWOOFers stumble over an impressive snake and try to manoeuvre it back into the wilderness. With a courageous "You're scaring the poor little animal!" Simone takes over the operation. That's just how we know our Mother Teresa of all animals. David has barely assured her that this is a non-venomous constrictor, which I wouldn't have readily believed him with his crazy humour by the way, when Simone simply grabs the python behind the head and on its tail and transports it affectionately into the next bush.

The guys are obviously torn between admiration and shaking their heads, and I can't blame them. The method with the stick also seemed more reasonable to me. But what can I say, we're just male...

Apropos snakes, on several occasions I would've almost died there due to snakes, not necessarily because of deadly bites but rather by a heart attack. When I had to go for a piss in the middle of the night, I would've almost twice, in a literal sense, stepped on one. In the case of tapping half-asleep only a few inches next to the head of a snake, which, to make matters worse, is coming towards you, you're suddenly really awake. The noises that escaped me in that very moment would've been worthy of a pubescent teenager, and in at least one case I jumped something like three feet up in shock. That, upon evaluation by David, it most likely would've been another python, isn't really comforting. The golden rule in Australia is that only the ones living on the ground are venomous. The ones that can climb are pythons, and by that not dangerous. That's the theory. However, it might be worth a mention that in the very moment one meets that beast in the grass, one most likely would not have a freakin' clue if it can also climb or not. When I met "mine" the second time, I observed it thoroughly after the first shock faded. Lo and behold, it truly winds itself up the smooth wall of our toilet house and should therefore be harmless, I would think. From now on the thought of having a carpet snake above me whilst shitting, is not helpful by any means. There is no trace left of the common relaxation, and instead I now accelerate when I follow nature's call, just to be on the safe side.

Snakes, by the way, are not the only reason why one should look very carefully where to put one's foot when making a nocturnal excursion visit to the toilet. Hundreds of frogs, which are the size of a hand, act as a hopping mine field. These are complemented by thousands of thumbnail-sized mini frogs, which are impossible to avoid due to the enormous amounts. Probably more than one would've died a painful death under my boots. As terrible as this may sound with all the snakes, frogs and other crawling critters, we've enjoyed our stay at David's farm. Still, I'm very sceptical towards the idea of working for strangers without pay, although it was real fun in this case. This wasn't only due to the motivational talent of our host, who was also generous and very approachable.

With only five months time at hand for this vast country, we have to balance our time very well. After this positive first experience, we agree that we would like to do another one or two weeks of WWOOFing. Whilst Simone dreams of saving donkeys and bats, my priorities move more towards the direction of the curious, such as the several gay nudist farms or B&B that offer WWOOFing opportunities, which, I believe, would be a really interesting challenge. Or should we rather do the only ecological true sea slug breeding station in Australia?

Great Barrier Reef

Snorkeling at the world famous Great Barrier Reef, which is the largest coral reef in the world with its entire length of 1,400 miles, is definitely an item on both our "Must-have-done-once-in-a-lifetime-list". There is truly no lack of operators in North East Australia, although their 1-day-tours don't vary much price-wise. The cruise with the sailing ship "Falla", which can exclusively only be booked online as it seems, comes with 57 USD per person at a fraction of the usual price. Somewhat dubious, we learn the reason for that shortly after. Namely the fact, that this exact ship has already sunk twice, explains the spectacularly low price and increases the adventure factor. A perfect deal for us. Two snorkel trips in different places are standard. Under water the Great Barrier Reef surpasses its reputation, and one is positively overwhelmed by the colourful variety of fish, corals, sea stars, turtles, stingrays and many more. The trip with the "Falla" is a real treat, which is also confirmed by a couple that has done the same trip with a modern, expensive speedboat only days before. Apparently it wasn't as good by far, and because of the higher passenger number it was apparently super packed at the snorkelling spots. Coffee and tea in the morning, a basic buffet for lunch and plenty of crackers, cheese and wine on the way there make our superb package complete. And then the captain describes in the most dramatic way the sinkings of both the "Falla" ships, why the boat was retrieved each time and why it was personally repaired by himself, a recommendable experience all in all.

An Intense Smell of Adventure

River-crossings truly aren't anything unusual for us, but this time Simone efficiently finds an underwater hole into which her front wheel fits perfectly. Instead of capturing the moment and her stable side position with the camera, including a cursing Simone, so to speak, silly me hurries in a reflex to the aid of my beloved one in order to quickly get the bike up again before the suitcases are filled with water. In the course of this, we stand knee-deep in water, which unfortunately and stubbornly remains in our boots for the rest of the day. Each step is now

accompanied with a loud "squelsch".
On our nightly bonfire we try to get our socks and boots dry, although only with limited success. An intense smell of adventure in the form of our wet socks dominates the usually romantic scene.

The Rebel Corner on the Cemetery

Cooktown will become our most northeast point in Australia and will remain in our memory because of the cool "rebel corner" of its cemetery. Whilst common with bikers, punks and other subcultures a "FTW" (fuck the world), which also decorates my skin in the form of an old school bomb, is not really something you could imagine on a gravestone in Germany. Not only the Catholic Church would put a strong veto onto it. Therefore it is pretty cool to see a photo of a biker on his tombstone, who is tattooed up to this temple with these insignias, including a tattoo machine and a V2 engine. There is a lot more to discover on this unusual cemetery, so make sure you take a look.

The One Who Travels on Four Wheels Saves Money

The area around Atherton is dominated by fruit plantations and vegetable fields, and we try unfailingly to find work as day labourers. With an hourly rate of 17 USD upward we would've loved to enslave ourselves for a few weeks doing piece-work, but our timing is crap. The avocados have just been harvested, and we'd have to wait until the next variety of vegetable is due, because of the unusual cold weather.
Once more we are annoyed that we cannot carry considerable supplies on our motorcycles, whereas four-wheeled travellers can again buy large amounts of vegetables for extremely cheap prices at any of the street stall or backyard shops. Our storage is only big enough for two pounds of avocados, which are available for a ridiculous 1.40 USD. The inability of transporting larger supplies on our motorcycles is not the only handicap due to the fact that you pay higher prices for larger amounts, but also because in some circumstances you have to stock up in expensive places when they run out. These two factors lead to the reality that motorcycle travellers spend significantly more on food supplies than overlanders with plenty of storage. Again, as so often, bicycle travellers have the toughest ticket in this case. In North Canada, Alaska, Patagonia and in Australia's outback they are often on the road for days until they have the opportunity to buy something. One can only imagine the prices that are charged in such remote areas.

Bat Orphanage

Simone's eyes light up at the bat's hospital, where in high season about 30 to 50 tiny, abandoned bats are admitted daily. When they are fully grown they have an impressive torso length of one foot and a wing span of roughly three feet. Simone would've loved to WWOOF here, but had already received a rejection via e-mail a few weeks ago, as they had no open positions. Therefore she experiences the visit at this awesome facility with mixed feelings.

At our breakfast picnic in the Mt. Hypipamee NP we are fortunate to observe a cassowary at arm's length. We have already seen it on countless warning signs on our journey through Australia, but not seen a living specimen until now. Caution is recommended, as the approximately three feet tall cassowary happens to be an uncomfortable contemporary, who can quickly react aggressively and cause great damage with his claws. We hold our breath when this flightless bird strolls comfortably past our table.

It is noticeably cooler in the tablelands, and we're mostly travelling between 2,600 and 3,300 feet. Heavy fog, which lasts long into the late morning, makes the entire experience even more uncomfortable. The

Innot Hot Springs come at the right time to warm us up, but the warm little stream is merely enough for our feet. A few enthusiastic Australians dig holes into the sand with their shovels in order to lie down into the artificial mini pools, but that looks neither graceful, nor cosy and warm.

As a general rule, one only sees living kangaroos either in the early morning or at dawn. However, those cute jumpers are sadly omnipresent as so-called roadkill. In this region it is particularly bad, and we ride past cadavers every minute. In places the odour of decomposition is constant. One or another wild pig also lies dead on the side of the road, and it must be said that the Australian humour can take on crude forms in the countryside.

Camp Drowned

Next weekend there's a camel race in the outback. We had originally planned to ride a large section of the stretch via dirt tracks, but the never-endingly drizzle keeps us from doing so. Dust can quickly transform into sticky mud here in the rain, making the many water-crossings impassable. Hence, we have no other choice than to follow the sheer endless asphalted major roads. Even a new attempt to travel off road fails due to poor weather conditions. West of Charters Towers it strikes the worst when we arrive at the rest area in the middle of nowhere shortly before nightfall. The heavens open and it pours down in biblical dimensions for 36 hours nonstop. In streams the rain runs down our collars when we set up our tent, and in the end everything is moist and the mood modest. 16 long hours we hold out in our little home, where we slowly don't know which side to lie on anymore due to severe back pains, until the rain finally becomes less, at least temporarily. We quickly run the 20 yards to the toilet without getting soaked. With great concern we see how the existing areas of water spread out around us, and wonder how long our location, which is situated 1.5 to 2.5 feet on higher ground, will be safe for at best. New travellers, who join us, report that the street we came from is now closed due to flooding and that the mud is one foot deep on the route we wanted to take on for our further travels.

I'm sure that if we look back on this otherwise unremarkable place, the memory will persist longer than any of the other beautiful moments of our journey. At least it is my experience that when everything runs according to plan, impressions are often less long-lasting than the ones in places, where one is stranded by force or where you had to struggle with mishaps.

On the third day silence awakens us, and no rain is pounding onto our tent. Instead we are greeted by a bright blue sky. In the meantime we lay out all our strong-smelling wet things and watch how steam clouds rise into the air. Barely two hours later everything is dry, the motorbikes packed and we're "on the road" again.

Wild Camels

60 miles before Mt. Isa the scenery changes, we have reached the outback, which is the epitome of Australia for us. In the town dominated by high furnaces, which is also surprisingly filled with garbage, we find ourselves again facing the decision to either take the single-lane asphalt road to Boulia or dare the dirt track? By the look of the thick clouds and overcast sky, it should generally urge us to behave responsible, but we're so keen to finally get the "real" Australia under our tyres that we decide to take the dirt track.

Our first night bush camping in the outback, and we are in high spirits. In the morning we travel onwards south in royal weather conditions. The sun is shining and with a temperature over 30°C (86°F) in the last two days, it has dried everything. Really everything? The further we move forward, the more frequent we come to muddy sections. The mud is so sticky that the profile of our tyres is filled immediately, resulting in us having no traction and getting sideways constantly. Having to take detours through the bush are also not for the faint-hearted and despite pre-investigation by foot, Simone gets stuck there and we can only get the bike out again together.

In hindsight we have to admit that it was quite naïve for us to take on this off road leg in doubtful weather conditions. The case of more strong rainfall alone would have had the roughly 50 creeks, which we were able to ride through in dry conditions, swell again and the track would've turned into a complete impassable mess. We would've had no other choice than to sit out that problem. Anyhow, at the end of the day we are then rewarded with a lucky snapshot, which is only granted to travellers every few months. To have wild camels ahead of our bikes is truly nothing that happens every day, and I have a broad grin from ear to ear.

Speaking of camels, they are one of many animal species that were introduced to Australia and whose population got totally out of hand. In the 1840's they were brought to the country as pack animals in the quest of making the outback accessible. In the 1920's they were made redundant due to the roll out of the railway and cars, and were hence released into the wild, where they reproduced magnificently despite targeted killing. Their number is estimated at roughly 600,000, and nowadays they prove a serious threat to the fragile flora of the outback.

Camel Race

The camel race in Boulia sounded so promising that we took a detour of 100 miles to watch it. When we arrive at the horse track on a Friday, already around hundred Grey Nomads have set up camp on the wide spread area, which is marked by the rainfalls of the last few days. We choose our campsite with the utmost care. It only lies a few inches higher than the rest of the area, but we hope that the marginal difference in height will save us if it should start raining again. The ride to this specific spot through gigantic puddles and deep mud is a little adventure. It requires intensive exploration and needs to be planned with military precision. We have merely set up the tent when the heavens open up again. By Sunday the water has climbed up so high that the bank of the flood lake has reached our awning, giving the term "Down Under" an entirely new definition. Now we're getting really nervous, and there are no alternatives. We're at the highest point for far and wide, and with the motorbikes we surely won't get away from here anytime soon. Now we can only sit and wait and hope.

To make matters worse we don't have any sedative beer on us. Luckily our nice sprightly pensioner neighbours, who are almost all travelling here with all-terrain vehicles and off road suitable camper trailers, take pity on us. Every evening there are some beers waiting for us, or even a port wine at times, we can charge our laptop and use their drinking water supplies, and on one occasion even receive an opulent dinner invitation. By this a superficial crap situation turns into a fantastic human encounter.

Annoying is, however, that the 12 camel races that were supposed to take place Saturday and Saturday, unfortunately have to be cancelled because the race track has turned into mud. What is extremely annoying is that the organiser blatantly refuses to reimburse the hefty weekend entry fee of 34 USD per person. We have heated discussions, but the event organisers were smart enough to add some small print to the posters, which passes on the entire bad weather risk to the visitors. What a mess! On the positive side, one has to admit that they're at least trying to put up a comprehensive alternative program, although activities such as gumboot throwing competitions rather remind us to a kids' birthday.

In Australia cowboys are called "stockmen". The bull rodeo is real fun, and the prize money as well as male honour seem to be excellent arguments to jump on one of the wild bucking young bulls. The potential of injury is pretty high, and more than once the audience sighs collectively when a rodeo champion in the making hurts himself big-time. At least the mud lessens the impact and increases the value of entertainment for the loud-mouthed audience like us.

Very entertaining is the so-called camel tagging, where the participants have to place a piece of duct tape on a camel lamb, run back to the referee, only to then rip off the duct tape again in a second attempt, which then again has to be brought back to the judge. Sounds simple, but it's far from that. Additionally, it is actually quite dangerous as the young camels kick quite nastily. We see one girl that receives one of those direct hits and is catapulted in full momentum in slapstick manner onto her behind, and she will most likely walk with a limp for days after.

On Sunday it surprisingly clears up and our tension in regards to "Down Under" lessens slowly. This wasn't a minute too early.

The organiser spontaneously sets a few consolation races for Monday, provided that the racetrack has reasonably dried by then. As we can't escape the morass desert with our motorbikes anyway, we hold out and are actually rewarded with a few entertaining camel races.

The Feared Roadtrains

The major road east has now also been reopened. Due to the floods that were occurring everywhere by heavy rain, it had also been closed over the weekend. The deepest water crossing is only 16 inches and therefore, thanks to a weak current, no real problem any longer.

Once again we're grateful for the signposts, which can easily be spotted on every road in Queensland, practically indicating the depth of the water when it comes to floods.

What causes us a little concern is that the asphalt road is single-laned. Should we meet a so-called roadtrain, we're fucked. Here, too, applies the common principle of the strongest. The smaller, which in this case would be us, has no other choice than to ride off the road to let the colossus pass. Unfortunately, as it so happens, the shoulder is nothing but dirt and mud, in which deep swerving marks indicate the exciting moments in the life of another defeated road user.

At a rest stop we strike up a conversation with the driver of one of these monstrosities. His has only three trailers, which makes it merely to 40 yards length and adds up to an overall weight of 110 tonnes. There are also the ones that have four trailers, are 55 yards long and have way more tonnage. The driver answers our curious questions willingly and swells with pride. Wee stops on his behalf have to be planned thoroughly long ahead, and the brakes are only used in emergency situations. To come to a halt from 60 miles/h the driver patiently goes down all 18 gears one by one in order to use the engine braking. This, by the way, is so loud that everyone can hear the monster coming. He needs a mile for the entire manoeuvre. Should one cross such a roadtrain, which are a very common sight in Australia's inland, a large safety distance should be maintained. This is also because the back trailers tend to swerve significantly here and there.

Despite their reputation amongst travellers, we have experienced the roadtrain captains as quite considerate in our encounters, if however possible, with the inflexibility by the monsters of the state roads.

Spare Jerry Cans Are a Necessity

Ideally our tanks cover 220 miles, and in adverse circumstances it can even be clearly less. As long as you're travelling on asphalt roads, this is no problem in the so-called hinterland and in the outback. There is a roadhouse at least every 120 miles, but the one who's travelling smaller roads has to be able to manage completely different distances. That's why our spare canisters are always filled to the brim, even if we have to carry an extra 20 pounds on both motorcycles, which again increase the danger of damage due to the vibration or breaks at the panniers.

Little Motorcycle Ailments

Meanwhile we have arrived in the state of New South Wales. Following the Great Dividing Range south more or less constantly, it takes us mostly through forest. In terms of the landscape, this is a huge difference to what we got to see in Queensland in the last weeks. We're mostly travelling on smaller side roads and enjoy the relaxing motorcycle journey to the fullest.

The only downer is that my motorbike announces smaller aches and pains daily. First and foremost this comprises of mysterious performance loss without a noticeable pattern to it. For days I try everything I could think of, which is a lot of effort without real result. That the problem seems to almost disappear at some stage could be pure coincidence or be related to some of my measurements. For now I won't be able to figure it out and hence decide to simply travel on and wait to see if it gets worse or better. Unfortunately I generally can't get those concerns entirely out of my mind, and therefore the enjoyment of this very relaxing leg is overshadowed a little.

Tyre Bin Scab

A motorbike retailer allows me to use his air compressor to clean our filters. This provides a good opportunity to rummage through his stock of old tyres. The things that are thrown onto the scrap tyre pile by retailers and tour organisers in rich countries, often still has enough profile to be useful for a few more thousands miles for such carefree low budget travellers as us. This is how I was able to wrestle another impressive 8,000 miles off my current back tyre, which was also second-hand.

Sadly, I puncture the tube when changing the tyre. Something I had heard often from others, but which had never happened to me until now. As I only realise the hole after mounting on the tyre, I have to do it all again from the start, arrrghhhhh! I hate tyre changes and twice consecutively really isn't something I need at all. But I fear it's my own fault, whinging doesn't help, only knuckling down and getting to work.

The next morning my first worried glance is dedicated to my back tyre, which is filled to the brim to my utter relief. In that moment I don't realise yet that my joy is premature and that I will be changing this damn' tyre a few more times over the course of this day.

Flat Tyres Nonstop

In the middle of Sydney my freshly patched back tyre suddenly starts losing air. It's a blessing in disguise that I wobble with a last swing onto the grounds of a petrol station. A new inexplicable hole is the origin of the misery, and there's definitely no connection to the issue of the day before. To top off the happenings of the day, the rim tape is also broken. I jump onto Simone's bike to quickly get a new one. Well, so was the plan, as somewhere I catch the wrong exit and find myself on the highway, which I can't get off for ages. Worried I check the satnav in Simone's tank bag, which is usually connected to my motorbike, where it is consistently supplied with power. It now runs on battery, and exactly that has become quite weakened by age. If this piece gives up on me now, I will never find Simone again as I, clever as I am, have not taken down the address but only saved the location as per standard in the GPS. After what felt like an eternity, I finally return to Simone with a new rim tape and breathe with relief. Done! Now I just have to quickly mount up the tyre and we can ride on. The task is barely accomplished when I hear a hiss, oh no! This can't be! It takes me forever to figure out that now also the patch from the day before is leaking. Treacherously this only comes into full effect at two bars and not when the tube is dismounted and hence not fully inflated. I have never had this before, and the annoying operation costs me around three hours all together. It is almost 5pm when we can finally move on, just in time for rush-hour traffic.

As I forgot to change the satnav from the for overland rides sensible "shortest-distance-setting" to the for major cities opportunistic setting "shortest time", we involuntarily take a stop-and-go-sightseeing tour of the inner city. The GPS takes us straight through Downtown, and I hope that the tube will last, as I don't really want to have a breakdown here. It finally dawns on me when we arrive at our host's place. When I get off the bike, I see it. There is a woodscrew going right across one of my tyre lugs. There is something entirely wrong with this day, and it is a miracle that the screw didn't go through all the way.

Sydney Sightseeing Deluxe

Geoff and Gus, who will soon be travelling for a year through South America by bike, are curious about everything that we can report about this region. They're full of questions, and such motivated listeners are especially fun for us. Their place is in a central location, and the next morning we're in the Downtown district in less than half an hour via foot. The "Central Business District", as it is called in Australia, is more pleasantly explored by foot than via motorcycle the day before. To see so many dressed-up people is slightly disconcerting for us. Each of them has a smartphone at their ear and a coffee-to-go in their hand. Hasty and with tunnel vision they hurry through the skyscraper canyons. How different has our world become, compared to this. That we haven't even switched on our for emergencies only mobile phones for the entire journey, is no sacrifice for us but rather life quality. Other travellers immediately get a local SIM card for each new country, we don't even have the wish to do so. Once per month we call family at home via Skype, and with hosts we communicate via e-mail. That's how we like it. To be always reachable, what for? Mobile phones and Powerpoint have become a symbol of my old life for me, and I'm actually quite happy without them.

But let's get back to our Sydney excursion. It is seldom enough that we find ourselves in a big city, and therefore we greatly enjoy exploring this foreign world by foot and check out all the sights. When we return to Geoff and Gus after a 10-hour-march, our socks are smoking. But it was nice to be the exception and explore the metropolis like totally normal tourists.

Geoff takes the next day off and chauffeurs us through the city with a car he borrowed from friends. We're spoilt with a sightseeing tour deluxe, especially as Geoff used to be a professional guide in this city. A picnic with bubbly and sushi is the highlight of this perfect day, where we have seen many a fantastic spots, which we probably would've never found on our own.

Blue Mountains

It is August, and in the Blue Mountains it is quite chilly at this time of the year. Ultimately it is just February here, compared with the scale of the northern hemisphere. Nonetheless we would like to do at least a short side trip to it. In bright sunshine and bearable temperatures in the upper 10°C we ride through eucalyptus forests. It is the essential vapours that has given this region its name. Presumably it needs to be a little warmer for the air to have a blue shimmer. We stop at some nice lookout points, and at the rock formation "Three Sisters" it almost feels like we're in Japan, as the close proximity to Sydney seems to obviously tempt hordes of Asian tourists. It is needless to say that the only enjoyment in their holidaymaking experience appears to be a record in photography taking.

It is a nice surprise when a Swiss Beamer stops and turns out to be Roland, with whom I had already exchanged a few e-mails earlier. Funny as it happens, of all the fruitless attempts to meet up, it finally happens by coincidence. Our conversation finds an abrupt end when I see that I have a flat tyre again. This just can't be true, for the sixth time in a very short period of time I have to take the tyre off the wheel rim.

Cold, Snow, Hail and Storm

At Perry's Lookdown one can camp for free, which is noteworthy, as wild camping is prohibited in many places within New South Wales. This has caused us considerable problems on numerous occasions, and it is in no comparison to Queensland, which receives five stars from us in terms of infrastructure and opportunities to camp free of charge.

The next morning it is cracking cold. The lady at the petrol station gives me a pitiful look and informs me that it is supposed to snow above 2,300 feet today. As we're currently on 3,600 feet, these evil tidings fill us with a certain nervousness.

Over the narrowest curves we ride through the Blue Mountains, which we can't really enjoy, and the reason for this is not solely the cold. Somehow this "eucalyptus-forest-mountain-landscape" cannot fill us with much enthusiasm, and a mere "quite nice" is about the biggest emotion I can bring up personally. However, one highlight awaits us when the single-laned road leads unexpectedly through a cave. This is something one doesn't experience every day, a tunnel, yes, but a cave? Motorcycle riding is no fun today. There is a sharp wind and the sky is full with grey-black clouds, which, as we now know, are full with snow. Concerned I watch the altitude indicator of the GPS. Instead of breaking through the magical 2,300-barrier downwards, it goes up on and on, and 4,500 feet becomes the record high of the day. Originally we meant to ride a gravel pass up here, but now all we want is get away from the frosty mountains. Until evening we actually make it below a bit under 2,300 feet, but even here it is freezing cold. When we set up the tent, it hails down on us from black clouds.

The next day we jump out of the frying pan into the fire, when, although milder at the coast, it is extremely stormy in return. We see tin roofs fly off and trees fall down beside us. In such circumstances motorcycle riding turns into a challenge. Fortunately, the wind becomes a little less in the afternoon.

We camp at the beach several times, including cute "kangaroo-mommy-with-joey-in-the-pouch" sightings. Another morning it then hits me again, when I see Simone's front tyre, my heart sinks into my boots. No, I don't want to, not another flat fuckin' tyre!!! One simply cannot have so much bad luck. This is the seventh time in a very short period of time, where I have the pleasure, I may add. I'm really fed up.

The Land of the Freak Animals

On the way to the Wilson's Promontory NP we see our first living wombat in a clearing. There is no escaping the usual hated adjective "cute" with this species. Locals, as per usual, see this completely differently, with reason being that wombats can quickly turn a garden upside down and hence aren't too popular.

We stay overnight on the NP campsite in Tidal River, and one can't get any further south on the Australian mainland from here. Mind you, our statistics mini record fades again in face of the plentiful animal life, which for us is definitely the strongest side of Australia. In terms of its landscape and motorcycle riding it couldn't really score with us yet. Apart from the outback, there was nothing really that we hadn't seen or ridden equally or even better in some other countries.

But in regards to its fauna, Australia is a real bonus. There are more strange animal species than anywhere else in the world, and for such animal sightings you don't even require to have a lot of luck as they happen pretty much everywhere. Even urban areas are full of animals, and not one day goes by that we can't tick off something on our freak list of animal sightings. Australia isn't only a paradise for children and friends of fauna, even animal grouches like me become enthusiastic and go into raptures about it.

But let's go back to our campsite in the Tidal River NP. Besides the numerous encounters with wombats, we are predominantly excited about the many colourful parakeets. Cheeky as they are, they land on our motorcycles and tent and try to steal anything that's not nailed down. A few days ago a king fisher flew onto our table whilst we were eating and tried to kidnap a considerably large piece of cheese, which being half a pound, was roughly ten times as heavy as the bird itself. Its operation was extremely bold and ridiculously hopeless at the same time. The wombats aren't less persistent by the way. When they smell food in the tent, they immediately rip a personal entry into the thin-walled home with their sharp claws to get to the origin of the smell. However, unlike North American bears they don't seem to have any interest in adventure fragranced motorcycle boots, or the like. Mind you, one just gets comfortable on Simone's laptop that's currently charging on the motorbike. We don't believe our eyes and assume that the juggernaut isn't scared off by the appalled Simone, because the device is pleasantly warm. The result of this very funny scene is a few exclusive scratch signatures on Simone's notebook. Laughingly we agree that these are more original than any Australia sticker.

Once Again without Juice

My motorbike won't start, damn it! The only thing that I have done even more often than changing tyres in the last half a year, is exchanging batteries between the two bikes. In light of the almost daily technical low blows of the last weeks, my frustration threshold is rather low. The good news is that already before testing Simone's battery, I am pretty sure that exactly that is the culprit. Obviously I managed to charge batteries and netbooks for too long on the motorbike so that this power pack is flat. Generally, I'm pretty measured on this daily process, provided that the battery is not affected. Good news, part two, is that after unsuccessfully asking various people for a jumper cable, I receive a jumpstart device at the information desk of the NP campsite, which reanimates my darling after a few initial difficulties.

Motorcycle Dream Road "Great Ocean Road"

The Great Ocean Road is commonly counted amongst the best asphalted roads in the world for motorcycle riding. We approach this rather sceptically but are quickly convinced. In the first third of the overall approximately 120 miles long Great Ocean Road it goes beautifully along the ocean, pretty much consistently. Despite still having crispy temperatures, we even get a bit of sunshine to our surprise, so that we can fully enjoy the motorcycle road legend. The middle part of the Great Ocean Road leads inland, and we turn off to Cape Otway, which is actually not worth the detour. But halfway between, we have one of the most spectacular animal encounters in Australia. The eucalyptus trees are full of koalas, and one can spot at least a hundred animals in the narrowest of spaces there. There is even one with a joey. We had one as a neighbour, when camping in the forest the night before that amused us greatly, for such a small animal they have quite a loud rutting sound. However, this is the first time that we have actually seen these cute little friends, who you are warned about on countless yellow signs throughout Queensland. That we haven't seen one as roadkill even once, might be evidence for the fact that it is generally really hard to sight koalas. In other respects the omnipresent cadavers on Australia's roads are a sad who-is-who of the local animal world.

Day two after a bush camping night on the dream road starts unfortunately with a drizzle. In addition to this the weather worsens by the hour, but we still manage to see all the tourist highlights in only light rain. Just at the end of the Great Ocean Road the fun starts, and it comes out in bucket loads nonstop. Within a short time we're soaked, and in temperatures of around 5°C (41°F) and thanks to the wind, it feels cold very quickly. The next one and a half hours ride to our new hosts is torture, where minutes turn again into hours and our stamina dwindles rapidly. We freeze awfully, the sight is miserable and the road floods are increasing so quickly in depths and figures that we worry if we can make it at all. When we finally reach our friends, it is not only the mood that is below zero. I had already forgotten how much stiffly frozen fingers hurt when their feeling returns. It is so painful that I'm not even capable to hold the usual welcome small talk with our host. Fortunately the aforementioned has his hands full as his garage is under water. The rainfall on this day is even a record for the heavy rains common to Australia. For us, we're just incredibly happy for now to get into the warm and dry. Very seldom have I enjoyed a hot shower like that, it is simply glorious.

A Disgrace to Sheep Shearing

We camp at the side of the road, which doesn't seem to bother anybody here in South Australia. The only vehicle that can be seen within two hours is one of a farmer, who stops for a quick chat and invites us to his farm for the next morning to watch him shear his sheep. Awesome, we're in.

When we arrive at the agreed time, everybody is already busy. It is a hard job, not just for the shearer but also for the helpers. Speaking of which, the shearers are actually paid on a piecework basis, they need approximately two minutes per sheep and hence can get to a good 500 USD per day. What they have to do to accomplish that, though, is not without demand, as you can feel it heavily on your back. Of course Simone suffers immediately for the poor sheep that are pinched bloody many times. It is incredible how stoic they endure it all and with how much patience they allow to be turned and fixated in the most impossible positions. We barely dare to ask if we can take some photos, because we always find it slightly inappropriate in such situations. But the three warm up quickly and agree quite happily. The price for our snapshots is only fair, meaning for us that we have to get at it, too. After a brief moment of hesitation, I whole-heartedly grab a big sheep from the pen and try to pull it out to get it into the formerly observed sitting position. The entire team laughs themselves silly when witnessing my clumsy attempts. To my shame the shearing itself is also not carried out as easy as with the professionals. I curse, the others cheer!

After a few rather not elegantly looking shearing strips I hand over to Simone, who initiates further bursts of laughter. Out of compassion she leaves behind quite a bit of coat, as in her opinion the poor sheep would surely be cold in such winter temperatures. It is great fun for everybody involved and a fantastic experience in a surprisingly casual atmosphere. Brilliant.

Back to the Outback

A second attempt to do some WWOOFing finds a quick end. Of all the spectacular things that we really wanted to do, nothing came of for one or another reason, so that we now sign on to flower and sheep farms. After a day of weeding in changing weather conditions I have had enough. Unlike Simone, I don't feel that these are tasks I would like to do without remuneration, and apart from that I have enough of the wet and cold weather in South Australia.

In the Flinder's Ranges we're finally back in the outback. We indulge in the improving weather and the more pleasant temperatures, and this is how motorcycle riding and camping should be. At the East and South Coast we had definitely been in the wrong season, but our timing is perfect for the outback as it is spring now. Countless kinds of wild flowers are blooming at the moment and give the desert an unusual spot of colour. We repeatedly see herds of emus, and settlements become more rare and smaller.

Our technical streak of bad luck continues to be undiminished, and a torn clutch cable can rather be counted in the more trivial issues.

A brown snake is sunbathing on the road and straightens up in a rather photogenic manner when I slowly roll towards it. My naïve and immediate thought is with the opportunity of the perfect "animal-motorcycle-photo", which is approaching, when I hear Simone's almost hysterical warning cry that this is a taipan, a highly aggressive and furthermore the most venomous land snake in the world. Or was it a common brown snake and by that the second most venomous snake in the world? At night Simone tries to answer this question in her familiar meticulousness with the help of her animal and plant field guide and debates loudly the pros and cons in the tent. I simply nod silently to her presentation and am incredibly relieved that this chapter ended well.

The Oodnadatta Track

The Oodnadatta track begins in Marree and is an interesting off road alternative to the boring Stewart Highway that cuts across the outback from north to south. Another argument to choose this route is the opportunity to see plenty of attractions along the way.
In the vast ghost town Farina we stroll around for almost two hours. The first of those two hours is a discovery tour, the second to retrieve a lost lens cap.

Pink signs mark the dog fence, which is with 3,437 miles long, the longest by humans built barrier in the world and keeps dingos from the North away from the farmland in Australia's South. It's partially desolate condition raises serious doubts in regards to its effectiveness.

With their rear vertically rammed into the ground, planes and several other bizarre sculptures are spread widely along the route in Alberrie Creed, which is a strange thing to look at. This would be the perfect setting for an Australian version of the Burning Man Festival.

We enjoy the nights in the outback, where we can camp wild wherever we like and are far away from other people. Every night we are spoilt with beautiful sunsets, whereas the stars shine on us later on. This is pure motorcycle vagabond romance.

As much as I like the desert, it can have minor handicaps at times.

Sometimes it's hard to find the privacy to carry out nature's call in the morning, so that you have to make do with the symbolic privacy screen. However, a closer look reveals that it is simply unusual and not really unpleasant.

Ahead of us shimmers in the sunlight the salt crust of the Lake Eyre South. Australia is a land of extremes, such as extreme rainfalls and extreme droughts. In the last years it has rained specifically a lot in Queensland, so that the lake is exceptionally almost full with water. This only happens very rarely and is quite interesting because of that. We would've preferred it entirely dry, but this seems to be our life. In comparison, we weren't even lucky in the dry season with the highest salt lake on earth, the Salar de Uyuni in Bolivia. Nonetheless Lake Eyre is well worth seeing, and to complement it all we are invited for coffee by an Australian family who camps here in the desert. Such small but nice experiences make us very happy.

It's just one hour to William Creek. The road has meanwhile become more arduous and my bike resuffers dwindling performance. I had hoped to have had eliminated the issue a few weeks ago, yet now it is back and to make matters worse, right in the middle of the outback. One couldn't ask for a place with less infrastructure, to be honest. I curse for a few minutes, but decide to reserve my rage, as it is boiling hot.
William Creek isn't much more than a petrol station and gives us a

shock with a record for petrol prices in the outback, with around 60% more than in more populated areas. Therefore we rather fill our canister reserves, which should take us at least another 25 miles into the next biggest city. On the parking lot we see a rented four wheel drive that has a BMW GS Adventure on its trailer. One of the team starts a conversation with us, and it turns out that it is a film team, who is doing coverage on the Oodnadatta track with a renowned motorcycle travel professional. Apparently they had driven up and down the road for hundreds of miles on the repeated hunt for perfect light in order to take down the bike and stage another film sequence. The finished product will then give the innocent audience the impression of a real motorcycle adventure, a Hello from "Long Way Around".

We would've loved following the Oodnadatta Trail further, but we're lured in by the underground town, Coober Pedy. Shortly after William Creek we turn off into its direction, and the first half of this dirt track is quite difficult. There are lots of nervy corrugated sections and sand passages, making crashes an inevitably for such sand twits like ourselves.

A lonely, dented motorcycle panier at the side of the road shows that another one went down less gently. We wonder about it as the box, which quite obviously seems to belong to a BMW due to its distinctive shape, doesn't seem unusable at all. Compared to this piece we've already seen way more tarnished examples on motorcycles of more daring travellers. Why would one surrender it, especially as the unlocked case still carries parts of the motorcycle and all its tools? Aside from drinking water, this would be the last thing I would throw away on a trip in general, but particularly not in the outback. Perhaps the case fell off a trailer, where you wouldn't realise the loss straight away? And so we go on guessing the riddle's possible solution, which we'd love to know but most likely will never do.

A difficult day draws to an end, not just for us but also for our poor motorbikes. Further to all the aches and pains of the last few days, we can now also add two leaking suspension struts and a brake fluid reservoir leak. A few loose small screws, which I can quickly replace from our reserve, don't even count anymore. After 80,000 miles under partially material-wearing conditions, our bikes feel the strains. However, somehow it always went onward so far. We both believe that our loyal bikes will carry us all the way home, and in this spirit we keep repeating mantra-like "We will make it!"

White Man's Hole

Coober Pedy's actual name comes from the Aboriginal term "kupa-piti", which means "white man's hole." When you look at the millions of molehills, which shape the landscape within a radius of something like 10 miles, one understands immediately where the name originates from. Everywhere there are signs that warn of deep open mine shafts. What the diggers from all over the world may look for, one wonders? Opals, of course. Over and over again we see the most adventurous self-built special purpose vehicles. In the beginning, abandoned mines were used as cool living spaces out of pure pragmatism, and considering an outdoor temperature of 50°C (111°F) in summer time, it's not a bad idea.

Since then not only underground living houses, so-called dugouts, are deliberately set up like that but also dugout shops and churches, which make for a much more pleasant visit with a temperature of around 24°C (75°F). There are extensive offers of underground hotels, and one can also find an underground campsite a few miles out of town. After a few minutes we turn our backs light-heartedly towards the latter, as it costs double the amount of a regular campground in town. The entire thing has the charm of a bunker, but most over all the manager is so outrageous and hostile that one could think his wife had run off with a motorcyclist. We set up our tent in the backyard of the "Opal Inn" and reward ourselves with a cold beer that we had been looking forward to for days. To our horror this seems to be worth more than gold in Coober Pedy. We have to put converted 16 USD per six-pack onto the counter of the local liquor store. At this point we don't know yet that we will be longing back to those prices, when we face 7 USD for a small can in remote roadhouses in the outback.

A visit at a mine is a tourist standard in Coober Pedy, and there are plenty of options to choose from, with pricing ranging from around 23 USD. With an admittedly not really similar sounding name, "Josephine's Gallery" offers interesting tours in their own house-owned mine for 4.50 USD. Although one doesn't get to see any mining equipment, the descriptions are very comprehensive and detailed. We like it. And for animal lovers there's a cherry added on the cake twice per day when the orphaned joeys, that are raised here, get their bottle.

Drunkard Tombstones and Anti-Drinking-Rules

The next morning we make a last escape to the cemetery. Similar to the bizarre death field in Cooktown, one can also find one or another extravagant grave here. Our favourite showcases a beer keg as gravestone with embedded wine bottles as ornaments.

Speaking of wine bottles, before we get back on track we quickly have to fill up our supplies, as from now on there won't be any chance for a while to buy anything affordable. In the liquor store, however, I almost suffer a crying attack. The employee points out politely but firmly the communal rule that 4 litres wine cartons (1 gallon), which we exclusively buy due to its outstanding value for money, can only be given out after 3pm. This might perhaps be due to the attempt of trying to keep all the alcoholics hanging out on the streets from getting wasted early, as they're most likely in no shape to buy any larger supplies in the early evening. And other sizes they simply can't afford, just like us. We are told that we could already have 2 litre cartons now, which are double the price. Let alone the bottles that are even more exorbitantly expensive. It goes without saying that I don't want to wait for four hours, and therefore I skulk out of the shop with a bowed head. A man, who had witnessed the scene, follows me and offers a banknote, which I obviously refuse politely at first. But he remains stubborn and tells me that it is his birthday today and he would love to shout a drink. That's so typical Australian. With the exception of the black sheep in the underground campsite, we got to know Down Under unanimously from this friendly and hospitable side. The inscription of the beer keg tombstone this morning befittingly said "Have a drink on me!" Could this possibly be a "Thank You" of the dead, because we liked his grave so much? Whilst bush camping in the evening, we light a birthday candle in honour of our donor and cheer in thought "Thanks mate, you made our day!"

Up to the Horizon Straight Ahead

We're now travelling on the Stewart Highway, the long asphalt road that divides the outback from South to North. Although the tarmac road leads straight ahead unattractively, we're not getting bored. Despite our standards of hot summer temperatures, it is only spring here. Because of this one can see colourful wild flowers shine everywhere and one of the many varied examples is the wattle flower, which is Australia's national flower. Bright yellow desert melons, which we can spot in abundance on the side of the road, look like a truck has lost its load of oranges.
Reptiles are continually sunbathing on the burning tarmac, and we're surprised that we don't see more of them as roadkill. The traffic is denser than expected, and every five or ten minutes a car approaches us. Seems like it is not such a bold deed to cross the outback on the Stewart Highway after all, contrary to the belief of many a Internet blogger. Admittedly, a breakdown would not be fun here and at least financially

a fiasco, but nobody would ever die here, if one remains faithfully close to the vehicle. The greatest danger is to fall asleep whilst riding due to the monotony. Countless rusty wrecks are a silent warning, and the significant damage and great distance off the road attest severe accidents.

Ayers Rock and the Olgas

Ayers Rock, which is named "Uluru" in the language of the indigenous people, may be the national emblem per se for most tourists in Australia. Correspondingly large is the influx of visitors. At the ticket booth of the national park we squeeze off a batch of money for the 3-day-ticket and head for our first destination. We would like to quickly look at the Olgas, correctly named "Kata Tjuta", then check out Uluru and take off again at 5pm at latest. That was the plan at least. Soon we come to realise that this doesn't make any sense whatsoever. There's simply too much to see, and therefore we take the time for a little hike at the Olgas and postpone Ayers Rock to the following day. Camping in the national park is prohibited and the official campsite with 16 USD per night is not an option, so we ride out onto the Lasseter Highway for a few miles. To find a spot for camping there is no problem. Over one of the many sand tracks, it takes us up on a small headland, from where you can look over the hilly landscape all the way to Ayers Rock and the Olgas. When the sun sets the horizon glows at a width of 120°. There is no red sunset but only the reflection of a gigantic bush fire, which we had already observed with great concern the night before. Should the wind turn, it would literally catch up with us in no time at all. We worry if the fire wave could surprise us in our sleep or if a sixth sense would warn us.

Safe and unburnt we enjoy the advantages of our VIP hill in the sunrise the next morning. Uluru just looks fantastic in the first light of the day, and Kata Tjuta can also be seen well in the distance. And the best of it all is that there are no loud tourist masses anywhere around us. There are certainly hundreds of cameras clicking in a race in this very moment at the Sunrise Viewing Points in the national park. We utilise the cooler morning hours to take a close look at Ayers Rock. The gigantic rock can be circled in a six mile hike or ride. It quickly becomes apparent that Uluru is more interesting than we had expected. What looks like a gigantic cowpat from a distance, turns out to be very diverse from up close. We practically stop every minute to take in new perspectives and surface structures over and over again.

And what we also love is that you can get free drinking water everywhere in the national park. In such extreme temperatures throughout the day, dehydration is a serious danger. There are plenty of warnings to drink at least one litre (1/4 gallon) per hour, and interesting boards in toilets assist to determine the stage of dehydration by the colour of your urine, which is pretty cool. We never make it above dark yellow on this day though.

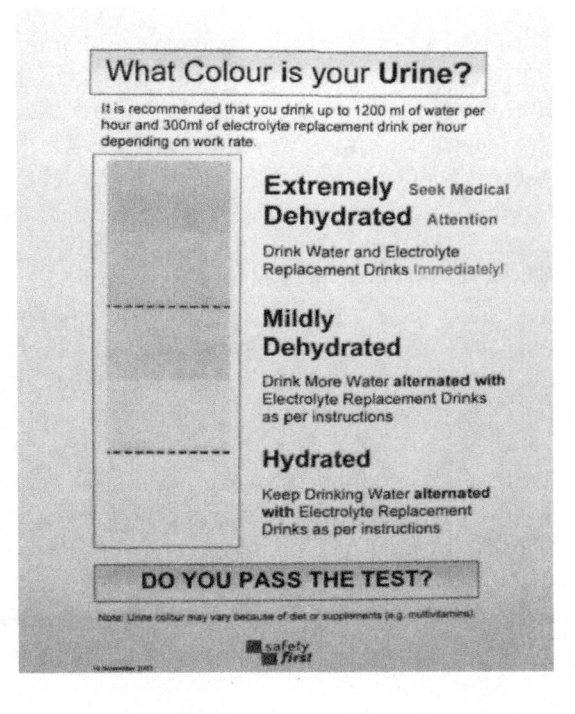

Drinking water is logistically a real challenge in the outback. In light of the clearly higher need of water in such environment, it is already difficult enough to transport enough of it on critical legs of the journey. Then there is the issue of procuring water as, contrary to the coastal regions of Australia where you have a tap on pretty much every corner, the situation looks a little different in the outback. In addition to this many roadhouses claim that well water, or tap water respectively, is not drinkable. In some instances this may even be the case, often though, it is just an old trick to mislead travellers to buy extremely expensive water bottles. The ones who fall for it will be losing a fortune in a few weeks in the outback. Hence we stick to the apparently non-drinkable tap water, but at the cost of a certain nervous foreboding in the bowels.

Alice Springs – in the Burning Hot Centre

The last 60 miles to the Stewart Highway are a nail-biting affair. In the end my motorcycle only rides 30 miles/h at full speed, damn! This really isn't the place to have such a problem. With the exception of the overpriced petrol station at the crossing, there is simply nothing whatsoever in sight. As per usual my bike runs better after a fuel-stop and, although feeling quite tense, we take on the last 120 miles to Alice Springs. When we arrive at Paul's and Tammy's place, we're relieved. We've made it. Everything else we'll be looking into after the first cold beer, or the second, or rather tomorrow? Paul has once participated in the legendary Finke Motor Race, but what has hero status amongst us, doesn't seem to be a big deal for him. The racetrack is his home and training track, so to speak, which he has ridden more often than he can count.

When he takes us to a nice sunset and beer on a hill west of town the next day, his off road skills become apparent. The steep, deep washed-out and in our eyes almost impossible track, seems to prove no challenge for Paul with his old four-wheel drive, which looks like it's going to die any minute. In awe and holding on tight to the door handle, we're rewarded with a magnificent view over Alice Springs and the West Mac Donnell Ranges, and also with a cold beer. Wow. We would've never found this spot on our own, let alone dared the ascent in the first place. Once again we're happy about the great experiences we make on this tour by specifically searching out contact with local motorcyclists. These encounters are the best part of our entire trip around the world.

To Get in Contact with Locals

Although it might not look that way in light of the amount of anecdotes I give about this topic, I really limit myself to a mere fraction of our encounters and hosts. That I still report often about our experiences with locals is because this gives us the opportunity to get to know a country and its people in a way that would otherwise not be possible, being a passing-by tourist only. Whether it be the secret sightseeing tips by locals as here in Alice Springs or in Sydney not long ago, or simply everyday life events of people who have similar interests to us. For us it is super exciting, although I would've not really categorised myself as sociable in my former life. On travels, however, opportunities come downright easier, be it online or on the street, where we are always talked to because of our number plates and motorcycles. As already mentioned, commonalities can help this greatly, as they break the ice and build bridges. It's not surprising that we're predominately guests at motorcyclists. Not that we're fixated on that, but it is often the connecting point, which starts a conversation. It is also helpful to travel as a couple, as my chances as a bold looking man to come in contact or even be invited, would surely be significantly lower. It seems to be more trustworthy and less threatening to have a woman on board, which other travellers will happily confirm. It is more difficult for groups beyond two people, especially when it's mostly men, and I dare to say that the chances of receiving an invitation, being three, four lads, are very close to zero.

Drunk Aborigines

Several motorcycle travellers in Australia had warned us of Alice Springs, where practically a state of emergency seems to prevail and where hundreds of drunken Aborigines were apparently lying around town in broad daylight. This may have been like this a few years ago, but nowadays the reality looks different in any case. No bums and no booze excesses in the street. Part of the reason for this might be the very restrictive alcohol release rules in the outback and in the Northern Territory, which we have already had to suffer under in Coober Pedy. And again I'm quite pissed off about the chicane of regulation here. Liquor stores only open at 2pm, and each day there's a policeman standing guard in front of it. Wine in caskets and port wine can generally only be sold between 6 to 9pm in two specific liquor stores. As one can imagine, it's really fun for the businesses doing that during the short opening hours. For good measure the pricing is much higher to what's common in the rest of the country, and to top it all off you also have to show your ID. The data is then entered into the computer, because each is only allowed to buy one 2-litre canister (half a gallon) per day. This also serves to identify the ones that breach their probation, who are officially supposed to be alcohol abstinent.

Albeit this would surely be demented officially, these rules are only in place to limit the massive alcohol problem amongst Aborigines. We can't help but think that this is only to experiment exclusively with the symptoms, but not really getting to the root of the problem. Besides our theoretical reservations against this method, we're totally annoyed by these alcohol handout rules, just out of sheer pragmatic reasons. The artificially high prices hit our tight travel budget hard, and it is far from funny when one happens to travel through a place after a few days without and is refused a red wine for a romantic bush camping night the next day, just because the handout ban for wine caskets still applies for a few more hours.

Escape from the Bushfire

The following day I get to grips with the internal fuel pump, located in the bikes petrol tank in Paul's garage, as I suspect the origin of the notorious performance loss to be located there. Everything seems clean and intact optically. However, when I see that the ventilation hose is blocked, I allow myself cautious joy. This could've been the issue, and it would fit perfectly to the error pattern. A few hours later the disappointment is great. It's a miss, the ventilation hose wasn't the problem and the performance loss is back.

Despite our still unsolved issue with the bike, we dare a day excursion to the West Mac Donnell Ranges. We ride through to the Glen Helen Gorge, from where we would like to work our way down the tourist sights backwards. The small lake in the gorge is literally an oasis in the usual dry outback, whereas the view onto the customary mountain panorama at the nearby Mt. Sonder lookout is concealed by black clouds of smoke.

There is a fierce bushfire that rages in front of us. We had already seen several large smoke clouds in the sky on our way here. From a safe distance we observe the exciting spectacle from our VIP spot. Suddenly the wind turns and freshens up considerably at the same time. The flames shoot up into the air and a firewall works itself in no time at all towards us. In only the few seconds we are required to put on jackets, helmets and gloves, the fire is already spanned across the last hundreds yards towards us. Draped in thick smoke we take to our heels. Phew, that was really close.

There is now heavy smoke everywhere on the way back to Alice Springs, and all turn-offs to the sights we originally had wanted to visit, are closed off due to the fire. The next day we read that 20 campers at the Ormiston Gorge, which was one of our stops on our sightseeing trip, had to be evacuated. Even the Lasseter Highway, which we rode on a few days ago when coming from Ayers Rock, had to be closed, because there was fire raging there, too. Our concern whilst bush camping nearby Ayers Rock had hence not been too unfounded. With the according wind, such a bushfire can travel enormous distances in a few hours only, so the imagination that many may have been surprised in their sleep whilst camping, comes to mind quite easily. We have even heard of cases, where cars at full speed were overtaken by the fire wave.

On a Visit at Helmut Kohl's

Back in Alice Springs, Paul has invited us to (Helmut) Kohl. Confused? Us too. The riddle's solution is that Kohl is the name of his German shepherd, which is de facto named after our great statesman, who brought us the European Union.
Paul and Kohl work in the prison of Alice Springs, and that's where we're heading to now. For three exciting hours Paul explains and

demonstrates his everyday working life as a dog trainer in prison, which is quite interesting. Amongst other things we learn how sniffer dogs are trained and used. The highlight, however, is Kohl who functions as so-called "general purpose dog", which includes the protection of his master. A colleague from the dog unit sacrifices himself as a dummy for a presentation. We are impressed and hope deeply that our arms will never end up between the unflinchingly slamming teeth of the slobber hurling Kohl.

In the UFO Capital

We leave Alice Spring towards north and take the Stewart Highway under our tyres again. Our destination is the at the North Coast located Darwin, from there we want to ship our motorcycles to East Timor.

Whycliffe Well is Australia's self-titled UFO capital. To be precise, the capital consists of a roadhouse with a campsite alone, but it is still a quite original place. Whilst we drink a surprisingly cheap coffee, coming as a bottomless cup, we study the countless reports of UFO sightings in the region and are amazed by the business sense of the proprietor, who prints aliens on pretty much anything you could think of in order to bleed tourists. In spite of the rip-off it is still a charming town.

In the evening we lie awake for a long time and think about aliens. Generally we don't believe in such a thing, generally…

The overdimensional Devil's Marbles, Karlu Karlu in Aboriginal, lie around in the hundreds in the middle of nowhere. Despite the brutal heat, the discovery tour by foot is great fun, and a not so shy dingo keeps us company. He makes a bolt for it when more and more tourists arrive. We meant to camp here originally, but there's too much going on here for us and so we ride on to the Devil's Pebbles, or Kunjarra, that are less spectacular. One has to follow a sand track for a few miles, however, this also means that we have the place all to ourselves at night.

Charred Country

We consistently see smoke clouds, and there are bushfires in all directions. Central Australia is only a few days short of the longest rainless period since the weather has been recorded, accordingly it lights up easily everywhere. What a contrast to the flood-plagued Queensland.
Bushfires are generally somewhat "normal" in this country and the vegetation has adapted to this phenomenon in various ways. Neither the eucalyptus trees, nor the termite mounds, which both dominate the local scenery, are affected by the fires. And for hours we ride through charred and smoking land.

Bathing Day

Towards the north of the Northern Territory it is full of wonderful bathing spots, which we use lavishly. The Mataranka Thermal Pools don't only seem like an oasis in the desert for their picturesque palm trees. Although they are warm springs, the water is a welcomed cool down. It doesn't attract human visitors solely but also many animals due to its unspoilt location. A kangaroo with a little joey in its pouch dares to come very close up to a few yards. Hundreds or maybe even thousands of fruit bats hang in the palm treetops and make a round through the air occasionally. Also for the good of others who do not recognise the snake in the tree, most of the bathing tourists would've escaped screaming from the water without fail, if they would've spotted it.

I would call the Mataranka Thermal Pools the most beautiful hot springs that I have ever visited, but the nearby Bitter Springs are even better. They're world class, the temperature is perfect and the site widely left to their natural state, which increases the attraction considerably. One can lazily float in the crystal clear water, which runs for a few hundred yards in the shade through the abundant green. To exchange this paradise with the merciless heat on the motorbike takes all our effort. The temperatures are that high that even the wind brings no relief.

Bathing day number 2, this time our favourite place in the Douglas Daly Park is called "The Arches". The cool river makes its rather photogenic way through rocks and has washed out a few pretty arches. Blue and red dragonflies buzz around, hundreds of small and cheeky lizards rustle through the foliage and in the water we spot zebra fish. In the shade of the whispering stream we enjoy our breakfast picnic. Half an hour later we tread Kneipp-therapy-like through the water of the nearby Douglas Hot Springs.
Hot springs are bubbling everywhere from the ground, which then merge with the cool stream. Natural pools invite you to splash around and offer all one could wish for, anything from refreshingly cool to unbearably hot.

The Most Spectacular Bush Camping Spot in Australia

The Litchfield National Park, which according to many is the best that Australia has to offer in terms of national parks, has its charms without doubt. Enjoyment is diminished by the large numbers of tourists that can reach the park conveniently due to its close proximity to Darwin. It gets terribly on my nerves that there are constantly and everywhere busses or rented cars, travelling at snail's pace on the road that pollute the air and disturb the silence. Numerous well-visited bathing opportunities offer a welcome cool down, but in face of all the people we just decline annoyed and leave the national park, heading north on a nervy corrugated road. It's more a dirt track that nobody except of ourselves wants to lay their hands on?A bit more comfortable is the tarmac east access road off the Stewart Highway. And the reward for all the shaking and vibrating is a place that beats everything in the Litchfield National Park. In the latter, there was a fenced field of compass termite mounds, which you could admire from afar. Here instead, one can view them from up close and even camp amongst them, which is brilliant. Apropos magnetic termite mounds, they are all strictly aligned south east and as flat as a tombstone. When the sun rises the next morning and the first red rays of light break through the mist, we feel like in a cemetery. It is eerie, fascinating and simply beautiful.
We agree, that deserves the first place for the best sunrise and the most

spectacular bush camping spot we ever had in Australia.

In Berry Springs I decline in shock, it is Saturday and sheer masses of people have found their way there from the nearby Darwin. Simone is not deterred by this and takes her sixth bath in three days with her usual enthusiasm.

Price Paradox – In Expensive Australia One Can Still Travel Cheap

We have to stay a few days in Darwin, North Australia's largest city, to whip our bikes into shape, order parts and organise our shipments to East Timor. As we don't know anybody here, we go from campground to campground, more out of necessity, and are shocked. 34 USD per day is the cheapest we can find, which makes it the second most expensive campsite of our entire journey. The most expensive one was in a real world metropolis, which Darwin is very far removed from. WiFi would cost an extra 18 USD per day, which is expensive even for Australian standards. The price shock continues at the Honda dealer, where discounted parts cost even far more than if we would order them from Europe, potential mailing charges included. Unfortunately we can't make it time-wise to have the stuff sent from Germany, so again we have to grin and bear it.

Food is generally expensive in Australia. Alcohol anyway. The only thing I can spontaneously think of that is cheaper than back home is the petrol, with the exception of a few remote places in the outback. In saying this, outside of Europe and pretty much everywhere in the world, petrol prices are generally considerably lower than back home. And the extreme distances in Down Under ensure petrol station bills that simply make you wanna cry. You could therefore say that Australia is an expensive country to travel in. For the ones, who like to sleep in hotels, eat in restaurants and drink in bars, this surely is the case. But it can also be different, as in the four and a half months we were in Australia, we only stayed on one private campground in Darwin. Drinking water is available for free pretty much everywhere and the free of charge camping infrastructure in this country is really of the finest quality. Hence, it is actually very possible to travel Down Under on a small budget, provided that you are willing to live modestly and manage to resist the temptation to explore every inch of this humongous country from your saddle or from behind the steering wheel. Namely long distances travelled, as in pretty much every country, are the travel cost number 1 for globetrotters. However, as we are very passionate about riding our bikes, we often find it difficult to take this wisdom to heart ourselves.

Working on Travels

If you need to fill up your travel funds "on the road", Australia is one of the best countries we have ever been to. For the ones under 30 this works out well and fully legally with a Work and Travel Visa for a year. For an illegal worker it is harder, but not impossible.

If it's all about making sheer money, the general rule of thumb applies to go working where the wages are high. And when it comes to this factor, Australia has a strong lead. We only experienced similarly good wages on our travel leg through Canada. The same applies for emigrants. If one works in countries with high wages and still puts aside a fraction of a wage, despite hefty living costs one can take a long break in a lower price country, such as South America or South East Asia, with no problems. But if one works in the latter countries, no matter if employed or in an entrepreneurial sense, one will have to save a higher income percentage until, for example, one can pay a flight home to visit family. If it is possible anyhow to put that much aside in the first place. Obviously this is only the financial aspect of it and herewith only one of many aspects when choosing a country to work from. For travellers it is most realistic to work for food and accommodation in touristy facilities, such as hostels. An alternative would be local or international charity projects, where you don't have to pay for anything else on top in the best-case scenario. These are both options to get to know a country a little more than via transit. However, one could write a separate book about this complex topic, I only wanted to demonstrate a simple rule of thumb for the financial sense.

All Just Bolts and Nuts

The search for a competent and mainly affordable garage in Darwin turns into a quest for finding the needle in the haystack. As in good South American fashion, so to speak, we are sent from A to B, who in light of our requests declines immediately and forwards us to C. C is named Tim in this case and is an incredibly positive and energy-filled lad. In terms of motorcycles he's not afraid of anything, and his slogan, which I get to hear several times a day, is "all just nuts and bolts!" His unbridled optimism reminds us once more to Latin America, but with him I really have the feeling that he knows what he's doing. In Central and South America the promised skills were often far from the actual deliverable ones.

The list of repairs is endlessly long. Tim services professionally our rear shock absorbers, which leak after the corrugated dusty roads of Australia. My performance loss is traced to a faulty petrol pump, which he can also exchange surprisingly cheap. To check the valve clearance on our bikes is a real act, which many a mechanics on our journey have always cringed about. Even "all just bolts and nuts" Tim starts sweating heavily when he gets to the back cylinders. The result of the entire operation is that after 90,000 miles, which is of course an amount way above the required service intervals, seven of eight valves have the nominal measure size. That's incredible! Bright smiles spread over our faces and we are more confident than ever to manage to get home with these reliable and incredible long-suffering motorcycles. Thereupon we leave Simone's bike be as the result would most likely be the same. Apart from that I believe in the superstitious rule to "never touch a running system!" Besides all the formerly mentioned repairs, which were all beyond my moderate skills as mechanic, the operation is also highly successful in other respects, as Tim lets me watch patiently over his shoulder, which should not be taken for granted at all. This helps me

to learn a heap of things, which can be very beneficial in desperate moments when I cannot fall back on a competent professional.
Over and above of it all I can also spend good time in Tim's shady and cool garage to work on the bikes.

Mounting and dismounting spring struts, changing tyres and brake pads, cleaning and oiling the air filter as well as many other items on the list are more pleasant tasks here than somewhere in the open in tropical heat.

Does a Traveller Need Mechanical Skills?

How much does one have to be able to repair by himself when going on travels? As so often, there is no definite answer to that. The one starting off with a modern vehicle should nowadays absolutely be able to hope for 30 to 60,000 miles without major problems, except of the usual wear and tear and unexpected crashes, whereas exceptions prove the rule. Therefore one can dare such an adventure without any mechanical knowledge, especially when travels are planned for predominantly popular residential areas in industrial countries. The other side of the coin is that in the case, where one is not able to fix anything on the bike, all repairs will have to be paid for, which can be quite costly when abroad. In addition to this, there is a great lack of know-how in developing countries, so that one is helplessly exposed to botched jobs and scams, often with fatal consequences in regards to the technical end of the journey. A realistic compromise is that one is at least capable to perform simple maintenance jobs, such as changing oil and oil filters, tyres, spark plugs, air filters, brake pads, light bulbs, chain and sprockets. Additionally one should at least be able to evaluate the necessity for other possible repairs, so that these can be initiated in time to avoid being overcharged, repairs such as steering and wheel bearings, spokes, and the like.

For most repairs one does not need any special talents and surely not a two-wheel or mechanic apprenticeship, it can be learned in a single day by specific courses. For the one who has at least a bit of basic knowledge, many a problem "on the road" can be solved itself, especially in situations in which one simply has to take care of it due to a lack of available help. Perfect solutions aren't required, what counts is that it can somehow go on, even if the pro at home would probably throw up his hands in horror and the TÜV inspector's blood pressure go through the roof.

Almost everything I know about motorcycles, I have learnt with real-time examples during breakdowns and faults. If that happens once, one definitely knows about it next time. And with every sense of achievement, confidence grows to tackle the next mishap that might happen. On one hand I would therefore say "Have the courage, it'll all turn out well!" On the other hand one should select their way of transport carefully. Newer vehicles tend to be more reliable. Although you often hear that one can do more on older models, this can turn into a boomerang when one can't do anything in the first place due to a lack of knowledge. In the case of the latter it would mean solely more required visits in the garage than with a newer one. This can quickly become the source for constant frustration and the end of a journey, as the one who is constantly overchallenged, ultimately has no fun.

Many motorcycle globetrotters have played with the idea to switch to a bicycle, including us. But even as a "bicycle" vagabond some knowledge must remain. The one who cannot patch up a tyre won't get far. Spoke and frame breaks or bearing replacements might yet be possible to be repaired in a garage abroad, but in terms of a gear shift or modern features, such as hydraulic brakes and springs, this might be an entirely different story in developing countries.

Hellishly Hot Days

Our shipping to Asia is in 10 days. To save money we leave the wickedly expensive Darwin and vagabond around. We try to travel from water hole to water hole, so to speak, as the brutal heat is not bearable otherwise. Even the few trees don't really offer any shade, as their foliage is rather meagre. When nothing else works anymore, we crawl under our tarpaulin at the hottest hour of the day.

There is no question of motorcycle riding in such conditions. We only ever set up our tent in the last rays of light to avoid it getting a chance to warm up. Nonetheless our sweat is running down in streams as soon as we crawl into our little home at night. That fact that we exclusively camp, doesn't' make it easier, as there is no quick jump under the cool shower available for us. We count the days until we can finally return to Darwin to move on.

Goodbye Australia!

Back in Darwin the stamping of the "Carnets de Passage" at customs and the submission of the bikes at the shipping company takes an hour, including all formalities. We can barely believe it, that's super! There are even good news with the Indonesian embassy, as our 60-day-visas were granted. With a palette box of German Öttinger Pils we get onto the bus that will take us back to the campsite. In two days our plane to East Timor will leave, and at night we celebrate our farewell from Australia, taking a look back and summing it up. In terms of the flora and fauna it is in a league of its own. There was constantly something to see there, which really was world class. In terms of the scenery our verdict is less positive. The mountains and costal regions rather earn the rating "quite nice", but would in our view not be worth the effort of getting motorbikes all the way to the other end of the world. The extremely sparsely populated heartland of the country has put its spell on us instead. The void space of this country, the enormous distances, the heat, the drought and the daily bush camping in the wilderness are the impressions that really make Australia for me personally and which I will be remembering for a long time to come.

We Surely Don't Have Enough Yet

Long-term travelling with all its sacrifices and its daily challenges is not everybody's cup of tea. Many, who enjoy the big journey enthusiastically in the beginning, change their mind in the course of months and years going by. We know many who have thrown in the towel eventually. The reasons for this vary. For some the vagabond life becomes a boring daily routine, touristy activities loose their appeal or the journey lacks meaning at some stage. Others can't cope with the social challenges, whether it be the inescapable constant proximity to a partner or the distance to beloved ones.
The one travelling low budget might eventually be fed up to have to

make every Euro go a long way and hence having to refrain from many beautiful and interesting things, especially if short-term tourists can permanently indulge in these in ignorant bliss right under their noses. Others again can't cope with the feeling in the long run of the endless list of unsolvable problems, which a trip around the world never lacks. These strains and doubts are no strangers to us, and it is not always sunshine and optimism for the motorcycle vagabonds. But the moments, in which one is very close to chucking it all in or in which one simply doesn't know what to do any more, fade in our perception against all the happy days, in which we manage to enjoy the moment or in which we realise that we live here and now exactly the way we always had wanted to. We still love the splendid motorcycle vagabond life! It is out of question for us that we will give it our all to make it home on our own wheels. We don't know at that point yet how hard this struggle will become, especially India and Pakistan will hit us heavily. With every additional mile the probability increases that something will fail on the motorbikes and the equipment. We're pretty sure that on the finishing straight the machines as well as the equipment will be whistling their last tune. And not only the technical and logistic challenges will grow, also mentally we will be facing great trials. But of this we don't know anything of yet, whilst looking longingly towards Asia from Australia's North Coast, where our travels will continue. Only one thing we know for sure:

WE SURELY HAVE NOT HAD ENOUGH JUST YET

Where to from Here?

In the second chapter of our trip around the world, we take you off the beaten track through South East Asia and over the highest passes of the breathtaking high mountain ranges in the Himalayas, to be followed then by travels through pretty delicate countries, such as Pakistan, Iran and Iraq.

Foreign countries and cultures open up a whole new world to us and also shape our "inner journey" with their diverse challenges, which we have more of than we would wish for. On several occasions the success of our trip around the world is at a tipping point, and the term "grit your teeth" becomes whispered words.

In the second chapter of our journey we also offer many descriptive insights into the highs and lows of a life "on the road", including the painstaking demands of travelling, bizarre anecdotes, concerns, frustrations and hardships, but also luck, freedom and overwhelming hospitality.

Where other travel books end, we don't remain silent or keep the last great challenge under wraps. Returning home and rehabilitating socially are pretty tough, and there will hence be no shortage of it in the second book of the motorcycle vagabonds.

See you on the road!

For the like-minded and friends: t-shirts, hoodies, sweaters, etc. with our original name Krad-Vagabunden (= Motorcycle Vagabonds)

Various designs and colours are available at:
www.motorcycle-vagabonds.com

Countless people have helped us "on the road" and many have supported us from home in various ways.

We say THANK YOU to all of you!

We couldn't have done it without you!

Only a small fraction of you could be mentioned in this book solely to keep a balance between the elements of a journey book.

Special thanks to Jannah, Rik and Pete, without whom the English version would never have been realised.
You did an amazing job!

Some Comments Regarding the Translation of This Book

Tales of adventure such as this are as individual as the people that live them. This is a story of two German people and their travels, and as such it is from their view point and perceptions. There is a danger therefore in translating to another language that the point of view of view and personality of the author can be lost.

To avoid this, care has been taken to only refine those things that did not easily and clearly translate into English. Many things have been left as English versions of what was written in German, and not translated as if an English speaker wrote them. This way the personality, the insights, and the humour of the author could still show through. All this was done by people who know the author and his sense of humour, his personality, fellow Europeans, fellow bikers, fellow travellers, who live in places other than where they come from. They hope you enjoy the book as a lot of work went into deliberately making the book read the way it does, with luck it will inspire you to go for a Vagabond adventure.

Do it now or forever wish you had!

Rik, the Frogman

Our ATW-Bikes

Honda Transalp XL700VA, built in 2008.
It was important for us to have two identical bikes, which gave us major advantage in regards to spare parts and the swapping of parts in case of defects.
The Hondas turned out to be an extremly reliable and tough bike. Both made it without nearly any significant defect - except things I would call normal consumption.
This praise is not in return for sponsoring. We had no discount and no support by Honda.
There are other companies, who build reliable bikes, too. And there are some who don´t.
I could fill a book about aspects of the „perfect travel bike".
In the end all rational arguments fade in comparison to one: with which bike are you most comfortable? Don´t listen to others´ „you have to" - just go with your beloved motorcycle. Any bike will do!

Printed in Great Britain
by Amazon